More Beautiful
and More Terrible

More Beautiful
and More Terrible

The Embrace and Transcendence of
Racial Inequality in the United States

Imani Perry

NEW YORK UNIVERSITY PRESS
New York and London

NEW YORK UNIVERSITY PRESS
New York and London
www.nyupress.org

References to Internet websites (URLs) were accurate at the time of writing.
Neither the author nor New York University Press is responsible for URLs
that may have expired or changed since the manuscript was prepared.

Library of Congress Cataloging-in-Publication Data

Perry, Imani, 1972–
More beautiful and more terrible : the embrace and transcendence
of racial inequality in the United States / Imani Perry.
p. cm. Includes bibliographical references and index.
ISBN 978-0-8147-6736-8 (cl : alk. paper) — ISBN 978-0-8147-6737-5
(pb   ) — ISBN 978-0-8147-6818-1 (e-book)
1. Racism—United States. 2. United States—Race relations. I. Title.
E184.A1P42   2010
305.800973—dc22   2010039826

New York University Press books

Manufactured in the United States of America
c   10 9 8 7 6 5 4 3 2 1
p   10 9 8 7 6 5 4 3 2 1

American history is longer, larger, more various, more beautiful, and more terrible than anything anyone has ever said about it.

—James Baldwin

For Issa Garner Rabb and
Freeman Diallo Perry Rabb and
in loving memory of Neida Garner Perry

Contents

Acknowledgments

It takes a village to write a scholarly book.

Thank you to everyone in my village. I see you on the street and in my home, I feel you in my heart, your humanity a testament to the righteousness of democracy, of fairness, of justice.

Thank you to my amazing editor, Eric Zinner, and to NYU Press for nurturing and believing in this project.

Thank you to my late aunt, Phyllis Perry Paxton, who was the first person in my family to merge commitments to racial justice, research, and writing. She is missed and admired by me and by so many others.

Thank you to my mother, Theresa Perry, for teaching me how to integrate empirical research into my theoretical analyses of race and for constantly keeping me informed. Thank you to my dad, Steven Whitman, for teaching me how to critically evaluate empirical research. This book is truly a reflection of the care and attention my parents put into the loving cultivation of values and intellect in their daughter. I am endlessly appreciative.

Thank you to my extended family. Every single one of you has inspired and motivated me in some way. Thank God for my late grandmother, Neida Mae Garner Perry, who created a family filled with resilient, creative, strong, smart, loving, and good people. Because of her, we are. Special thanks to my aunts Thelma Perry Brown and Jaqueline Perry and to my uncle William Brown for providing essential family support as I worked on this book. Additionally, the communities of the House at Pooh Corner child care center, the Germantown Friends School, and the neighborhoods of northwest Philadelphia nurtured my family as I worked on this project.

Many friends provided intellectual and emotional nurturing and support in this endeavor. I want to especially thank Farah, Michele, Simone, Cheryl, Sarita, Theo, Daphne, Robin, Eddie, Mark, Salamishah, Janet, Anita, Regina, Mike, Freager, the Rabb family, the Jones-Walker family, the Vaughn-Cooke-Ewell family, the Davis family, the Thomas-Hartzog family, the Linneman family, the Wingard family, all of my colleagues and students in CAAS, everyone who babysat my boys, and all of the FB friends who offered virtual support in the wee hours.

I received important institutional support as I worked on this project. Many thanks to the Princeton University Center for African American Studies, the Princeton Program in American Studies, the University of Pennsylvania Law School and Department of African American Studies, the Columbia University Institute for Research in African American Studies, the American Studies Association, the Japanese Associaton for American Studies, Rutgers School of Law-Camden, and the Minority Section of the Association of American Law Schools.

Thanks to the many scholars whose work I cited and read and learned from. I have had the great fortune to have studied at the knee of many influential scholars, and I have also had the great benefit of having been influenced by many scholars of varying degrees of acclaim in many fields. It would take too many pages to name them all.

Thank you to my co-parent, Chris Rabb, for constant encouragement and countless hours of listening and discussing.

Most of all, thank you to my children, Freeman Diallo Perry Rabb and Issa Garner Rabb. The joy you give is endless. Your brilliance and promise are breathtaking. Every day you sharpen my sense of purpose and responsibility. The world as it is not good enough for you and your generation, but I am trying to do my part to prepare it for the revolutions you will bring.

Preface

or "A Method to the Madness"

God gave Noah the rainbow sign, no more water, the fire next
time.
    —"Mary Don't You Weep," African American spiritual

John knew I was serious about what I was doing, and I knew he
was serious about what he was doing.
    —Sonny Rollins, discussing the recording of "Tenor Madness"

Every scholarly project begins with an inspiration—to uncover a
pattern, to illuminate or explicate a time, place, or thing, to pose or solve a
problem. Mine is this: to understand our ongoing embrace of racial inequality in the United States, despite the fact that we are a society that formally
and colloquially decries racism and proclaims equality.

For the better part of my life, I have grappled on a daily basis with this
thing called race and, more specifically, Blackness, especially my own. As
a scholar who studies and writes in multiple fields—law, literature, cultural
studies—I feel confident in saying that race is everywhere and that it is a
many-headed beast. Cut off a head, another lashes out, while the previously
amputated spontaneously regenerates. This makes it rather hard to write
about, not to say anything of actually addressing, the politics and practices of
race in day to day life.

To be frank, it sometimes seems that the abstractions allowed for in the
arts (music, literature, painting) facilitate a more robust description of race
than do the most meticulous academic inquiries. Listen to Nina Simone,
read Toni Morrison, and you will "get" race in America. And so you can
understand why I (a scholar, rather than an artist) avoided writing this book
before I finally decided to heed the call.

My decision to heed it I attribute to James Baldwin, whose *The Fire Next Time* was neither comprehensive nor weighed down by footnotes, caveats, or anxieties. Rather, it cut across modes of writing and reading to make a ground-breaking yet cogent set of explanations about race the United States. That book transformed me as a reader, thinker, and person. When I revisited it, years after my first reading, I found it pushing me to put my fingers to the keyboard. Maybe, I thought, my years of thinking and reading and thinking some more about race across academic fields, and in and out of art forms, might actually make me a reasonable candidate for attempting to compose a twenty-first-century story about race "after the flood,"[1] as it were, that could cut across the boundaries of discipline. I'm no Baldwin, but I have plenty to say.

Just as Baldwin inspired the spirit of the book, a song inspires the composition. In 1956, two young tenor saxophone players dialogued with their horns on a song called "Tenor Madness." These two men, John Coltrane and Sonny Rollins, would become jazz giants, and this would be the only recording of them sharing a soundscape.

This important moment in jazz history functions as a key metaphor for me in this project. In answering the questions I have posed, I am also attempting to create a dialogue between distinct bodies of scholarship with different methods of inquiry but with the shared terrain of trying to make some sense of this social construction that we call race.

"Tenor Madness" was recorded two years after the first *Brown v. Board of Education* decision, which outlawed state mandated segregation in public schools, and one year after the second *Brown v. Board of Education* opinion, which backed away from rapid implementation of desegregation with the infamous phrase "all deliberate speed." It was a period of possibility but also a period of frightening rage against the prospect of full equality for all American citizens. That was the social context of tenor madness.

There is something similar about this moment in history, the second decade of the twenty-first century. We have turned a page in American history by electing the first African American president. And yet, race still shapes our lives, divides our communities, and warps our collective projects. There is a frightening rage displayed by a critical mass of Americans against the reality that our president is a biracial African American and Pacific Islander man with a complex past and present. Behind this, there are real questions as to how much meaning we should place on the identity of political leaders and how much on the reality of ordinary citizens' lives when we evaluate the state of race relations.

We need a wide range of tools to apprehend and comprehend this evolving and, in some ways, devolving racial landscape.

The aesthetic brilliance of jazz is matched by some philosophical illuminations provided by the musical form. The repetition and internalization of skill, knowledge, and technique can propel the artist(s) into extraordinary improvisation, experimentation, and conversation. Imagination and creativity are enriched by a rigorous foundation. And it is not uncommon, in jazz, for musicians to "sit in" or "jam" with a band that is not their own.

I am inspired by jazz wisdom and practice. In these pages, I have cited many of the giants (and the Lilliputians) of the study of race who have applied the methods of their respective disciplines with rigor and diligence. And I have them jam with one another on these pages. I use this impressive body of work to ask, What is the common story and what are the consistent themes across these inquiries? In light of the shared terrain that emerges, I argue, we can imagine new and even deeper ways of approaching the study of race and, most important, addressing the challenges race poses in our lives. The Baldwin quote that gives the book its name is particularly apt because in the contemporary United States we routinely fail to acknowledge how terrible things actually are with respect to race. It is indeed more terrible than what we say. And so, this is a sober book. But it is also a hopeful one, because, in the midst of all that is terrible, there is still beautiful possibility.

Introduction

That Justice is a blind goddess
Is a thing to which we blacks are wise.
Her bandage hides two festering sores
That once perhaps were eyes.
　　　　　　—Langston Hughes, "Justice"

In 1932, Langston Hughes published a volume titled *Scottsboro Limited: Four Poems and a Play in Verse.* This slim, gorgeously furious book was a work of protest literature. By weighing in on the infamous trial of four Black young men[1] facing capital punishment for the alleged rape of two White women on a train in Alabama (one of whom recanted, the other of whom provided inconsistent testimony), Hughes followed an established tradition within African American arts of providing social and political commentary through creative expression.

His poetry remains illuminating even as we approach fourscore years since the Scottsboro trials. The poem "Justice," part of this five-piece meditation on Scottsboro, imagines the blindfold worn by the Greek goddess not as a deliberate gesture of fairness but as a bandage hiding wounds inflicted against her principle. Hughes, with this provocative imagery, foreshadowed a powerfully troubling relationship among the concepts of blindness, fairness, and race, several decades before the U.S. Supreme Court would interpret the principle of color blindness to mean that American law should reject any attention to race, even in efforts to address racial subordination, in all but an increasingly narrow class of cases.

In this era in which we proclaim a national ethos of racial egalitarianism[2] and yet find race qua inequality rearing its ugly head in place after place, we see the festering sores of (in)justice in many sectors: housing, poverty, imprisonment, health, education, and on and on. On one hand, the humane person feels a certain urgency about addressing these inequalities. But that emotion exists in the midst of a long legal and policy retreat from remedies for current and past racial discrimination. On the other hand, we feel compelled to also ask why a social transformation as profound and deep as the civil rights movement could not divorce American democracy from the blood money of racial caste with which it purchased its stability.

In the fall of 2007, the case of the "Jena 6" entered the public eye. Six young Black men were aggressively prosecuted in small-town Louisiana after allegedly beating up a White peer. This occurred in the midst of a series of altercations that began when Black teenagers had the "gumption" to sit under what was designated a "White tree." Nooses were hung on the tree—perhaps the closest thing to a death threat that could be issued by the use of an inanimate object. When some pundits termed the experience of the Jena 6 a modern-day Scottsboro, I took pause. Sure, the parallels were there, but it concerned me. This isn't 1932. And, while we shouldn't be antihistoricist in the manner of the Jena, Louisiana, school officials who referred to the noose as a "silly prank,"[3] that is to say, while we should understand the role history plays in constituting symbol and in shaping present reality, it really isn't 1932. And we have to grapple with what that means. This book is written, in part, as an argument that a mid-twentieth-century framework for understanding race and racism handicaps our comprehension and action in the twenty-first century. Our experience of racial injustice has a derivative, but distinct, zeitgeist.

At the same time, the fact that tens of thousands of protesters arrived at Jena in September of 2007 indicated a tide turning. There was a brewing call for movement that ultimately manifested in the grassroots energy that surrounded the campaign and election of Barack Obama to the presidency of the United States. And yet confusion followed the cheers of sweet progress. In fact, any honest assessment of race in the early twenty-first century should make us remark that "these are strange days indeed." Barack Obama is a biracial African American president who grew up in Hawaii and Indonesia. Beginning on January 20, 2009, the White House was occupied by an African American family. From November 5, 2008, forward, the chatter about a postracial America was everywhere, and yet six months into Obama's presidency a critical mass of Americans hysterically proclaimed the president a noncitizen and decried the very destruction of the United States under his leadership. We have been told by pundits that we are moving beyond race, and yet the media have displayed a renewed interest in talking about race. Who can tell what exactly is going on?

Similar to the way Michel Foucault noted that Victorian mores about sexuality offered an opportunity to talk about sex, a lot; the "postracial" discourse reflects both anxiety and confusion about what race means and doesn't mean now. In order to answer these questions, we must approach the enterprise with great rigor and sophistication. At each point, we must consider the ambiguity of terms and the transformation of ideas and identify that which is fresh and that which is stagnant. And, if we are to be at our best, we must sustain and expand the hope that excited us about the 2008 election.

Those are tall orders. My ambition in this book is much smaller. This book seeks to pursue a very specific question, which nevertheless demands a complex body of information and analysis: how does a nation that proclaims racial equality create people who act in ways that sustain racial inequality? I suppose a second question is pursued, too: what can we do about it?

I have chosen to focus our attention on what I have termed "the practices of racial inequality," by which I mean actions that individuals take that researchers can identify as being clear decisions to disadvantage others on the basis of race. Identifying these as decisions based on race is made possible largely by empirical social science research that reveals trends and makes comparisons between how different groups of people are treated. When we see the cumulative effect of the choices people make about how to treat others, we recognize that there are undeniable patterns of racial privileging and disadvantage that are part of contemporary American culture. As an interdisciplinary scholar, I have, in my work, always drawn upon a range of scholarly fields. However, I would argue that efforts at understanding race and how race operates hold special demands for those doing interdisciplinary work, and require an openness to reading across disciplines. Within fields like sociology, psychology, and media studies, there are constantly growing bodies of important research on race. Also, within disciplines, while each has its own rules and practices, the most important efforts to contemplate race have also engaged in critical practices vis-à-vis the disciplines themselves, which, without exception of note, have been shaped around notions of humanity, objectivity, and normativity rooted in White (largely male, largely affluent, largely Western European) experience. And so, to talk about race with rigor has also meant using new tools, creating new norms, and challenging flawed or limited methods within each respective discipline.

A key part of the method of this book is the application of cultural studies analysis to social science research. Such a use of social science research does not necessarily fall within the orthodoxies of social scientific argument. At various points, I argue that "the evidence" shows something greater than or different from what many of my social science colleagues would say, perhaps with the exceptions of sociologists of culture and anthropologists. But I take risks with fields that are not my own because my hope is that the method cobbled together here can be a critical intervention, one that challenges the resistance to and suspicion of empirical data that exist in much humanist race theory even as it shows how cultural studies can be useful to address questions about race that get lost in the gaps of quantitative social science research (as a function of the constructions and imputed meanings of categories).[4] At the root of it all, my fundamental belief is that figuring out this race thing requires us to become "bricoleurs,"[5] notwithstanding the pressures of specialization, professionalization, and the disciplines. Obviously, I am not alone in this belief, and a noteworthy group of scholars and intellectuals precede me in a "bricolage" approach to studying race, including but not limited to Patricia Hill Collins, Robin D.G. Kelley, Hortense Spillers, Gloria Anzaldua, Ronald Takaki, George Lipsitz, Eduardo Bonilla-Silva, Herman Gray, Philip Deloria, and Cornel West.

Race and racism are lived by virtue of encounters, real or virtual, with "raced" bodies. (And we all have "raced" bodies; even those of us who are seen as "racially ambiguous" are raced by virtue of our culture's fascination with our "indeterminacy.") In the moments of these encounters, individuals read, evaluate, and judge others. This means that even though we can measure racial effects or racialized phenomena, there are myriad immeasurable ways in which race is experienced or given meaning in the midst of social life. While using aggregate data of the sort provided by social science research in some ways collapses the diversity of racial experience into a few modes of analysis, that collapse is necessary to a certain extent in order avoid the danger of the overrepresentation of an individual and/or nonrepresentative experience or of a questionable interpretation of a representative experience. In a book like this, which aspires to provide a theory and a remedial framework that can have broad application, the useful individual interpretation or racial anecdote must coincide with the existence of patterns. Although telling individual stories about race can be extremely illuminating, examining empirical evidence about race gives necessary and critical information about what is happening with race today.

In recent years, the analysis of cultural patterns in relationship to race have more often been of two sorts: either discussions of the culture of particular racial or ethnic groups and how they are related to, and resist, the dominant social order or analyses of the cultures of people of color, which have far too often been shaped around diagnostics of what is wrong with those people (through their own fault or because of the conditions of their lives). Culture talk in the twenty-first century has especially centered on debates about how disfavored or favorable "ethnic traits" and behaviors impact the outcomes of groups.

Instead of talking about "colored" culture, I want to talk about racial inequality as a national cultural practice.

In explaining what I mean by saying the practice(s) of inequality is a cultural practice, I find the description of culture provided by the anthropologist Ulf Hannerz particularly useful. He describes culture as having two locations, in human minds and in public forms. He goes on to say:

> The three dimensions of culture, to be understood in their interrelations are thus:
> 1. ideas and modes of thought as entities and processes of the mind—the entire array of concepts, propositions, values and the like which people within some social unit carry together . . .
> 2. forms of externalization, the different ways in which meaning is made accessible to the senses, made public . . .
> 3. social distribution, the ways in which the collective cultural inventory of meanings and meaningful external forms . . . together is spread over a population and its social relationships.[6]

Applying these dimensions to race in the contemporary United States, I argue that we have common ways of thinking that are reflective of a racial ideology and that sustain a belief in or an assumption of White superiority. Our active practices of inequality are means of externalizing these beliefs and assumptions. Importantly, we can identify a belief in White superiority as having concrete material impact in some contexts and other kinds of impact—civic, emotional, perceptual, philosophical—in others.

My decision to focus on racial inequality as a cultural practice today, rather than starting with the conditions of inequality that we have inherited, may be troubling to some readers. There is widespread agreement that a history of racial inequality has shaped current inequality. We live with the baggage of history. As well, there is an all-too-common yet profoundly incorrect belief that racism is no longer practiced[7] and that the inequality we see today can be largely attributed to the legacy of our racist past. While I acknowledge the former (history *has* shaped what we find today), I reject the assumptions of the latter. The practice of racial inequality is sustained. It is sustained in ways that are important for the maintenance of inequality. It shapes markets for employment, law, public policy, and the media and our experiences as citizens and residents of this and other nations. I believe we should be historically sophisticated, aware, even humbled by historic knowledge and yet not shackled by earlier interpretive frameworks. Moreover, we must avoid the danger of looking back in order to avoid looking at the present.

The applied value of this book, I would argue, is rooted in a position I take—that efforts to remedy what I would call the static picture of inequality (the snapshot vision of how inequality is) cannot be effective without attention to the active practice of inequality. The active practice serves the status quo and sometimes even takes us backwards in our move toward racial equality. Moreover, practices of inequality even infect our best-intentioned efforts to remedy the static, historically shaped picture of inequality. Therefore, these practices must be unraveled and exposed.

But first they must be identified. In a national context in which very few people want to be seen as "racist" and in which we profess a commitment to racial equality, how do we explain the persistence of practices of racial inequality? We have two choices routinely offered to us. We can call the nation and its inhabitants hypocrites who say one thing and mean another. Or we can focus on the fact that a given practice of racial inequality is unintentional (i.e., that it happens through structures of inequality, that human agency is subservient to the wheels of inequality that operate like a driverless engine). While both of these options are partially true, they are deeply unsatisfactory and insufficient. I hope to provide a more satisfying answer to this troubling dynamic.

In order to describe how and why practices of racial inequality persist in the midst of an egalitarian ethos, we must be rigorous with the languages of race. What do race and racism mean? Who are we talking about? One could argue that a society like ours, where people report far less intentional racist sentiment than in the past,[8] is one that is moving closer to an eradication of race and racism and toward the less fractious categorization of people by ethnicity. The problem with this idea is that the absence of a *necessary* hostility to an ascriptive racial group does not mean the absence of a *likely* hostility to members of an ascriptive racial group. For this reason, we can find in recent history a majority of Americans saying they are not racist *and* a majority of Americans reporting that they believe the traditional racist stereotype that African Americans are lazy.[9] By the same token, the fact that people have generally rejected racial determinism by saying that an individual is not *necessarily* possessed of some negative trait because he belongs to a particular ascriptive racial category doesn't mean that people have rejected the idea that he is *likely* to be possessed of some negative trait because he belongs to that group or is perceived to belong to that group. Tanya Hernandez refers to this as the "Latin Americanization" of race in the United States,[10] referring to how racial inequality in the United States is beginning to operate the way it has historically in much of Latin America, where, while it is not deterministic and not shaped by a rigid system of classification and articulated ideology, it is nonetheless widespread and demonstrable through economic stratification, aesthetics, and bigotry.

Racism is not deterministic these days, and it is frequently unintentional or unacknowledged on the part of the actor. Race is not even a static category. Individuals and even whole groups can be seen differently in different times and places. And the agents of the practices of inequality are not necessarily White and may even be members of the group against which the inequality is being enacted. That is the most profound example of why I say that the practices of inequality are a matter of our collective culture. We all learn to participate in the practices of inequality, even though members of racially disfavored groups may be better equipped in certain instances to withstand this negative socialization.

This work focuses heavily but not exclusively on the practice of inequality as it impacts African Americans. The socialization with respect to the practice of inequality vis-à-vis African Americans has deep roots in U.S. history, and it is a national acculturation. Notwithstanding the popular eagerness to focus our attention on southern acts of racial discrimination against African Americans and therefore implicitly to absolve the rest of the country, racial discrimination against African Americans has always been a national matter. The fascination we have with Blackness in American culture can be traced to the manner in which the encounters between the Black subject and the American project have throughout history been the grounds for the public expression of both the fallacy and the promise of the American ideal, often in the most public fora available. And so that a Black man is the first person of color to be president of the United States is at once most improbable and unsurprising.

Today, among people of color, African Americans are the most visible in media, formal education, and public history. The minimal visibility of non-Black people of color is ambiguous. On one hand, it creates significant difficulty in garnering interest or outrage in conditions of profound inequality or simple suffering faced by those groups. On the other hand, limited visibility has the benefit of allowing more space for self-identification or self-fashioning without the influence of the powerful forces of media representation and ubiquitous popular narratives of the group. It is nonetheless critical to investigate the references in our popular culture to Asians, Latinos, and Native

Americans. Because they are relatively few, they can easily become overdetermined and grossly representative and therefore fuel largely unchecked stereotypes.

In contrast to the national culture of racialization that affects African Americans', Native Americans', Latinos', and Asian Americans' encounters with practices of inequality are more often shaped by specific regional histories, as well by moral panics around geopolitical configurations in particular historical moments, economics, and/or the presence of a critical mass of a certain group in a specific space or place. Insofar as I am offering a national picture of the practice of inequality, I am focusing heavily on African Americans. However, this does not reflect a political stance that assumes that the practice of inequality has an exclusive or majority Black subject. Rather, it reflects my observation that, with respect to identifying a specific set of cultural practices based in disadvantaging on the basis of race, all of us in the society are trained, socialized, and guided much more explicitly regarding our perspectives on African Americans than we are with relation to other ethnic groups. At the same time, there are trends in how inequality and bigotry are manifested that are found in the experiences of more than one racial or ethnic group, and I attempt to identify these, as well.

One might argue that growing awareness of the diversity of the United States and the greater acknowledgment of multiracialism and in-racial-group diversity, along with higher rates of interracial marriage and increased conversation about non-Black people of color in the public arena, means we are moving toward a fuller understanding of the social construction of race, disavowing biological notions of race, and accepting that race is not a black-and-white matter. But widespread recognition of certain demographic facts and growing intimacy across the color lines alone do not necessarily move us to a better place, racially speaking. Across the globe, racial inequality and racism have been expressed in a plethora of ways, ranging from color hierarchies to the drawing of racial distinctions between people who are phenotypically indistinguishable. In some places, race and class are inextricably linked; in others, race is more intensely connected to forms of civic and political membership.

Even in the United States during the Jim Crow era, a period historians have understood as solidifying the "one-drop rule" of African American categorization, there were isolated individuals who were able to traverse the boundaries of the color line, formally or informally, due to access provided by wealth, color, intimacy with figures of power, and the like.[11] And, of course, there is a very long history of interracial intimacy in the United

States that, although not juridically recognized in the form of marriage for most of our history, occasionally found expression in other legal relations.[12] Even when American race rules were at their crudest, they were not simplistically fixed. They played out in distinct manners in a wide variety of social contexts. In an earlier era, sometimes when an African American person passed for White, the person's mixed heritage was a well-known secret rather than one fully shrouded.[13] In an earlier era, we could have spaces in which Asians were categorized with Whites and others in which they were categorized as "colored."[14] In such instances, we could see inklings of a working of race that has broadened to what we have today. The holes in the sieve that allow for the incorporation of more people of color into full social, political, and economic membership are much wider now; after all, one could barely have imagined an Obama presidency or the presence of Oprah Winfrey on the *Forbes* list of the wealthiest Americans a generation ago. Still, we should be cautious about thinking that we are inevitably marching toward equality or that the sieve is gone.

The Chapters

The first chapter of this book introduces two intellectual frameworks. The first asks that we think of race in a way that takes us beyond the notion of intent as being necessary for the existence of racial discrimination. The second describes how racial discrimination can be rooted in concepts of "correlation" between particular characteristics and racial groups, rather than in the idea that there is a "causal" or necessary relationship between membership in a racial group and particular attributes or qualities.

In chapter 2, I discuss what race is and move into a narrative overview of research that demonstrates how racial inequality is a cultural practice in the United States. This cultural practice creates a devastating accumulation of disadvantaging experiences. Although it is based in individual actions, these individual actions are all part of a consistent yet diversely expressed cultural logic. The identification of this practice sets the foundation for the subsequent chapters' analyses of how and why the practice exists and persists.

In chapter 3, I argue that racial narratives are fundamental to the practice of racial inequality. They intervene into the processes of individual and group deliberation and decision making about how to treat others and how to distribute resources. Racial narratives shape practices on affective, rational, and moral bases. Racial narratives are constructed as both positive and negative evaluations, as well as general and specific ones. Moreover, although the cumulative instantiations of racial narratives about people of color can be quite destructive, the generative human potential for narrativity means that we should be attendant to how the practice of deliberately "shifting narratives" was important historically in making progress in the pursuit racial justice and that we should accept that it has ongoing possibility.

The work of the third chapter is extended in chapter 4, in which I describe how categories are used as the terms upon which to practice inequality because facially neutral categories operate as proxies for race. These categories elide commonalities and heighten distinctions between groups, yet also trigger information about how to treat individuals within those categories. Moreover, the categories, often brought to us through our political discourse, policy initiatives and research methods, truncate human experience in ways that allow for dangerous presumptions about groups of people. To demonstrate this, I do a close reading of the term "fatherless" in policy literature. This chapter also explores the concepts of merit and standards as framing devices that simultaneously exclude and offer opportunities for transgression.

In chapter 5, I use the examples of means-tested entitlements and the police power as the entry point to an investigation of the relationship between surveillance, privacy, and voyeurism in African American life. Further, I attempt to provide ways of understanding the connection between the experiences of African Americans and Latinos in racialized surveillance. The alienation from the right to privacy through surveillance practices leads to a widely accepted yet deep inequity in the protection and punishment distributed by the police power and destroys the accountability structures essential for any ethical surveillance practices.

I argue, in chapter 6, that the presence of "exceptions" to dominant racial rules and narratives about non-White people are essential for the maintenance of a racially egalitarian rhetoric in the midst of widespread inequality. An examination of such exceptions reveals that they may be individuals or groups and that they may or may not identify themselves through the formation of symbolic boundaries against other people of color, but, importantly, they are distinguished to a great extent on the basis of their differentiation from other people of color. However, they are nevertheless subject to constraints resulting from both individual kinds of racial surveillance and the rules of exceptionalizing narratives. I then provide a theoretical analysis of how to move past exceptionalism into broader incorporation.

The relationship between race and value is the subject of chapter 7. In it, I argue that the history of formally using race in property valuation and the theoretical concept of Whiteness as property are part of a much more comprehensive practice of attributing value to or of devaluing things, places, and concepts because of their high levels of association with people of color. This process becomes a self-fulfilling prophesy on an economic level and also makes cultural artifacts, institutions, and geographies harder to protect for people of color. The chapter concludes with a discussion of how discomfort with ascribed racial designations can and should be understood in light of the mechanics of "value," rather than simply "esteem."

The final chapter of the book begins with a recuperation of the concept of "freedom" as essential to the conceptualization of remedies to inequality. Using Elizabeth Anderson's critique of the supposed conflict between freedom and equality that has emerged in American jurisprudence, I present arguments that are imagined as identifying pathways to freedom, equality, and enriched democracy. I identify twin aspirations that emerge from this vision. One is building capacity in groups that experience the practice of racial inequality in order to counteract the impact of these practices. This capacity building is essential to supporting a participatory democratic vision. At the same time, I argue, we must aspire to build our capacities, as citizens and as residents of the United States, to diminish our practice of racial inequality through educational, civic, political, legislative, and social interventions.

"It Wasn't Me!"

Post-Intent and Correlational Racism

> Today, there is no longer any single articulating principle or
> axial process which provides the logic required to interpret the
> racial dimensions of all extant political/cultural projects.[1]
> —Howard Winant

Since the mid-1960s, Americans have lived within a nation that announces racial equality, democracy, and fairness as fundamental to its creed. During the same period, Americans have witnessed little movement in the most egregious signs of racial inequality. Although the percentages of African Americans and Latinos in professional schools and occupations have improved over the past several decades, these groups are still significantly underrepresented in virtually all professions relative to their percentage of the general population,[2] and, while Asian Americans and African immigrants have become distinguished as two of the most highly educated sectors of the U.S. population,[3] these groups are minorities within minorities. Ongoing and dismaying racial gaps in health, employment, education, wealth, and imprisonment persist. The American Dream is not lived by all hardworking and upstanding residents of the United States. While the borders to achieving that dream are more porous than ever, the forces diverting many from the dream are extremely powerful.

In the early 1990s, scholars studying race began to alert the nation that we were failing in our equality mission.[4] Their accounts were divergent, even competing or conflicting, but few could neglect the reality that the twenty-first century would arrive with the problem of race unresolved. Although academic interest was high in the 1990s, this message hadn't translated to an understanding in popular culture for the most part, with the general public reporting a belief that racism was dead or dying.[5] But things began to turn at the dawn of the twenty-first century, and while 9/11 forged a thin nationalism across our differences, it also highlighted our hysterical fears of difference.[6] The deep partisan division in American politics reignited debates about race and racial ideology. And, by 2006, the public at large acknowledged that we were faced with some sort of race problem, as evidenced by the decision of CNN (a cultural common denominator of sorts) to run a special series on race[7] and, in 2008 and 2009, to offer featured programs titled "Black in America" and "Hispanic in America."

Most of us, from our various points on the political spectrum, look to the current state of Black and Brown people in the United States—the persistent gaps in income, education, health, crime, and other measures—with frustration. Yet we are divided, in the midst of our shared frustration, about where we place blame, why we are frustrated, and what we think ought to be done about the situation. These divisions do not fall along simple race, class, ethnicity, gender, or political party lines. However, in the midst of a complicated set of responses to this landscape, there are two dominant explanatory frameworks provided in both the academic and the popular literature to describe why racial gaps persist, despite our nation's transformation under the moral authority of the civil rights movement. One says that racism has been largely ameliorated in our society but that gaps persist because of deficits (moral, cultural) among these particularly low-achieving populations (especially poor Blacks) and because of misguided remedial efforts that encourage dependence and victim complexes rather than striving and achievement. The other argument says that the civil rights revolution failed to resolve the structural inequalities that are responsible for ongoing poor outcomes for people of color. We are still seeing the effects of a historically, as well as contemporary, racially discriminatory society with inadequate policy and judicial responses to racism.[8] Although universities today are filled with those who have devoted entire careers to presenting sound evidence of persistent racial inequality, our popular culture sways in the direction of the former explanation. We are all quite familiar with the argument that, given that the society no longer embraces formal or philosophical racism and yet gaps persist, they can best be explained by behavioral failures or lack of human capital among sectors of communities of color. Depending on the political perspective of the authors of these explanations, the inequality may result from moral or cultural problems inherited from the oppressed generations past or from paternalistic social policy that offered handouts and expected little responsibility.[9]

Mainstream media conversations about racism in the twenty-first century have frequently been episodic responses to celebrity episodes of one sort or another. Sometimes public figures make racially inflammatory statements that hearken back to old-fashioned racist discourse and yet also prompt accusations that the subjects of racist language are "too sensitive" or "can't take a joke" because, after all, we aren't really a racist society anymore. Other episodes are framed around the treatment of a public figure who is a person of color. The treatment looks undeniably like racism to some and like innocent or easily explained behavior not involving racism to others. In both scenarios, what follows is a headache-inducing soup of outcries, humiliations, hysteria, public apologies or standoffs, a flurry of anonymous hate speech, cries of unfair treatment of Whites, abstraction from individual episodes to general truths for people of color, public outcries from civil rights activists, right-wing backlashes, and then the proclamation of racial exhaustion. These moments, which have the potential to be highly instructive, often leave us simply confused, angry, or self-satisfied (either because we are not like "that" or because "that" is unusual). The reality is that the media and most educational institutions do not train us to think about race in its complexity. We don't learn how to put together our understanding(s) of race in terms of material realities; everyday race talk; new, old, and corporate media; law; religion; geography; patterns of consumption; economic competition; and human interaction.

Sure, Americans generally disavow a belief in an ideology of racism.[10] But we must understand the terms of that disavowal. What, precisely, is being disavowed? What is the definition of racism that we have rejected in our purportedly racially egalitarian society? In U.S. race talk, we generally define racism as comprising two components: intentionality and determinism. More specifically, racism requires both the intent to disadvantage someone on the basis of race and the belief that a person must necessarily be a particular way or have particular characteristics because he or she belongs to a specific racial group.

Likewise, in constitutional law, with the exception of the employment discrimination context, in order to prevail, one must show intent to establish racial discrimination.[11] This is an extraordinarily difficult standard to meet and often requires a "smoking gun"—virtually irrefutable evidence of intent to discriminate. Rhetorical gestures (e.g., "judging by the color of your skin," "color-blind society," "I'm not a racist," "White guilt") reflect the way constitutional interpretation has dovetailed with the popular interpretation of the messages of the civil rights movement. Racism, in the minds of many, is a question of blame, what is in someone's heart, and the impoliteness of race altogether. There is an analogy to this popular perception in our constitutional law. In constitutional law, courts fixate on a concept of equality that depends upon treating "like" in "like" fashion, that is, treating person A in the same fashion as person B, irrespective of differences in race or national origin. The absurdity is that, in our culture, we know that our behavior isn't consistent with the principle that we are all fundamentally (a)"like." Federal courts have not completely abandoned the idea that remediation of cultural and institutional practices of discrimination is lawful, but they are seen as barely legitimate departures from the principle of equality.

The dependence on "likeness" as a principle central to equality also creates discomfort for many people over the differences we see and about our awareness of the aggregation of certain "differences" in groups. Who can deny the concentration of certain ethnic groups in service jobs and their invisibility in other professions, the state of disrepair in certain neighborhoods, and the rarity of certain types of people in others? In acceptance of a narrow multiculturalist poetics that was adopted in the late twentieth century, we can generally celebrate differences in food, clothing, traditional music, and (sometimes) language, but the differences that aren't decorative or entertaining aren't so easy for us to engage.

To say "I don't see color" not only is likely to be inaccurate but also reveals a central anxiety about race. Indeed, it is perhaps the fact that "no one wants to be called/considered a racist"[12] that animates our mainstream sense of racial justice. And yet the disparities and distinctions between groups are so visible that they cannot be denied. As a result, no explanatory frameworks for the "seeing" and "not seeing" of race emerge. In this vein, one deeply troubling trend is the proliferation of what Howard Winant has identified as a civil privatist vision of racial equality. This "civil privatist" vision is one in which "equality is strictly a matter of individual actions, of striving, merit, and deserved achievement on the one hand; and of intentional discrimination against specific individuals on the other."[13] Hence, the apparent disparities appear not because we "see" race in ways that lead us to act in a racially discriminatory fashion but because of the accumulation of behavioral failures in the underachieving "group" or the accumulation of behavioral successes in the achieving group.

But, as shall emerge over the course of this book, social scientists continue to demonstrate that in fact people do act in ways that reveal both "seeing" and distinguishing and advantaging or disadvantaging on the basis of race. And so the civil privatist vision is clearly false.

In truth, the racism we see in the United States is more appropriately called "correlational" racism, in which disfavored qualities or, for preferred groups, favorable qualities are seen as being highly correlated with membership in certain racial groups and dictate the terms upon which individual members of those groups are treated, as well as the way we evaluate the impact and goals of policy, law, and other community-based decision making. Correlational racism is communicated in a plethora of ways that provide powerful counterscripts to the idea of "racial equality." Certainly, the fact of disparities in education, wealth, and power can and do support correlational racism so long as those disparities are not explained in the light of historic and current practices. Additionally, the ideology of correlational racism is communicated outside the formal talk about beliefs in race and in informal ways that people can easily write off as not reflecting sincere racial beliefs but rather as offering entertainment or emotional release, such as jokes, pornography, comics, the talk of intimate association, adolescent social banter, and workplace chatter.[14] There are clearly both external and internal evidences of this practice. An external example can be found in research that shows that people associate Black faces with primates, even though it is socially unacceptable to walk around now saying, "Black people are monkeys."[15] An internal example can be found in the evidence of the impact of stereotype threat and stereotype lift[16] on student performance, even though it is unacceptable to walk around saying, "Black people are intellectually inferior."

That said, while biologically deterministic ideas of race (i.e., the idea that "Black people are stupid") may be out of the mainstream of popular currency, they intermittently recycle back in through publications like Charles Murray's *The Bell Curve*,[17] which identified Black people as having lower levels of intelligence in general, and through the comments of DNA pioneer James Watson about the intellectual inferiority of Africans. Although public outcries ensued over the work and comments of these men, the construction of their statements needs to be watched for indications of an increasingly popular riff on racial determinism; indeed, these statements can arguably be reconciled with the antideterminist and correlationally based racism of today. This is a result of the idea, present in both arguments, of "in-group difference." Neither has said that people of African descent *cannot* be intelligent—in their eyes, there is the prospect of intelligence among Africans—but both believe that the levels of intelligence among Black people as a group are significantly lower. For example, Watson has said that, while he hopes everyone is equal, "people who have to deal with black employees find this is not true." But he also says that people should not be discriminated against because of their color, because "there are many people of color who are very talented."[18]

The search for subcategories of Black people who possess deficiencies through practices like looking for a "crime gene"[19] indicates the presence of a form of "new biological racism." At the same time, the concept of in-group difference allows a logic to emerge whereby people consider themselves nonracist even when they feel disdain for the overwhelming majority of the members of a racial group.

The kind of racism that we currently generally decry but that had broad currency in an earlier era includes the following elements: a belief in the inherent racial inferiority of non-White people, a belief based either in biology or theology or some combination thereof, along with the belief that such distinctions should find expression in our social and political lives, through mandated or informally practiced segregation and domination. In the social science literature, this kind of racism has been given several names, including redneck racism,[20] blatant racism,[21] and classical racism.[22] While there are distinctions between biological/theologically rooted racisms and other kinds of racial bias, there is a murky space in which "behaviors" are attributed to racial groups without accounting for whether the cause is found in biology or in culture. Here is a sphere in which correlational racism exists and even draws in believers with widely divergent political perspectives. The stereotypes of Black people as lazy, stupid, amoral, loud, violent, and out of control have been in circulation for many years even as popular explanations for these traits have changed.[23] Even those who believe that such behaviors reflect social inequality may be likely to believe that social misbehavior has greater currency among African Americans or within African American culture than in the majority population.

There have been many theories developed about "new racism," including symbolic racism,[24] modern racism,[25] subtle racism,[26] racial resentments,[27] ambivalent racism,[28] laissez-faire racism,[29] and aversive racism.[30] And these theories have their critics. One line of criticisms has questioned whether racism today is actually any different from what it was in the past, suggesting that those with racist attitudes have simply learned to superficially mask their attitudes. Others have said that focusing on the sentiment behind the racism is a troublesome diversion, because it doesn't matter whether the racism is rooted in biological or in cultural arguments if the negative impact of the racism is the same. This approach is philosophically consistent with the "victim-centered approach" to problems of racial discrimination espoused by the critical race theorist Alan Freeman as early as 1978.[31] It suggests that the immediate causal explanation for the discrimination is less relevant than the impact of racial inequality and the structure of racial hegemony, which may take different forms at different moments but ultimately supports one particular ideological position—the superiority of Whites.

While impact is of paramount importance, if we want to move through remediation and ultimately achieve a society where racial fairness and equality are the norm, we have to look at how to stave off the perpetuation, the practices of inequality. And we have to do so in both practical and informed ways. One problem with ascribing old-fashioned racism to these times is that it implies that little has changed since the social transformations of the civil rights movement, and, whether one is satisfied or not with the current state of affairs, it is undeniable that significant changes have taken place with respect to racial inequality. Moreover, given that no one wants to be called a racist and that few will admit to being racist, why would we remain committed to a definition of racism that is dependent upon a self-consciousness about racist beliefs? Do we try to force people to admit they hold racist beliefs that they don't believe they possess because we have an inapt definition of racism? Do we encourage people of color to always assume that inequality has conscious malice associated with it?[32] As an ethical matter, if we imply that the practice of inequality is nothing more than a contemporary manifestation of old-fashioned racism, then we run the risk of accusing millions of Americans of deliberate hypocrisy, rather than developing opportunities to revisit how we define and respond to racism. Another problem with holding fast to the concept of old-fashioned racism, and even the term "racism" generally, to describe practices of inequality is that it limits our interpretive frame. Dave Chappelle's ironic skit about the blind black racist is satirical as well as instructive. We consider it absurd for a black person to be racist against black people. But, in fact, it is not so unusual for African Americans to hold negative in-group stereotypes about African Americans. African Americans have countercultures around race but are part of the larger project of racial socialization and so participate in the practices of racial inequality even as their efforts have been key to eradicating many of the most egregious forms of racism. Or, take for example this response to Glenn Beck's accusation that President Obama is a racist, which I read on many a message board: "He is biracial, so how can he be racist?" This, to me, is an illogical response, although I was sympathetic to the expressions of support for the president. One's parentage, lineage, and intimate associations do not determine the existence or nonexistence of practices of inequality. They may have an impact upon them, but that impact cannot be assumed, given how complex our lives and relationships are. We must look to how people make decisions to treat or respond to others, not just how they are situated.

Moreover, if we identify racial inequality exclusively in terms of impact, institutional formations, and unconscious bias, we limit our belief in our capacities to change the society in which we live. If we locate the problem outside our conscious actions, we also move it beyond the realm of individual or small-scale community intervention. In order to advance racially democratic principles, we have to maintain some belief in will, deliberation, and agency. Research in the fields of metacognition and "critical thinking" are established enough that we should all know that we have the capacity to think about and revise both our thinking and our learning. There is ample ground for hope in human agency and capacity for change. So, while our definition of racism need not be dependent upon intent or determinism, we must be intentional and determined or, in other words, willful about addressing racial inequality. We have to challenge the assumptions that accompany "correlational" racism and racial narratives in all their guises. As Banaji and Bhaskar write regarding evidence of unintentional bias, "Unawareness of the discrepancy between intention and behavior as well as the discomfort that accompanies awareness of such discrepancies cannot justify the characterization of these errors as anything but errors . . . conclusions about decision-making that are disturbing ought not be mischaracterized as benign or correct."[33]

The demands of addressing race today are distinct from those of a previous era. It is clear that the civil rights generation understood that the terms of the particular social, cultural, and historic moment had to be considered in strategizing action. For instance, the movement changed significantly after the *Brown v. Board of Education* (1954) Supreme Court decision because, for the first time in nearly sixty years, advocates enjoyed the prospect of having the law on the side of racial justice. Likewise, part of working for racial justice in the twenty-first century is developing a nuanced understanding of the politics of race in this particular moment.

That said, the fact that I am arguing that we should look beyond intent and determinism as signature elements in the definition of racism does not mean that intentional racism and racial determinist ideas are gone from the American consciousness. Any look at an online message board that has even a marginal reference to race will reveal extant old-fashioned intentional and deterministic racism. Even though the cyber world allows angry individuals to overrepresent themselves through repeated entries, the ubiquity of these assertions cannot be ignored. Following Obama's election to the presidency, White supremacist militia activity dramatically expanded.[34] Old-fashioned racism is still around, but that's not the normative form of practices of inequality.

We should no longer frame our understanding of racially discriminatory behavior in terms of intentionality. It is too unsophisticated a conception of discriminatory sentiment and behavior. It doesn't capture all or most discrimination, and it creates a line of distinction between "racist" and "acceptable" that is deceptively clear in the midst of a landscape that is, generally speaking, quite unclear about what racism and racial bias are, who is engaging in racist behaviors, and how they are doing so.

If articulating a deep antipathy for a people is against the rules, not just as a matter of politeness but as an ethical norm, that doesn't mean the antipathy necessary disappears. Rather, it means that the terms according to which that antipathy is ordinarily communicated and taught are no longer a matter of simple articulation. Our continued devotion to defining racism by the simple articulation "I don't like X people" reflects two things: a resistance to really addressing the antipathy and an anxiety about how diligently we must monitor the simple articulation precisely because the ethical norm of racial egalitarianism seems so frail in American society. Both situations demand a better toolkit.

To say we must think post-intentionally is also a means of escaping a problem with what is meant by intentionality. One could read post-intent as simply referring to the growing body of cognition research showing that there is a great deal of unconscious bias. But, at the same time that there is unconscious bias, there are quite conscious racial narratives about groups and places that are expressed all the time, in our humor, our entertainment, our schools, our news, our government, our places of employment, and on and on. When Martin Luther King Jr. said, "Let us be judged not by the color of our skin but by the content of our character," perhaps he wasn't prepared for the widespread impugning, in the twenty-first century, of black character, not on a deterministic basis but through what appears to be race-neutral evaluations regarding behaviors, culture, and morality.[35] As Glenn Loury notes, "It is a politically consequential cognitive distortion to ascribe the disadvantage to be observed among a group of people to qualities thought to be intrinsic to that group when, in fact, that disadvantage is the product of a system of social interactions."[36] It is not a simple matter to assess whether we, collectively or as individuals, are saying or thinking what we mean when it comes to race. So, rather than say that racism is now unintentional, I am saying that intentionality isn't a good measure any longer, in part because the notion of intentional racism truncates the realm of intent. An employer can intend to hire a particular person and make that decision while being highly influenced by racial stereotypes and yet not intend to be "racist."

One can promulgate racist imagery and ideas without having any interest in identifying oneself as a racist. One can decry racist jokes and opinions as morally untenable while acting in ways that diminish others on the basis of race. Americans have a long tradition of reconciling inconsistencies between professed values and cultural practices. These inconsistencies have existed in arenas as diverse as domestic norms, sexual mores, economic policies, political rights, and democratic principles. Therefore, we do not experience cognitive dissonance when such inconsistencies arise; rather, we cultivate explanations that allow them to operate in tandem.

In sum, our cultural logic allows us to easily distance ourselves from both the people who make mean-spirited racist remarks and the inequality of the society we live in. The problem is that such a neat package neglects a great deal of research that has been accumulating for decades about the persistence of race-specific inequality, its operation, and its meaning, research showing that our habits, attitudes, behaviors, entertainment, and a plethora of choices we make actually work to support racial inequality. The question with regard to this evidence can no longer be "What is wrong with the Black and Brown poor and how can we fix it?" Rather, the question must be "What is wrong with a nation where people act against the racial equality we trumpet, and how can we fix it?"

It's All of Us

The Practice of Inequality

The people must know before they can act.
—Ida B. Wells

Race, like sexuality, is a place where power masks itself as nature.
—Anthony Farley

To identify the practice of racial inequality, we must also have a framework for understanding what race is. We cannot talk about race or racism without good common definitions. As already discussed, we do have something of a (not very good) common definition of racism in our society that is largely shaped by our legal framework and our "poetics of citizenship." But what about race? Any collective definition can be produced only in fits and starts, full of partial ideas that are not taken to their logical conclusions.

One piece of this seems to be that we consider race to be an immutable characteristic (cogently expressed in the traditional Black saying "I don't have to do nothing but stay black and die," noting two unchangeable elements of human existence). We use the term "color" as a shorthand for race, but, given the physiognomic diversity of racial groups, particularly African Americans, and the racialization of genealogically and nationally diverse Latinos, we know that the term "color" is nothing more than a shorthand for membership in an ascriptive group. In truth, while we assume race is immutable, it is experienced in ways that are contingent upon some combination of history, identification, identifiability, moment (in time), and geography. In the epigraph, Anthony Farley offers a revision of the implied spectrum theory of sexuality to be applied to race, one that understands its structure as contingent upon situs and power. Race, like sexual orientation, is produced by social arrangements and political decision making. And these arrangements, along with self-identification, are generative of the persistence of certain conceptions of race and the introduction of new conceptions of race.

All of this is to say that we should take a phenomenological approach to race. The meaning of that is simple: race is something that happens, rather than something that is. It is dynamic, but it holds no objective truth. In the academic world, we often talk about "the social construction of race." The "social construction of race" is the idea that race is not something that has any logical meaning in biology but rather is something that we have created in our social worlds. If there is a consensus in most of the academic world that race is socially constructed, that consensus is at best a grudging compromise. Some of the many scholars who accept that race is a social construct make that point in order to say that we should eradicate race because it is a terrible fiction. Others say that it is not race but racism that is dangerous, that race, albeit entirely created, in fact has usefulness as a category, not least as a way to measure the existence of inequality. Still others argue that the simple fact that we believe in race makes it meaningful. Obviously, even among those who agree that race is socially constructed, there are important cleavages. What is irrefutable is that race has an impact on individuals outside their control. As Appiah and Gutmann note in *Color Conscious*:

> Once the racial label is applied to people, ideas about what it refers to, ideas that may be much less consensual than the application of the label, come to have their social effects. But they have not only social effects but psychological ones as well; and they shape the ways people conceive of themselves and their projects. In particular, the labels can operate to shape what I want to call "identification": the process through which an individual intentionally shapes her projects—including her plans for her own life and her conception of the good—by reference to available labels, available identities.[1]

Race is dynamic, and so, at a given moment, "racial meaning" may be in transition or may be in the process of retrenchment because of the impact of new or changed social forms or products. That said, if we look at the empirical evidence, we see that racial inequality persists today as a practice in the decision making of people at all levels of society. Or, to view it from another perspective, for people of color, many, most, or all major life events have a significant likelihood of being shaped by the practice of racial inequality. This means neither that all people are making choices that disadvantage people on the basis of race nor that people who do make such choices do so all the time; nor does it mean that every person of color necessarily experiences this disadvantage all the time, most of the time, or at any time. These practices are not absolute, but they are ubiquitous.

Although the concept of the social construction of race has not been articulated in a widespread mainstream fashion for the American public, the academic compromise mirrors the compromise over race that the larger society has embraced. When we accept the idea that there *can* be diversity in all kinds of traits within racial groups, we reject simplistic racial biological determinism. But even avowed racists today will acknowledge that individuals can in certain instances diverge from the norms of the group, and so the potential for lying counter to stereotype has been established. Some say that racial differences that nevertheless persist are a result of culture or cultures, whereas others say they are the results of economic or historical variables. Still others may say that there are genetic predispositions that highly overlap with but are not in total union with racial groups. This last perspective is least fettered when it is associated with positive stereotyping, ostensibly because it is not seen as "bad" to compliment an ethnic group,[2] but usually the flip side of every positive stereotype of one is a negative one for another group. Moreover, "positive" stereotyping can have an ugly underside for the groups positively stereotyped. The positive stereotype about African American athleticism diminishes academic expectations for black male students. The contemporary sexual politics of Orientalism in the United States, in which Asian women are "idealized" (and assumed to be nonfeminist and subservient) is tied to particular kinds of gender discrimination against Asian American women. The romanticization of Native American culture comes with an imagery that Native Americans are noble primitives, an ancient people, spiritual and yet not "real," and therefore the poverty and disenfranchisement of Native Americans in real time and space go disregarded.

Moreover, even though the norm may be to accept that race is not deterministic, we do express some confusion about the matter, likely in part because of our committed beliefs that race is an immutable trait and persistent ideas about inborn gifts and proclivities. Rather than relish the notion of race as biological, however, I believe Americans experience a constant sense of uncertainty and perhaps fear that there *are* some biological differences attributable to race, fear that is titillated by the sporadic outbursts of biologists like James Watson who don't believe that race is a social construct. This is especially troubling in the United States because it lies contrary to our professed democratic ethos. The idea that everyone has a fair chance in a competitive world as well as our belief in the appropriateness of electoral democracy presumes, at least in some arenas, that we are appropriately seen as and treated as fundamentally equal.

To read race phenomenologically is partially about the social construct of race. It insists upon a further step, a step of the sort taken by Appiah and Gutmann. Race is not simply created; it lives. And so, for example, with it come certain associations found in expressive culture: language, dress, style, and regional affect "associated with" racial groups. Race acquires meaning through and with all of these things. Race is also highly defined by stereotype, so that, even though an individual may reject or counter the stereotypes that go along with his ascriptive group, his experience is nonetheless shaped by the impact of stereotypes, both positive and negative.

These environmental realities and social practices are part of what marks individuals as parts of a "group." Indeed, while texts like Charles Murray's biological racist treatise *The Bell Curve* demand that we continue to engage in the nature/nurture debate about race, that debate may be a deceptive one as we learn increasingly about how social forces have physiological consequences, including: the effects of environmental racism, varying rates of HIV infection, incidence of nutritional deficiencies and low infant birth weight, slow physical development and increased exposure to toxins, and reactions to stress that are evidenced in brain development. There is no clean line between nature and nurture, although politics demand that we often speak as though there is. Rather, we might distinguish between that which can be impacted by the environment and that which cannot. And the category of that which cannot be impacted by environmental forces seems quite small. In short, biological or physiological phenomena can occur more frequently within certain racial groups without having any genetic basis. This is all because of the myriad ways in which race is lived, acted, performed, diagnosed, and treated.

Add to this an incredibly diverse racial landscape in the contemporary United States, one that is constantly informed by our global diversity because our nation-state defines itself against and in the context of other nations. To fully understand how this works, we must see race not simply as the line of categories described in law and popular rhetoric. Rather, there are a number of divisions that demarcate racialized insider and outsider status, self and other, that lie along multiple axes and have a variety of metaphoric expressions. And this is where power, as the epigraph from Anthony Farley argues, is intimately aligned with race.

In the field of cultural studies, much work has been devoted to developing an understanding of power not merely as structural or governmental but as something that permeates social interactions, institutions, and personal lives. Individuals have power, some much more than others. Wealth and position translate into greater power over other individuals and over the operation of society, both for groups of people and for individuals. However, people all along the economic and social spectrum exercise power in their interactions with others. Race is a key terrain for the exercise of power. The choices of how and when to exercise power over people are influenced by race and by people's drawing every day upon the culture's racial toolkit.[3] This toolkit is, of course, shaped by a historically rooted philosophy of race. However, it is not bound to that philosophy in simplistic terms. Even though the most powerful fault line of race in U.S. history has been that of Black/White, a descendant of the slave/free split in the antebellum era, it is important to theorize racial architecture in a more complex fashion, in ways learned from Patricia Hill Collins's essay about the "matrices of domination."[4] It has often been noted, for example, that non-Black people of color are often cast as being either "like Blacks" or "like Whites."[5] But that is not the entire story. In fact, there are multiple categories of racial difference into which people are cast, determined by nationality, exceptionalism, class, hybridity, geographies, and contingent physiognomies. As well, there are many metanarratives of race, a number of which will be discussed here. The term "metanarratives of race," used by the historian Evelyn Brooks Higginbotham, is descriptive of how other kinds of social distinctions have actual or imputed racial meaning. Social relations produce racial ideas and vice versa.

For example, there are at least two principles of social organization that have racial meaning: insider/outsider and high status/low status. We can use these organizing principles to imagine race being mapped on a two-dimensional graph. On the y axis, we can imagine the left side as "insider" (i.e., citizen), and, on the right side, "outsider" (i.e., noncitizen). On the x axis, we can imagine the upper half as "high status" (solidly middle class) and the bottom half as "low status" (working class or poor). Now, I have identified the categories by material and legal facts, but just as salient are perceptions. So, for example, Asian Americans and Mexican Americans are often presumed to be "noncitizens" even if they are citizens, or even native-born Americans. To take another example, African Americans are generally perceived as "low-status insiders." even though there is a sizable Black middle class. Furthermore, on each axis, the stereotype about distinctions between the categories has meaning for how race and racial inequality manifest. Distinctions between high-status and low-status insiders are often described in terms of work ethic, culture, social contributions versus social costs, productivity, and achievement. Distinctions between high-status outsiders and low-status outsiders are often drawn on the basis of immigration status (e.g., visitor, permanent resident, undocumented immigrant) and conception of social benefit or detriment. High-status outsiders may not experience the most debilitating forms of racism, and yet they are often cast as potentially threatening; in addition, like their low-status counterparts, they are often the targets of perceived scarcity. "They're taking our jobs" is a mantra born of that fear. Low-status insiders are formally guaranteed a set of rights and remedies that outsiders often do not. However, the distribution of access to those rights and remedies is asymmetrical, as class and race profoundly shape law, economics, and politics. Another important distinction is that outsiders are often framed in terms of their economic role, rather than their civic or political one. This is relevant because it frames immigrant "race talk" in a manner distinct from the "race talk" that surrounds low-status insiders.

Gaining access to high-status insider status is far easier for high-status outsiders than for low-status outsiders. Immigration policy for a number of decades has preferred immigrants of high status from other countries, re-creating a stratification that translates to very different realities in the United States. Being here legally affords one much broader access to the society and its institutions; being here in an undocumented status is an extremely vulnerable position. And that vulnerability is far greater than the "threat of deportation" that the popular media tend to emphasize. Exploitation, violence (outside or inside the home, from strangers or intimates), food insecurity, lack of access to health care or education—these are all problems to which undocumented status leaves one particularly vulnerable.

In contrast, there is also a small multiracial group of high status economic elites that function transnationally. Their wealth crosses the borders of nation states, they are the greatest beneficiaries of global capitalism, and they benefit universally from the economic exploitation of the poorest people on the globe. These individuals are a multiracial group. Those among them who are public figures may be "racialized" (i.e., seen in a popular light in terms of their race), and the way their images are deployed may have an impact on the social meaning of race, but their individual experiences cannot be seen as representative of any racial or ethnic experience or group.

Insider/outsider status and whether one is of high status or low status are two axes of race, and many others could be mapped. But, with nothing more than a rudimentary discussion of those two, we can see how inequalities exist between groups of people of color and that the nature of those inequalities can vary. It is not enough to identify Whites as an in-group and everyone else as a member of the out-group, even if we acknowledge that we practice preferences for Whiteness in our society. In fact, the perception that all non-Whites suffer inequality in identical ways obscures a good deal of the practice of inequality. There are distinct relationships to privilege and access between, among, and within groups of people of color. What is consistent is that being financially secure and White almost always is the location of the greatest racial privilege. But, as the nation gets "Browner," it is also worthwhile to observe how the category of Whiteness itself is changing.

The New Whiteness

Historically, the category of "White" was policed by the rule of hypodescent. Any person with known African ancestry was considered colored, and Whiteness was constructed around images of racial purity. However, this is no longer an accurate description of racial categorization in the United States. As the cosmopolitan elites of the United States have become increasingly heterogeneous, both culturally and genealogically, the category of "White" has become more porous and reputational, rather than genealogical. And all racial group membership in daily life increasingly hinges on the intersection of identifiability and self-identification, rather than on proof of bloodlines.

When the celebutante Nicole Richie pantomimed Black women on her television show *The Simple Life*, the show was canceled immediately thereafter. It was an illuminating cultural moment. In clothing, speech, and behavior, she adopted a behavioral blackface, all the more fascinating because, in adopting the behavioral blackface, she marked herself/was marked as something other than a Black woman. To be a Black woman was, for her, a fiction. And yet, she has been quoted numerous times as saying, "I'm Black."[6] "African American" is her formal racial self-identification.

And yet, if new media chatter is any indication, she isn't seen by the American public as a member of her self-identified group. She possesses a collection of attributes that bring her closer to the category "White" in the minds of many, if not most, Americans: light skin, straight blond hair, wealth, social intimacy with affluent Whites, a West Coast White female speech style, and an indeterminate genealogy due to her adoption.

Contrast Nicole Richie with the mid-twentieth-century celebrity Carol Channing. Carol Channing's African American father was a light-skinned man who passed for White. She kept her African American ancestry a secret until the twenty-first century, when she published her memoir. Upon publication of the memoir, the CNN trailer at the bottom of the television screen read that Carol Channing's father had "African American ancestry." Had she outed herself or been outed racially in the mid- to late twentieth century, it is likely that she would have not only experienced an adverse effect professionally but "become" Negro, Colored, Black. Today, she can be defined as someone who is twice removed from Blackness, the child of someone who had some African ancestry, without losing her Whiteness.[7]

In Bliss Broyard's memoir, *One Drop*, she recounts the revelation of her journalist father's African American ancestry. For Anatole Broyard, the secret of this ancestry was so painful that he was unable to share it even when he was on his deathbed. His wife was the one who told their children. The response of his two post–civil rights generation offspring was the following: "I burst out with a laugh. 'That's the secret. Daddy's part black?'

'That's all?' Todd asked."[8]

It was not a life altering revelation. At least not at first blush, largely because it did not have to cause a dramatic transformation in their life experiences or identity the way returning to the other side of the color line would have done for their father a generation earlier. Bliss Broyard spent years researching and writing a book about her identity and her father's history and race. But she could do so without an external transformation in her status or category. In her recounting of the revelation, she describes how her brother defused the situation with a joke: "'What a great pick-up line,' he said, 'I may look white but I'm really Afro-American where it counts.' The guys in my office are always giving me such a hard time for being so white bread.'"[9] The joke is instructive. The potential for adopting a positive characteristic (although one related to a destructive sexual stereotype) associated with African ancestry without relinquishing Whiteness, perhaps even gaining a cosmopolitan White status, is available today in a manner it wasn't when the rule of hypodescent was, if not absolute, virtually so.

This is a dramatic and significant transformation, but, as Tanya Hernandez points out,[10] the Latin Americanization of U.S. race relations (in which the categories are more fluid) does not mean much in terms of the distribution of inequality, beyond providing greater access for a small group of elites who would historically have been considered members of an out-group. As Patricia Hill Collins writes:

In this context, one can not only celebrate racial and ethnic mixtures of all sorts. One can even develop positive feelings about the music and dance styles of impoverished Black American youth. Privatization masks these relations. By making the marketplace the final arbiter of all social relations, the segregation and racial hierarchy that does remain can be attributed to the good and bad qualities of people who compete in the marketplace.[11]

Collins makes an important point. While we can delight in our ethnic and racial admixture, that public celebration obscures the way race functions. It makes race and its attendant features appear to be far more a matter of choice than they are. The facts that the general public tends not to be overly concerned with the genealogy of a racially ambiguous public figure, at least not as a matter of negative interest (multiracial young starlets are often fetishized for their exotic admixtures) and that we don't witness the same obsessive worry about racial admixture that existed in previous generations are further indications that we are abandoning notions of biological determinism and intentional racial animus. These signs are supported by growing rates of interracial marriage. People who oppose interracial marriage are generally perceived as racist unless the opposition is rooted not in race but in ethnic, religious, or cultural identity. It has become increasingly popular for people to speculate as to why a biracial person who is Black and White is easily defined as Black but almost never defined as White. These are all signs of flux. And yet, even if the category of Whiteness itself expands dramatically, it does not necessarily mean that Whiteness and other structures of racialization have decreased significance. So, what I am describing is a change in the terms of membership, not a change in the relevance of membership. Future chapters discuss the various means by which racial distinctions and privileges are drawn. For now, I want to discuss where, notwithstanding changes in race, evidence shows that the practices of racial inequality are alive and well.

Where Can We Find Practices of Inequality?

People engage in practices of racial inequality in a wide range of contexts, including individual, interactive, collaborative, and administrative decision making. Often it boils down to choices made in the context of asymmetric power relations, where one party must choose how to distribute resources or opportunities that impact others. In contexts such as employment, health care, education, law enforcement, housing, and more, the evidence demonstrates that, in the aggregate, people make choices that tend to advantage Whites.

The race-neutral justifications offered in each of these contexts are often accepted as legitimate despite the collective evidence that suggests that bigotry drives behavior. This legitimation derives from two factors. First, in our late capitalist culture, we have a conception of choice and preference rooted in consumption as a foundational right. Although we have a very long history of fetishizing property in the United States, in our recent history we have also come to fetishize choice. We assume that choice is good. However, race is influential and embedded in the process of making those choices.

The other legitimating force is the way that decision making is quantified and therefore seen as neutral. This quantification (either anecdotal or professional) takes place in the form of assessing risk, value, odds, and likelihoods and ultimately supports the static state of inequality, because a member of a privileged group is almost always presumed to be the "safer bet."

Because of Americans' resistance to acknowledging the existence of racial discrimination and because of the widespread availability of race-neutral justifications for the practices of racial inequality, those who "see" bigotry as shaping American culture and those who don't often remain at a standoff, both relying on what they perceive to be good information. And so, I will attempt in what follows to provide good information, using many different modes of analysis, to demonstrate that racial inequality is undeniably a widespread social practice.

At the Cognitive Level

As quoted earlier, Ulf Hannerz described culture as having two locations, within the human mind and in external forms. The culture that drives the practices of racial inequality in the human mind has been identified through a growing body of research in the field of social cognition. Here I want to discuss two articles, both of which were seminal pieces in American legal scholarship because they brought cognition research to bear on the question of how the principle of equality should be interpreted in American constitutional law.

In 1987, the Georgetown law professor and critical race theorist Charles Lawrence published "The Id, the Ego, and Equal Protection: Reckoning with Unconscious Racism" in the *Stanford Law Journal*. Lawrence argued that requiring a showing of discriminatory purpose before invalidating legislation as unconstitutional under the Fourteenth Amendment ignores the fact that racial discrimination is often the result of unconscious racial motivation.[12] Eighteen years later, Jerry Kang, a law professor at UCLA, published an article titled "Trojan Horses of Race" in the *Harvard Law Review* that had the same underlying theme. Kang drew on the substantial body of cognitive research on race that had grown in the intervening years.[13] He used the data to show how much racial bias is unconscious and applied that information to challenge recent FCC rulings that allowed for media ownership consolidation and did not enforce diversity measures.[14]

Kang cited data from a range of researchers, covering everything from word associations based upon pictures of individuals belonging to particular racial groups[15] to interpretation of behaviors (e.g., likelihood that someone would be holding a gun) according to membership in different racial groups.[16] The picture that he presented is quite substantial and suggests that most people in the United States have racial biases that operate on an unconscious level. Interestingly, while Kang didn't focus much attention on it, one of the studies he cited also demonstrated that members of a racial minority group might have biases against their own group members as well, evidence of an internalization of the biases of a society at large.[17] While we should not overstate what evidence of unconscious bias tells us, it does suggest that we might act on racial associations and biases at myriad micro levels on a daily basis. These quotidian interactions impact the way we experience life.

Cognition may be an individual process, but it has social dimensions. Cognition is both physiological and sociocultural. Our conceptualizations of things emerge from both sociocultural factors and neural processes. Moreover, the brain is altered by the social environment, as we can see in studies of development and impairment and trauma. Cognition is even political, including both "victims" and "perpetrators" and all the valences of the signs and symbols they use to organize the world.

However, there is a danger in the language of unconsciousness, even as researchers pursue such work with great skill and integrity. For the nonacademic or nonsocial scientist who adopts the language of unconscious bias, there may be an inclination to identify all bias as unconscious rather than to connect the very conscious and present discourses about people of color to unconsciously biased practices. Lawrence's critique of the intent standard in antidiscrimination law in this seminal article was important particularly because it provided a means for people to think about how racial discrimination had shifted since the days of open animus. Although the intent standard remains in antidiscrimination law, Lawrence's work provided a model for thinking about the practical application of cognition research as a way to move the society toward greater racial equality.

In "Trojan Horses of Race," Kang quite compellingly connects unconscious bias to conscious discourses about people of color by advocating media policy that expands opportunity for people of color to decide what we see in mainstream media. As Ulf Hannerz notes, "The defining feature of the media is the use of technology to achieve an externalization of meaning in such a way that people can communicate with one another without being in one another's immediate presence; media are machineries of meaning."[18] The challenge of thinking about both the media and the unconscious as sources of the practices of inequality is that they both easily nurture a sense of impotence. But, in truth, there is agency to be had. Although the consolidation of corporate media has diminished the possibility of all but one-way communication in their "machineries of meaning," there are democratic possibilities that abound as the world goes digital; the scarcity of "space" on the airwaves is not an issue, and the Internet has become ubiquitous and more democratic than the traditional media. Likewise, one way we can respond to the unconscious biases is to identify the choices that they motivate, with the goal of changing our behavior.

In the Choices We Make

If we are focused upon how present and decisive discourses and practices and choices regarding people of color produce and re-produce bias, then we can imagine individual and collective demands to undo that work. Unlike some advocates of the theory of structural racism, I argue that the individual decision maker's role in inequality is extremely important. The academic tendency to look at structures rather than at individual will is rooted in the profound influence of Marxist modes of analysis. But even Karl Marx understood the importance of individual consciousness in producing or sustaining these structures. Moreover, the cultural and critical theory developed from the Marxist analytical tradition has depended upon an understanding that there is ample human agency present in the choice of either confirming or resisting the status quo.[19]

An academic conflict between two important race scholars is useful to illustrate the point I am attempting to make. One scholar, David Theo Goldberg, criticized another, Jennifer Hochschild, for locating responsibility for responding to the "plights and problems of the racialized poor primarily with those closest to the problems: the individuals directly in touch with those whose values are seen to need transforming. These include parents, schoolteachers, social workers, police, potential employers and local politicians."[20] He negatively contrasts Hochschild's work with that of Elijah Anderson, who is interested in structures of inequality. Goldberg identifies this line of thinking with the "individual responsibility account."

I am sympathetic to Goldberg's concern that we may neglect large social forces when we focus on individual actions. And I find his and Anderson's work to have been critical for my own scholarly development. However, Hochschild is correct in observing that individuals make choices that sustain inequality. The problem is that individual roles are often assumed to translate to individual responsibility or blame. I am arguing that recognizing individual roles is not about assigning responsibility and blame; rather, it allows us to recognize that we have a cultural practice that is diffuse. It is not a top-down problem, orchestrated in insidious ways. If we don't look to the actions of individuals—social workers, police, parents—how do we believe in the capacity of citizens to effect change? If we rely completely on state action, don't we run the risk of delimiting agency or else locating it only with elites and bureaucracies? The accumulation of practices of inequality, internal and external, must be confronted. The problem is not that we disregard material consequences if we attend to individual action. There is a problem if we imagine only individual solutions to material problems. Solutions must also be pursued in and through the political process and in communities.

Race in Our Life Journeys

Let's consider the major factors in a person's life. You are born into a body that has certain facts about it: color, shape, organs, senses. The fact of what your body is and what it will become has no meaning independent of the society into which you are born. It is inherently arbitrary. But, of course, since you are born into a society, the fact of your body has almost immediate meaning applied to it. What is more arbitrary than the color of one's skin? And yet, not just between but within racial groups, it is apparent over the course of life that there is an economic value to having lighter skin.[21] There is meaning applied to the circumstances of your birth and to whom you belong. If you are born to someone poor and Brown or Black, you are at risk of being separated from the people you love at a very early age because of the operations of gray economies in poor communities of color, labor markets that demand the labor of the undocumented but punish their presence, and a dysfunctional social welfare system that applies child removal policies in a discriminatory fashion.[22]

You grow and live in one, two, several, or many communities. All of this happens inside the arbitrary body you were born into, which faces its own obstacles as you journey from birth to death. Your path through life is an interactive one, and the results of your life are shaped by a dynamic set of variables, including choices made by you and the many people you encounter and share life with.

If you begin this journey as a Black or Brown child in the United States, from the very beginning of your life you are less likely to receive decent medical care and a quality education from teachers who have high expectations of you,[23] and less likely to live in a safe community. You are more likely to be exposed to environmental hazards,[24] to live in poverty, and to experience food insecurity.[25]

If you are on this journey as an Asian, Latino, or Black person in the United States, once you enter the employment market you will likely earn less than your White counterparts with the exact same credentials,[26] and you will be less likely to be identified for promotion regardless of your skill.[27] You may go to purchase a home. If you are Black or Brown, you may experience discrimination from your realtor on the basis of your voice or speech pattern.[28] Because of where your home is, who your parents are, and their ability or inability to provide you with financial support,[29] you will likely find it much more challenging to purchase a home as a person of color, will be charged a higher interest rate for your mortgage, and will see less appreciation in the value of your home in the years following your purchase.

You may become ill. And in that illness you might find that doctors are less likely to order necessary tests or to investigate your illness fully; regardless of your class, they may assume you will be noncompliant with treatment.[30]

Perhaps you do something illegal. The likelihood that your car will be stopped because you were speeding is much higher if you are Black than if you are White.[31] In addition, the likelihood that your car will be searched is much higher.[32] The likelihood that a prosecutor will decide to pursue the case is much higher.[33] The likelihood that you will be convicted of a crime is higher and your sentence will likely be longer.[34] And, if you are a dark-skinned Black person, it is likely even longer than if you are a light-skinned Black person; if your features are African, it is likely to be longer than if your features are European.[35] If you are Black, a criminal offense is more likely to lead to the denial of your right to vote for the rest of your life.[36] If you use drugs,[37] get in an altercation, fail to attend to your child,[38] or play your music too loud,[39] the consequences are demonstrably greater if you are Black or Brown than if you are White.

But maybe you aren't a person who ever gets into trouble. You simply go about your daily life in clean-cut fashion. You turn on the television and see that people like you are overrepresented as criminals, jokesters, and social deviants.[40] You buy a car, a house, some other consumer good, and you are charged more because you are Black.[41] If you work in the service economy, you get tipped less than Whites,[42] and if you are seeking a service, the quality of services delivered is poorer.[43] You may find that the hair you are born with, the name you were given at birth, your features, your accent are all sources of discrimination that you experience at work and in your daily life.[44]

If you superimpose on all this the intergenerational transfer of wealth available to Whites and the paucity of economic resources, the lower rates of quality health care and education, the poverty, and the problems caused by immigration status that are present in African American and Latino communities, you will see the presence of inequality exponentially grow. But, even if we just limit ourselves to observing a contemporary active practice of racial inequality, one can easily recognize that daily life and life outcomes are shaped by race. But the greater question is how and why?

All of these things I have identified are the product of choices made by individuals in response to other individuals. Doctors choose which tests to order, Juries choose whom to convict, producers choose which news stories to run, studio executives choose which projects to greenlight, teachers decide which kids go into accelerated classrooms and which go to special education, social workers choose who stays with their families and who doesn't, restaurateurs choose to exploit cheap labor and hire undocumented people who cannot risk complaining when they are cheated and abused. Choices, choices, choices. Chances are the individuals making these decisions would not identify themselves as bigots even though we can see the racial preferences embedded in their choices. Many are likely to be people who identify themselves as victims of discrimination themselves. This story about the inequality encountered in the life journey and the data that I have cited is offered as evidence that there are cumulative patterns to be found in the choices that individuals make, patterns that are often not readily identifiable if one looks at the actions or beliefs of an individual but that emerge when one looks at how many individuals choose to act in the same way. In subsequent chapters, I will go into further detail about certain patterns of disadvantaging decision making, but I hope the general point is made here.

By focusing on the accumulated effects of individual decision making, I invite a consideration of the practice of inequality as an interactive reality. It rarely happens outside an interaction between the decision maker and the decided-upon. There is a substantial body of literature describing how people misread physical and linguistic cues depending on their race. In the following chapters, I will consider how racialized speech, style, and other cues operate in practices of inequality. However, because I am specifically concerned with how choice and power translate to inequality, rather than with questions of cross-cultural communication, I think the interpretive value of the literature on cross-cultural communication is to consider it part of the pragmatics of race, by which I mean that not only do people misunderstand each other, but much more is communicated than what is literally said, and, in those communications, both spoken and unspoken, we "read" actions in order to fit our preexisting racial frameworks.

Preferences and Ideas of the "Us," "Them," and "We"

These practices of racial inequality indicate that, even though most of us have rejected crude racism, we have maintained an underlying ideology of White supremacy and other hierarchal notions of race. It is not simply that White is a normate. It is a preference. It is also the case that in each arena, decision makers are acting inequitably and that their individual decisions have a cumulative impact. These practices of racial inequality are also clearly unfair. They reveal that acting in ways that are unfair is part of a cultural norm. This action is diffuse, and, importantly, it is not limited to Whites. In fact, perceived or actual labor and social competition among groups of people of color effectively encourages this practice between historically marginalized groups.[45]

Moreover, although people may not often acknowledge it, they do think in terms of their groups and group interest, and those notions of group membership coincide with ascriptive categories. The sociologists Lawrence Bobo and Vincent Hutchings have been leading scholars in understanding the relationship between group identities and contemporary practices of racial inequality. Bobo has described the transformations in the practices of racial inequality as a shift from "Jim Crow racism" to "laissez-faire racism." He argues that, while "we have seen the virtual disappearance of overt bigotry (at least in polite society), of demands for state imposed segregation, of advocacy of anti-Black exclusion and discrimination in the labor market, and of adherence to the belief that Blacks are the categorical intellectual and temperamental inferiors of Whites," that Jim Crow racism has been replaced by laissez-faire, racism which "involves a persistent negative stereotyping of Black Americans, a tendency to blame Blacks themselves for the Black-White gap in socioeconomic standing, and resistance to meaningful policy efforts to ameliorate America's racist social conditions and practices, with the latter views substantially rooted in perceptions of threat and the protection of collective group privileges."[46]

In the context of laissez-faire racism, Bobo has described how group position fuels prejudice. In his group position theory of prejudice, he links the decision making of individual actors to the larger social structure in which they participate. Importantly, Bobo identifies competition as well as symbolic racism as the source of the existence of racism. Applying Blumer's group position theory of prejudice, he "theoris[es] how social structure comes to shape individual psychology and socially consequential behavior. It is neither a sociological approach interested only in the macro-level, structural dynamics of race, nor one that defines individual psychological dynamics as relatively unimportant." This recognition brings an agency to the construct of laissez-faire racism. It is not simply a structural or instrumental phenomenon; it is acted upon.[47] Bobo pursues his theory by conducting research on competitive threat from the perspectives of multiple groups and examines the impact of competitive threat on policy attitudes and preferences. Finally, he uses the group position framework to theorize changes in Whites' racial attitudes in the United States.[48]

One interesting idea that develops from group position theory is that, while discriminatory actors might not intend to perpetuate racism per se, they might in fact intend to disadvantage the other. By that I mean that this may be a framing issue. The decision to "help people like me" need not be articulated in the mind of the actor as "disadvantage Latinos," but the resulting action might have that effect. Hence, this is another instance in which we must avoid putting too much stock into the concept of intent to discriminate according to race.

Social cognition researchers have considered group preferences as a basis for the practice of racial bias, as well. In their work, Gaertner and Dovidio have demonstrated that people will avoid acting in ways that are generally acknowledged to be racist, especially if they are political liberals.[49] However, when there is a space for discretion and when there is no public statement that such bias is evidence of racism, they will show preferences for Whites or members of what Gaertner and Dovidio have termed "in-groups" for the evaluating parties.[50] Two things are notable with this evidence: first, people interpret the racial implications of their actions according to narratives that are popularly held about what racism is or is not, and, second, parties may disadvantage people of color, even while vociferously stating that they are not "racist" and without showing evidence of any form of deliberate racial animus.

Moreover, Gaertner and Dovidio show that the bias is more likely to be present when it is possible to justify it with an alternative race-neutral reason. This brings us back to why Lawrence's argument about the turn to intent standards and race-neutral justifications in antidiscrimination law was so critical. In our antidiscrimination law, discriminatory intent can be inferred through a series of actions, but if the discriminating party can find a rational (and race-neutral) justification for the action, he or she is safe from having to take responsibility. As a result, our legal standard[51] actually serves a form of racial discrimination that is, according to Gaertner and Dovidio, quite common.[52] In particular, the creation of norms that are proxies for races (rather than rational ideals) serves a discriminatory purpose, according to the findings in these cognitive and sociological research studies, even if race is not explicitly referenced.[53]

In order for a court to begin to be able to account for this kind of discrimination in antidiscrimination law, it would have to do a multivariable analysis not only of race neutrality and rational basis but also of the relationship between the neutral factor and the presence of members of the suspect class and whether the neutral factor actually allowed a justification for discrimination, not only in the specific case but perhaps even in a larger social context.[54] This is an unrealistic scenario. Given the complications of doing such an analysis and the challenges of doing it effectively, it makes much more sense to allow states to remedy inequality through race-conscious programs, rather than force victims of practices of inequality to prove not just that they were victims of the practices of inequality but that the perpetrator intended to act in a discriminatory fashion.

This work on group preferences and identities adds another important piece to the puzzle. There may be some fundamental conflict between the way members act in the interest of their group, and their proclamations of egalitarianism. In particular, it may demonstrate why White Americans, when surveyed, may acknowledge the existence of racial inequality and yet be resistant to remedial measures for their "unfairness." In addition to what George Lipsitz has described as a "possessive investment in whiteness," it reflects, as Bobo says, a laissez-faire attitude toward inequality that is motivated by feelings of group competition that trump the national ethos and that is compounded by an easy reliance upon "neutral principles" in making evaluations of what should happen to groups of people.[55]

In theoretical treatments of sociological patterns such as Bobo's laissez-faire racism,[56] Gaerter and Dovidio's aversive racism,[57] and Michele Lamont's symbolic boundary formation (which is discussed in greater detail later), we see how racialized concepts of "us" and "them" shape interactions among the "we" of the nation. This us-them vortex doesn't have to be based in broad racial categories in order to be racialized. It could be middle-class-assimi-lated-Black as us, poor-Black-and-ghetto as them, native-born as us, immi-grant as them, light-skinned South American Latino as us, dark-skinned Caribbean Latino as them. In each case, the distribution of power makes those who are closer to the position of the insider/high status person (the financially secure White citizen) better able to have their preferences trans-late to material benefits or losses.

This all occurs in the midst of our discourse of liberal democracy. We have an articulated belief in individual responsibility and support the unfet-tered aspirations or attainment of individuals in a free market. Our popu-lar culture generally rejects any communitarian responses to evidence of inequality—social programs and the like—which are seen as not respecting the individual responsibility to sink or swim. And yet millions of individu-als are hampered by an ascriptive categorization that acts as a weight upon their achievement at every turn and that is not based at all in their individual qualities.

Changing the Lens

We cannot legislate away diffuse practices of inequality. But, by the same token, they are not beyond treatment. One way to approach this problem is to consider our intellectual history. We are part of a tradition that places great value upon reason. The civil rights–era strategic descriptive of racism was often based upon a concept that it was irrational, ignorant, and illogi-cal. The problem with such a conception, of course, is that, depending upon what one wishes to accomplish, racism may be very rational. It may offer an easy way to cut some citizens out of the job market; it may justify the exis-tence of a huge labor force denied civil and political rights in our country; it may facilitate the continued cultural social and economic dominance of your community in your town, city, or county. But, more than that, the logic we bring to decision making is always shaped by the epistemological framework in which we exist.

When we make choices about whom to hire, how much to charge some-one for a good we sell, or whether to sell (or show) a home, these decisions are made not on the basis of simple like or dislike but in the context of a decision-making process that we have learned through our socialization, our professional training, and other education, both formal and informal. Our decisions are shaped by what we know, what we think we know, and what we choose to learn or choose to use in a given moment. I would argue that the process of decision making that leads to the practice of racial inequality is influenced by visceral responses to assumptions that operate within the process of reason and analysis and that insidiously lead to inequitable and illegitimate discrimination. Certainly, practices of inequality cannot explain all intergroup disparities, but they cannot be discounted as a huge influence upon people's opportunities and outcomes. For example, research shows that physicians treat Black patients worse than they treat White patients.[58] At the same time, hospitals serving poor populations have less money and fewer resources than those with largely White clienteles. So there is a resource gap in health care, as well as differential treatment in individual interactions. However, then we must also consider how poverty itself is reproduced as a function of practices of inequality in employment and education. It is hard to think of a context where a present inequality isn't, to some greater or lesser extent, sustained by practices of inequality.

The other piece of this picture that must be reformed is our notion of the dynamics of discrimination. In academia, we often talk about structural or institutional racism versus personal racism. This distinction takes on several different manifestations. One is the idea that, even as personal racism has subsided, structural or institutional racism is sustained. What is often meant is that resource gaps and information gaps and institutional policies account for inequality of opportunity. The problem with the discourse around structural racism is that it codifies the stasis of inequality in such a way that it appears impossible to challenge it without revolution or at the very least, massive reform. The discourse of structural racism in my mind has lost much of its usefulness. It absolves responsibility and dampens activism. The language I have chosen, "practices of inequality," may not ultimately be embraced, but it is my hope that, in whatever new terms we choose, we deliberately shift our attention from thinking about personal versus institutional racism to focusing on how the accumulation of practices of inequality—engaged in by professionals, average citizens, and residents, as well as by groups acting in a common interest—translates to large-scale institutional, social, economic, and political inequalities. If we are to make that shift, with the ultimate goal of changing the practices of inequality, we must investigate how we learn to "be that way" and how to "be different."

3

Telling Tales Out of School

The Work of Racial Narratives

> A low theory, a despicable view of a given group must usually be thrown ahead like a barrage before we can follow with the outrage and mistreatment of that group. We make them hydra-headed in theory so that we may be inhuman in our practices toward them. Humanity that has climbed to places of social and economic authority must learn how to trace the rainbow tint over the life of the lowly, and to interpret the swelling and ferment at the bottom of society as a healthy and beautiful essay of one's fellow men in the direction of fuller life.
>
> —Vernon Johns, "Transfigured Moments"

Stories have been told about racial groups since the invention of race. Human beings use stories, or "narratives," to process information and to order the world. As older conceptions of race and racism have been cast aside, so have some of the stories we tell about race. Others are more firmly entrenched. Like many other stories within a culture, racial narratives garner an accepting audience in part because of their familiarity and in part because of the perception that they allow us to make sense of the world, and they are therefore replicated and repeated. In this chapter, we are concerned with inequality qua narrative, how racial narratives teach us to engage in practices of racial inequality.

Racial narratives can be produced by anyone and serve a wide variety of purposes. However, the resilience of certain widespread racial narratives can be traced through social and legal history as well as through the technological developments in media over the past two centuries. There are also racial narratives that have limited scope, geographically, temporally, and in terms of audience. Racial narratives can be both positive and negative with respect to the race or ethnicity being described and may be based in myth or documented realities. They are transmitted through many communicative tools. Most important, they are stories that do explanatory work and instruct.

Racial narratives are different from schemata. There is abundant and convincing research on race and schema. But schemata aren't stories. "Schema" refers to the mental structures we use to organize, sort, and simplify our worlds. Racial narratives are stories that, I would argue, facilitate schematization of race and individuals as racialized subjects.

The appeal (for my purposes) of using narrative to talk about race rather than schemata (which are very compelling and useful in many bodies of research) is narrative's mutual intelligibility across so many fields, including neurocognition, history, literature, psychology, theology, sociology, geography, architecture, economics, and the visual arts. Even though the study of narrative is put to various uses across fields, the meaning of any narrative generally remains the same. Moreover, narrative can encompass the rational, the affective, the physical, and the spiritual dimensions of human experience. It can allow for the fact that a novel can be more profoundly affecting than oodles of data.

A theorization of racial narratives is useful, but so is an understanding of how narratives contest each other. An understanding that narratives shape our behavior is important for understanding how race works, but equally important is an acknowledgment of the human capacity to tell and learn different stories with socially transformative possibility. In *The Literary Mind*, Mark Turner argues that "procedures and modes we think of as 'literary,' like metaphor, story-telling, parable, are not exotic or peripheral to cognitive life but in fact pervasive, central, and fundamental to it."[1] Other cognitive and literary researchers have shared Turner's thoughts about the role of narrative in how we acquire knowledge. Narrative is fundamental to the way we as humans structure our lives and operate within the world as individuals and members of communities. The use of parable, metonym, and metaphor allow us to project a given story into new contexts. Nowhere is this more salient than in the precedent-based structure of Anglo-American law. Narrative literally shapes the way we are governed.

The stories that are told about members of racial groups in daily conversations, in print, through the broadcast and new media, in literature, and in child rearing, are a fundamental piece of how we acquire knowledge about those groups. They also are part of how we make decisions about how to treat individual members of those groups. There is nothing unusual about this. Story-making and story-telling are fundamentally human. So, while racial stories may be subjective, cultural, and contingent, the power of narrative is universal.

What does it mean to acknowledge that racial narratives are not all cut of one cloth and yet tend to produce certain kinds of attitudes or behaviors? Perhaps it is enough to say there are narratives and even metanarratives of race but no singular creation story to make sense of it all. In an article titled "Culture and Cognition," the sociologist Paul DiMaggio argues that research at the intersection of the sociology of culture and cognitive science shows that cultural schemata provide cognitively efficient means of interpretation that are contingent, mediated, and often fragmented. Hence, our cultural practices around race may be reflected in cognitive research and may show the various practices of inequality, without our having to find a universal story that has trained us in these behaviors. Importantly, for the goals of this book, DiMaggio and the literary cognitivist Ellen Spolsky both recognize the potential to change culture even as culture is dynamically connected to cognition and cognitive development. Spolsky has argued that the genetically inherited epistemological equipment we share actually provides a means of avoiding cultural determinism because we can reshape norms and interpretations through our access to narrative and schemata.[2] Spolsky, then, sees within the cognitive dimensions of narrative the possibility for transforming the cultural manifestations of it. To state it simply, racial narratives have the potential to be changed. As such, while this chapter focuses on the destructive impact of racial narratives, it holds out the generative liberatory possibilities of racial narratives, as well.

In this discussion of racial narratives, I am distinguishing narrative not only from schema but also from stereotype. To tease out this distinction, I want to analogize to the difference the literary theorist Roland Barthes identified between metaphor and metonymy. He wrote: "Metaphor sustains any discourse which asks: 'What is it? What does it mean?'—the real question of any Essay. Metonymy, on the contrary, asks another question: 'What can follow from what I say? What can be engendered by the episode I am telling?'"[3]

While metaphor tells you something about something else—it tells you what something means—it does not tell you what follows from that meaning in the way metonymy does. Stereotype is as to metaphor as narrative is to metonymy. Take, for example, the observation of the Russian formalist Roman Jakobson, who cites a classroom experiment in which schoolchildren were asked to react to the word "hut." Some said that a hut was like a cabin (metaphor), whereas others that it had burned down (metonymy). Racial narratives not only give you a particular image; they tell you something consequential that will follow in the lives of people or characters in ways that are presumably reflective of their membership in a particular racial group.

Racial narratives say: "When Black families move into a neighborhood, they run down the quality of the homes and increase crime, and that leads to depreciation of home values" whereas stereotypes say: "Black neighborhoods are poor and dangerous." Stereotypes, while pervasive, are also more easily challenged because they have a totalizing quality that we are increasingly uncomfortable with. On the other hand, racial narratives have a greater potential to intervene in deliberation and decision making because they both operate in people's minds as knowledge and also seem less ideological. Additionally, racial narratives transcend partisan divides. For example, while the statement "Black people don't care about their neighborhoods" is more likely to come from a conservative perspective, a liberal narrative such as "African Americans have low rates of home ownership and high rates of poverty and so they feel alienated from a sense of ownership in their communities and don't keep them well maintained" and a more conservative narrative such as "Black people spent so many years relying on the government for handouts that they stopped meeting responsibilities to keep their neighborhoods clean and safe" both lead to the same core fact: "Black people don't care about keeping their neighborhoods clean." But often, neither the liberal nor the conservative narrative includes the following factors that may be relevant to the story: frequency of trash pickup and other public works, environmental racism, or the presence of drug trafficking and addiction, both of which impact neighborhood cleanliness. And there are many more factors that could be relevant. Narratives seem as though they are giving you more information than stereotypes, but they also entail the pruning of a lot of information, highlighting certain details and diminishing others, and a willing suspension of disbelief as long as you accept the narrative without skepticism.

Importantly, not all racial narratives are negative, and the malleability of racial attitudes evinced in some social science research may simply reflect the variety of narratives that are available for Americans to choose from.[4] Hence, Martin Luther King Jr. and the civil rights movement provide the foundation for a positive narrative about African American history. Another example of a positive racial narrative tied to "positive stereotyping" might be "Asian Americans come to this country with little, work hard, and excel above all others, and so they are more deserving people."[5] Additionally, one stereotype can lend itself to multiple racial narratives. In one example, Asians' success may be used as a counternarrative to racist thought, while in another it may be a means of heightening White Americans' anxieties about their relative underachievement: "Asian Americans are high achievers and so are more likely to accumulate wealth and complete with whites for benefits." For exceptionalized Blacks, the Barack Obamas and the Oprah Winfreys of the world, the rhetorical shape of their successes are often "success against odds" stories that operate as positive, yet exceptionalizing racial narratives. Their stories can say, "If you work hard, racism will not affect you" or "Look at the ascent of this person; clearly there is no racism." Rarely are they deployed to say, "African Americans are doing great things for this nation." But they could.

We use stories to make assessments and choices. As Schank and Berman argue, the knowledge that we use in our "day to day lives is stored in our memory structures as stories."[6] The stories we hear channel our attention and our relationship to the story is shaped by our identities.[7] When people identify as members of groups already, their willingness to accept and adopt stories that distinguish between in-group and out groups, or stories that negatively depict the in-group or out-group, is determined in part by who they think they are. Schank and Berman describe how we sort the thousands of stories we hear in our lives, and when we hear the stories of others "we seek to match what is being told to us to ideas we have already stored in our memories. We are essentially attempting to confirm the beliefs we constructed earlier."[8] Therefore, racial narratives can be, and presumably are, buoyed by the repetition of "evidentiary support" in the form of visible differences among groups. However, if we have difficulty incorporating stories with our confirmed beliefs, according to Schank and Berman, "we may learn something new or we may revise a belief."[9] On the one hand this points again to the transformative potential of narratives that do not support practices of inequality. On the other hand, the ambiguity and complexity of all kinds of stories means that if there is something within a particular story that coincides with pre-existing beliefs, that belief is likely to be confirmed even if there are other elements within the story which challenge pre-existing beliefs. As Schank and Berman argue, richer stories have more details that can trigger recognition of a familiar story. So, for example, the HBO series *The Wire*, which depicted the lives of police officers and drug dealers in Baltimore, was critically lauded. The show was unique in the diversity and emotional depth of its representations of Black men. But it is also possible that, despite this depth and complexity, a viewer who strongly associates Black men with antisocial behavior will experience the show as an affirmation of the stories about Black male antisociality that are already in his or her mind, while another person might recognize in the show the diversity of Black life that he or she is familiar with. Increasingly, popular media representations of people of color are more ambiguous, which makes sense because they can be more engaging to more people if there are multiple triggers of recognition. But what this means is that while I, in my African American left-wing experience, may see a television show or movie as an artifact that challenges biased assumption, another person might see the same show and experience it as a confirmation of stereotype. This complex ambiguity has made racial satire and comedy especially difficult to assess, as evinced in the public furor over the departure of the Black comedian Dave Chappelle in the middle of taping the third season of his show. He described doing a "pixie" sketch. In this sketch, pixies appeared over people's shoulders, egging them on to act according to racial stereotypes. Performing the sketch while dressed as a blackface minstrel, Chappelle described a crew member who laughed and said, "It was the first time I felt that someone was not laughing with me but laughing at me."[10]

Evidence of Narrative Impact

But how do we identify racial narratives, and how do we know they influence deliberation and evaluation? The realm of media and politics is good for answering these questions. The media are often a convenient straw horse for racial images, yet aren't necessarily a causal factor in racial narratives. They probably reflect racial ideology far more than they guide it. However, racial narratives can be measured much more easily in media than in many other contexts (although I think ethnographies of racial narratives in social life would be a wonderful research area). As the sociologist and cultural critic Herman Gray has argued, "television is a dense site of struggle over the symbolic meanings of blackness in the production of the nation."[11] The backlash against the civil rights movement may have begun as early as 1965, but it became widespread in the early 1980s, and its most powerful symbols were stories told through media representations. As Herman Gray writes, "The conservative claim on American national identity depended on the production and circulation of specific representations of blackness that could function as the centerpiece of manufactured resentments, moral panics and fears."[12]

And, if we look to presidential elections over the past twenty-five years, we can see how racial narratives have influenced outcomes for both Republicans and Democrats. Ronald Reagan's campaign stump speech, in 1980, about "welfare queens" tapped into an emotional reaction among recession-wounded Whites to the civil rights movement's remedial measures. And

Reagan's policies reflected that orientation as he moved the nation from pursuing remedies for racial inequality to punishing Black Americans on the margins of the U.S. economy. During Reagan's presidency, the U.S. prison population nearly doubled, and by 1990 the United States had the highest incarceration rate in the world. African Americans made up nearly half of the U.S. prison population in that year.[13] As Jimmie Reeves argues, "The war on drugs . . . succeeded in defining social problems that grew from global transformations in late capitalism (deindustrialization, job migration, the vanishing 'family wage' of a vanishing manufacturing economy, the flexible exploitation of fragmented labor markets in a burgeoning service economy, the rise of transnational corporations, etc.) as individual moral problems that could be resolved by voluntary therapeutic treatment, compulsory drug testing, mandatory prison sentences, and even the penalty of death." The narrative was that the behavior of damaged and morally deficient Blacks had failed and even worsened in the wake of remedial efforts that only served to debilitate them and encourage them to be lazy or criminal. The reasonable response proposed was no longer to reward behavioral and moral failure.

Media generally provide a powerfully influential narrative about race. For example, in a five-year study of stories on poverty in magazines from 1988 to 1992, the authors found that "Overall, African Americans made up 62% of the poor people pictured in these stories, more than twice their true proportion of 29 percent."[14] Comparable results were found in broadcast media. Moreover, in this media representation they found that "blacks are especially overrepresented among the least sympathetic groups of the poor, and comparatively underrepresented among the most sympathetic poverty groups."[15] (The most sympathetic were groups like the elderly and small children, and the least sympathetic were adult men.) The author goes on to argue that "Such a consistent pattern cannot be explained by the differential accessibility of the black and nonblack poor, and suggests instead that judgments of 'suitability' . . . shape the pictoral representation of poverty in the national news."[16]

Interestingly, the basic image of the welfare queen (a greedy and lazy succubus), like many of the most powerful racial narratives, was not new. Nor were those of the bad Black mother, the Black thug, and the Black rapist. These were images that could be traced to the antebellum era, when they were used as justifications for the control of African Americans in the form of enslavement and to the postemancipation era as explanations for the inappropriateness of radical reconstruction.[17] Just as, arguably, the civil rights movement could shift and create new racial narratives, the Moynihan Report could bring back old ones.[18] The nostalgic return to objective social values in the 1980s, which has continued currency today, combined with the narrative depiction of Black people as not possessing desirable qualities and values, provided a means for Whites of avoiding thinking of oneself as racist while maintaining discriminatory attitudes. Hence, colloquial formations such as "Blacks need to stop whining" could coexist with the thought "I'm not a racist." Also, values talk could obfuscate oppressive practices; thus, Mexicans at the bottom of the economic ladder could be valued for their "good work ethic," a purported compliment that was rooted in the grossly asymmetric power relations between employer and employee and the relative lack of negotiation power of poor and often undocumented Mexican employees measured against that of their native-born counterparts. However, when activists draw attention to the exploitative structure of economic relations and demand a modicum of rights in exchange for economic labor and taxation in this country, the narrative can easily be displaced with one about "illegal immigration" and the threat it poses to our livelihoods. Because Latinos constitute a substantial voting bloc, politicians are careful about how they deploy racial narratives in their campaigns, but the "long-suffering, humble, and hardworking" immigrant and the "illegal immigrant taking our jobs and living off of our tax dollars" are two consistent stories that both reflect and produce practices of inequality.

Thomas and Mary Edsall argue that both the competitive threat and a racially shaped moral narrative played a decisive role in presidential elections beginning in the 1980, writing that "Republican dominion over the terrain where religious conviction, the work ethic, backlash over social reform, conservative egalitarianism, anti-black feeling, and racial conservatism met, gave the GOP, by 1984, a decisive advantage in the competition over values, providing access to both a general election majority and to those specific groups of white voters most directly affected by conflicts over race."

As a specific racial narrative, the Willie Horton[19] imagery that was prominent in the 1988 presidential campaign between the Republican candidate, George H. W. Bush, and the Democrat Michael Dukakis did not simply say that Democrats can't protect you; it said something about how to expect Dukakis to act if he were to be elected; that is, he would advocate furlough programs that let rapists and murderers come to communities like yours to commit violent crimes. It was a story that led to interpretation and evaluation. It was sensationalistic and provoked a visceral response, but underneath that it had a logic that went something like this: "If you are concerned about crime coming to your community, then you probably should not vote for someone who will advocate policies that allow this to occur."

Racial coding and linguistic proxies for race like "inner city," "fatherless-ness," and "crack baby" extended the racial narrative by alluding to race without any requirement for specific reference. This allowed for a further protection against claims of racism based in determinism or intentionality. As Howard Winant argues, "The increased use of 'coding' was itself a reactionary response to the upsurge of minority movements of the 1960s, which discredited the use of overly racist appeals without obviating their effectiveness. The 1988 Bush presidential campaign's incessant hammering on the theme of law and order and its scurrilous use of the image of a black rapist to mobilize white voters exemplifies the ongoing efficacy of racial coding in the mainstream political process."[20] While coding in elections is explicitly used to this day, to manipulate voters, the reference points for coding are no longer dependent on explicitly racist narratives. They can confirm racial narratives that are presented as innocent knowledge without animus.[21] At any rate, the issue of prison furlough programs raised by the Willie Horton story was a significant factor in moving George H. W. Bush from the underdog position he held early in the general election campaign to victory in November.[22]

Despite the dominant discourses in which race is broken down along political party lines, the use of racial narratives in deciding elections has not simply advantaged Republicans. Bill Clinton, beloved by so many African Americans, also saw the benefits of using racial narratives, often in the form of picture-stories but also in speeches, for increasing his constituency. The coding began in his speech accepting the Democratic Party's nomination for president, in which he stressed "individual responsibility, using the term more than twenty times.[23] The party platform that year was "tough on crime" (Clinton left the campaign trail to witness the execution of a lobotomized black defendant in Arkansas, his home state) and promoted workfare instead of welfare; in the southern primaries, the Clinton team circulated a flyer showing Clinton shaking hands with a White prison warden in front of a group of huddled Black prisoners.[24] This image told this story: "Despite Clinton's Democratic Party membership, he will affiliate with the White working man and will also control Black criminals." In 2008, a Lubbock County, Texas, judge posted a photograph on the courtroom bulletin board of nine people, seven of them Black, wearing Obama t-shirts and being arrested. He later apologized, but the racial narrative transmitted the message that this Black president was the choice of Black criminals and was therefore a poor choice to lead the nation.[25]

Hillary Clinton engaged in this same strategy when she referred to her popularity among "hardworking White voters" during the Democratic primaries prior to the 2008 election. Those who would interpret Barack Obama's winning of the nomination as a triumph over this brand of politicking should remember that this strategy brought her a string of victories toward the end of the primary season. Moreover, Obama also employed racial narratives about the need for Black men to be better fathers and for Black children to take school more seriously, narratives that potentially confirmed the civil privatist belief that Black people are responsible for many, if not most, of the social challenges they face, while simultaneously engaging voters of all races by framing his campaign in terms of uplift and progress positively associated with the civil rights movement. Interestingly, this combination allowed for the embrace of civil rights values without re-engaging the question of what we should do to actualize the goals of the civil rights movement that Reagan cut short by translating the messages of his racial coding into policymaking and judicial appointments. Early in his presidency, Obama seems to have developed a strategy that makes high-achieving people of color highly visible in unconventional arenas, therefore producing a new set of public stories, while hesitating about pursuing any policies directed toward responding to racial inequality. It will be interesting to see what impact the stories of the Obamas and these other new public figures have on our consciousness. The CNN reporter Rick Sanchez interviewed his mother when Sonia Sotomayor became the first Latina nominated for a seat on the U.S. Supreme Court. He asked his mother if the nomination had any special meaning to her as a Latina. She responded, in Spanish, that it inspired her because "she did it by herself, without any help." Sonia Sotomayor has described herself as a beneficiary of affirmative action, as someone who succeeded because she was offered opportunities that were infrequently available to someone of her class and ethnicity. And yet her narrative, in this case and in many others, was reinterpreted in bootstraps language. This is in part because the dominant narrative of affirmative action is one that posits it in conflict with excellence and labor. The unquestionable excellence, hard work, and achievement of Sotomayor automatically drew her out of the affirmative action narrative for many viewers. Moreover, the unfortunately effective racial narrative that depicts African American as wanting undeserved benefits also often posits other people of color as morally superior because they are more "self-reliant." Also importantly, Rick Sanchez is Cuban American, an ethnic group that tends to be more economically successful, more regionally powerful (in Florida), and more conservative than Puerto Ricans, who share lots of social characteristics with African Americans. All this to say that the stories that were triggered for Mrs. Sanchez by the Sotomayor nomination were likely framed by ethnicity and culture and politics. And so, if we hope that public figures can undo existing racial narratives or offer alternative narratives to counteract the ones that encourage practices of inequality, then we must be deliberate, consistent, and diligent about telling stories that discourage the practices of inequality.

To return to a previous example, one that provides a less deliberately manipulative context than politics, we can look to the role racial narratives play in physicians' response to Black patients. This provides an example of the destructive work of racial narratives that cannot easily be attributed to racial animus. With some sensationalism, news reporters in 2004 provided readers with a truncated version of research suggesting that physicians respond to Black patients differently from Whites and provide Blacks with inferior treatment. The Board on Health Sciences policy report *Unequal Treatment* reveals that part of the phenomenon of racial inequality in medical care had to do with the shorthand work necessary for deliberation in medical contexts:

> The assembly and use of . . . data are affected by many influences, including various heuristics that introduce significant problems for recall and weighting. In conditions such as these, it may be assumed that cognitive shortcuts have significant value to any decision maker. Physicians, in fact, are commonly trained to rely on gestalts that functionally resemble the application of "prototypic" or stereotypic constellations. That is, physicians use clusters of information in making diagnostic and other complex judgments that must be arrived at without the luxury of time and other resources to collect all the information that might be relevant. These conditions of time pressure and resource constraints are common to many clinical encounters and map closely onto those identified as producing negative outcomes due to lack of information, to stereotypes, and to prejudice.[26]

In addition to reporting studies of physician showing features of unconscious bias and aversion, these authors also argue that the response physicians have to patient vignettes and encounters vary along racial lines. The interpretation of patient symptoms and behavior is shaped by physicians' sense of what members of those groups will do, and the responses of members of those groups are shaped by previous encounters with the medical profession.[27] The research shows that part of the physicians' decision making has to do with assumptions they may make about the likelihood that patients will comply with their directions or about patients' ability to follow those directions.[28] This is not a negative narrative per se, but, if the evaluation is being made along the lines of race, rather than on the basis of other signifiers or behaviors, it may have the effect of being systematically disadvantaging regardless of the physician's intent. It is also a quite normal, although disadvantaging, human response to the process of categorization, which tends to minimize distinctions within groups but maximize distinctions between groups and shapes how information is recalled about members of groups.[29]

There has been some public debate over the use of racial categorization in medicine and epidemiology, highlighting the potentially stigmatizing effect of such categorization. And yet, there are very real demographic distinctions that make collecting data on race extremely important in order to provide adequate care for communities of color. It is important to know, for example, that African Americans have higher rates of death from breast cancer. And this must be distinguished from the operation of negative narratives upon treatment decisions. That is to say, ignoring race isn't the appropriate response to the persistence of damaging racial narratives in medicine. An important feature of narratives that is also relevant for our purposes here can be brought from literary theory. The literary theorist Jacques Derrida describes text as a tissue of signs. There are multiple valences to the text. Often, we cannot simply say that a racial narrative means X; this is why the same narrative has different political and social interpretations for different parties. The problem we must confront is that our social practices guide certain ways of responding to a particular narrative and offer primacy to certain narratives and certain interpretations of narratives. The statement "When Black people are prescribed medicine, they often do not take it" could mean that Black people reasonably don't trust doctors, Black people don't care about their health, Black people often cannot afford to pay for prescriptions, or something else altogether. But if one acts to deny the medicine because of the logic of the narrative, the unequal effect is present irrespective of supplementary information.

Some of the sensationalized episodic outbursts about race in the contemporary United States are invocations of racial narratives. These narratives are less likely, I would argue, to receive censure than simple name calling or stereotyping; in fact, they are often defended as straightforward "truth telling." I want to use one such outburst, in this instance Bill Cosby's commentary about the names of young Black people to think more deeply about the work of racial narratives.

Naming and Race

> With names like Shaniqua, Taliqua, and Mohammed and all of
> that crap, and all of them are in jail.
>
> —Bill Cosby, quoted at the NAACP gala event
> honoring the fiftieth anniversary of *Brown*
> *v. Board of Education*, May 17, 2004

In this quotation from Bill Cosby, Black names are identified with social pathology, poverty, undesirability, low status, and physical unattractiveness. And such storytelling about naming and race has discriminatory consequences. For their article "Are Emily and Greg More Employable Than Lakisha and Jamal?: A Field Experiment on Labor Market Discrimination,"[30] Marianne Bertrand and Sendhil Mullainathan conducted a study of response rates to resumés sent to potential employers in Chicago and Boston. The fictional resumes were assigned either very African American or very White-sounding names.[31] The results showed that White names received 50 percent more callbacks for interviews. For Whites, a better-quality resumé elicits 30 percent more callbacks, whereas for African Americans it elicited a far smaller increase. The authors created addresses for the resumés as well, and their study showed that an address in a wealthier (or more educated, or more White) neighborhood increased callback rates significantly for Whites but not for Blacks.[32] Moreover, they found that federal contractors did not discriminate less than other employers,[33] despite facing more rigorous requirements under equal-protection laws.

The authors also examined whether race-specific names were a proxy for social class, judged by the education of birth parents. The Black names (generally African names) associated with higher socioeconomic class didn't trigger less discrimination than the lower-class black names (Latonya, Leroy).[34] On the other hand, the "White names" suggested above-average class in general (i.e., on average, the Whiter the name, the richer the people).[35]

The authors did find some differences among occupations. The highest discrimination ratio happened for administrative supervisors, in which case Whites were 64 percent more likely to get a callback. Executive positions elicited the lowest discriminatory response, with Whites having only a 33 percent greater chance of getting called back, and the second lowest gap was for clerical work, at 38 percent.[36] With respect to industry, the callback rate gap was greatest in finance, insurance, and real estate and smallest in health, education, and social services.[37] Interestingly, business-related professions and mid-level professional jobs elicited the highest level of discrimination. However, there was discrimination across the board.

How you interpret the social practices that might explain these findings depends in part on your theory of how racial inequality operates. One who believes that new racism is nothing more than old racism with a veneer would probably read this as a rather blatant effort on the part of employers to keep Blacks out of the interview pool or at least to minimize the number of Black candidates that have to be considered. Perhaps. But to know whether that is an accurate assessment, we would need information about what happens in interviews. Are the Blacks who get interviews and come into the office (the ones without racially identifiable names) thrown out of the hiring pool, and are they subject to some other weeding mechanism? Research by David N. Figlio in the Florida public schools has suggested that children with distinctively African American names are less likely to be recommended for gifted programs (although more likely to be promoted).[38] He theorizes that teachers associate the Black names with low parental involvement or socio-economic status and therefore don't recommend the children for gifted programs. Yet the fact that the students with distinctively Black names are more likely to be promoted suggests that some positive racial identity comes along with the distinctively Black names that increases school success.[39] In contrast, he finds that Asian children with racially distinctive names are more likely to be recommended for gifted programs,[40] indicating that the name's "Asianness" is connected to positive assumptions about intelligence or school success. Moreover, the fact that, within families, if a child has a distinctively Black name, he is less likely to be recommended for a gifted program than a sibling with a more mainstream name[41] further indicates that what is at work is a negative association with the Blackness of the name, rather than some familial feature or all Black people. This research indicates that the aversion is not a thinly veiled form of old-fashioned racism but rather a negative association with something that is distinctively Black. The names may be a sign of undesirability because they are associated with Black people, and this association may well have a significant disparate impact on Black students or employees without being intentional or absolute or even eliminating all Black people from consideration. On the other hand, the experiences of an individual party with a "Black" name may be unfairly influenced because of people's reaction to that name, which, while not an immutable characteristic, may be a powerful racial proxy or signifier.

An article by Roland Fryer and Steven Levitt considers, however, why the authors' research doesn't confirm that having a distinctively Black name creates economic disadvantage.[42] The outcomes are virtually the same, regardless of how "Black" a person's name. They theorize that names reflect socioeconomic status (and also skills and marketability), rather than cause it. To make this point, they cite the concentration of distinctively Black names in the most segregated and impoverished communities.[43] How, then, do we account for David Figlio's research, which suggests that, even within a family, a name can operate as an educational disadvantage? Perhaps it would be useful to think of the name-based discrimination as just one of many proxies for race that operate in a person's life, along with language, dress, address, and so forth. While a child named Michael (an extremely popular name for African American boys of all social classes) may not be disadvantaged by his name, there may be some other distinctively Black feature that he carries that operates to disadvantage him according to a racial narrative.[44]

The name narrative is tied to the practice of inequality and should alert us to a need for antidiscrimination law to revisit what we mean by discrimination. How should this be treated legally? Should claims be allowed on the basis of name-discrimination as a proxy for race? How do you collect the evidence? How do you distinguish between the names? Is Monique (a very popular African American names) to be treated the same way as LaKeisha? Should Arabic names, so popular among African Americans, be given the same treatment as those that are of African American vintage? If those with Arabic names are being discriminated against, do we assume that discrimination is based upon national origin or race? How should the disadvantage faced by a White person with a Black-sounding name be treated? What becomes clear rather quickly is that any resolution would not protect everyone; it would also be quite difficult to show what exactly the Title VII violation was and to figure out how to establish a class, case, or controversy. How many different iterations of this kind of problem could one find? The possibilities are seemingly countless because of the myriad correlations between race and other factors. For example, researchers have found that employers have used neighborhood, address, or city or suburban school attendance as screening devices for employees; all of these operate as proxies for race and class.[45] While it is useful to maintain standards of review in order to enforce social norms, it is unclear how we would create a coherent framework in law that could address such inequalities. In fact, what is clear is that affirmative action is one of the few clear ways to address disadvantaging behaviors that are based in racial proxies or signifiers.

Interestingly, while Bill Cosby participated in a classist discourse about Black names, he has also been the principal agent of positive narratives of working and middle-class Black life, which quite explicitly embrace African American high and popular culture. Such representations in shows like *The Cosby Show,* the subsequent *Cosby,* and the children's program *Little Bill,* however, are rare. The majority of representations are quite different.

There is also the problem of representation. Race stories often emerge as stories about people of an ascriptive group that are taken as representative by virtue of their frequency or prominence or because viewers are encouraged to see them as representative. In mainstream hip hop as well as in reality television, claims to ghetto authenticity operate as encouragements for viewers to take those particular individuals as representative examples of residents of poor urban communities of color. The sensationalism of those media, however, encourages the exaggeration and caricaturing of stereotypic behavior in ways that belie the very authenticity claimed. The viewer (or listener, in the case of music) is encouraged to make generalizations in ways that may be unfounded. It is hard to measure the impact of such imagery, beyond observing its popularity. It taps into something by garnering a substantial audience and the cultural imagination. We should also note that there are loci of control in all popular media entities that are not simply dictating imagery but marketing products on the basis of longstanding biases, prejudices, and stories.

Like stereotypes, racial narratives are not always objectively negative. They may contain a negative underside to a positive face. Asian American critical theory explores the question of whether discrimination against Asians often occurs because the presumption is that Asian Americans are too compliant to speak out against discrimination, at the same time as that stereotypic compliance has historically been used as part of "positive" stereotyping of Asian Americans as different from other troublemaking people of color.

The question of the truth of racial narratives must depend upon what we mean by truth. Some racial narratives are blatantly false, others are overdetermined, and others have a high correlation but certainly not a perfect correlation with qualities of the ascriptive group. Others have a high correlation not only to the ascriptive group but also to other groups not weighted with that story. The impact of such narratives as race stories is potentially quite significant beyond their perceived truth, because certainly narrative shapes the truth that people experience. The problem with the narrative presented as truth is that it often turns into a deterministic and exceptionalizing account of individuals and groups.

Moreover, racial narratives in the marketplace are also often commoditized. The products of the media version of racial narratives (television shows) bank upon a saleable image of ascriptive groups. The market winners of the sale of these images may be of any color. We should be careful not to assume because the images may be sold or profited from by a member of a disfavored ascriptive group that they are not racist. Chris Tucker and Jackie Chan's presence in the *Rush Hour* films do nothing to discount the deep racism in the representations of Asian and Black people in the movies. At the same time that we acknowledge that individuals operate as representatives vis-à-vis the impact of racial narratives, we should not make the mistake of believing that individual experience with a particular artifact that entails a racial narrative tells us whether it is a good or bad thing. For Chris Tucker and Jackie Chan, there may be great personal advantage to participating in stereotypic images. It doesn't hurt them individually. However, the cultural life of Tucker and Chan and the extra images coincide with narratives that operate in the conscious or subconscious minds of many individuals who choose to advantage or disadvantage Black and Asian individuals on the basis of racial group membership.

Getting from Punishment to Skepticism and Narrative Shifting

The punitive application of racial narratives is always ethically suspect and should be confronted. By punitive I mean an application that denies opportunity or services or resources, diminishes the range of someone's humanity, and fails to recognize individuals and groups in the sense in which "recognition" is used in political theory—as indicating respect and an acknowledgement of civic participation. Confronting the punitive application of racial narratives can occur in many different kinds of context.

It can occur when a professional association responds to a report showing widespread practices of inequality by revising or re-establishing standards of care that address the practice of inequality. It can occur when bureaucratic structures maintain oversight of differential treatment within administrative and policymaking agencies.

It can also occur if individuals and groups dedicate themselves to maintaining deep skepticism about all racial narratives that are attached to denying access, resources, or services. Imagine a teacher is hired to work in a school in a poor community of color. Imagine that this teacher sets up a parent-teacher association. She schedules a series of PTA meetings, and almost no parents show up. Her fellow teachers and the mainstream news media and film industry may tell her, "The parents don't show up because they do not care about their children's success." And she may decide that her efforts to involve parents in their children's education are all for naught. Or, she may embrace a skepticism about this racial narrative. A skepticism about this narrative would demand certain kinds of investigations. She might ask parents what keeps them from coming to the meetings. She might try to determine their work schedules and access to child care and schedule meetings that accommodate parents' schedules. She might encourage grandparents, extended family members, older siblings, and other adults who are involved in the kids' lives to come to the school if the parents are unable. She might make a concerted effort to explain in a detailed way how even parents who are overextended can nevertheless support their children's academic achievement. She might encourage families to create a buddy system whereby they can work together to support their kids academic achievement if the challenges are too great for one or two adults to effectively pursue on their own. She might ask parents, "What do you want for your children" and then offer them ten concrete steps that facilitate reaching those goals. All of these possibilities open up if the teacher remains skeptical of the racial narrative that encourages disengagement or judgment rather than increased engagement and creative and concerted problem solving.

Skepticism about racial narratives is also warranted because of the evidence showing that in many instances racial narratives lead us to trust bad evidence over good evidence. President Obama and many other public figures have decried the phenomenon of African American children who believe that doing well in school is "acting White." Anecdotally, people rally around this claim, especially high-achieving or middle- and upper-class African Americans who feel as though their authenticity has been challenged by other Blacks because they are successful. The scholarly origins of this idea were found in the work of the sociologist John Ogbu, who studied eight African American high school students. However, the majority of subsequent researchers studying the phenomenon have shown that this argument that Black youth do poorly because they think that doing well academically is "acting White" is not substantiated. Darity and Tyson write, "Social scientists have produced little empirical evidence to substantiate the claim that an 'oppositional peer culture' or 'a burden of acting white' is pervasive in the black community or that either explains the underachievement of black students or some part of the black-white achievement gap."[46] Yet, the anecdotal is relied upon as good evidence, even making its way into Barack Obama's speech at the 2004 Democratic Convention, in which he said, "Go into any inner-city neighborhood, and folks will tell you that government alone can't teach kids to learn. They know that parents have to parent, that children can't achieve unless we raise their expectations and turn off the television sets and eradicate the slander that says a Black youth with a book is acting White." This is an anecdotal truism that runs counter to the evidence. But people readily believe it (including many Black people) because of the mainstream narrative, promoted in popular film and television,[47] that Black people don't value education, despite abundant research and history to the contrary.[48] What impact does this truism have on teachers, guidance counselors, and employers who encounter young African Americans? And, in turn, how does the treatment of young African Americans perversely produce results that appear to confirm the stereotype?

Indeed, the narrative is a very convincing one in the eyes of many Americans. But then there are the kids associated with The Young People's Project in Baltimore. The students (a multiracial but largely African American group) of their own volition began to protest the inadequate education they were receiving in the Baltimore city schools, including the lack of advanced placement courses, expert teachers, and equal funding and the failure of the state to comply with the 2002 legislation mandating improvements in funding and curriculum in Baltimore's public schools.[49] These students tell a story that is supported by the social science research and that runs counter to the anecdotal mythology. They *do* want to achieve academically. They shift the narrative by acting as citizens, as members of the social contract, and the narrative shifting is both internal and external. They exemplify how, at any time, communities can choose too "shift narratives" or, as Theresa Perry describes it in the context of education, provide "counternarratives." Not only do these young people adopt a group membership and a self-definition that are framed by aspiration and engagement rather than by failure but also they identify themselves to others as those who long for achievement. It provides a way of being and acting that has resonance for those students and, one hopes, for the world at large. This strategy is rooted in traditional activism in African American communities. During the civil rights movement, activists performed citizenship even as benefits of citizenship were denied. The Mississippi Freedom Democratic Party chose delegates for the national convention in 1964, having conducted a freedom vote, even when the state party as a matter of policy and practice did not count Black voters. In that process, Black Mississippians redefined their citizenship by rewriting the democratic process leading up to the election. And such practices go back even further. When the abolitionist Frederick Douglass broke from Garrisonian abolitionism and decided to embrace the Constitution (Garrison declared it fundamentally illegitimate because it allowed slave ownership), he told a different story about the meanings of freedom and liberty and personhood, one that included Black people who were then noncitizens.

In 2006, marches across the nation advocating for reform in immigration policy with respect to Mexico and Central America were framed around the concept "A day without immigrants," a riff on the theatrical production *A Day of Absence*, Douglas Turner Ward's satirical social commentary about what would happen in a southern town if all African Americans disappeared one day. In using the civil rights strategy of marching, in arguing that the distinction between legal and illegal residents was a false one when it came to contributions to the society, and in engaging millions of marchers of varying immigration statuses and ethnicities, the marches offered alternative racial narratives to the standard ones about Latinos. This narrative was about denial of rights to members of our social contract, not whether or not "illegals" should be given all the benefits afforded to citizens. This was a powerful narrative-shifting moment that awakened a new politics around race and legal status for many Americans.

I don't mean to suggest that these moments of narrative shifting have immediate transformative impact. Rather, I am arguing that we need to explicitly revisit them as a part of the project of racial equality, both at the level of government and law and at the level of community-based activism and family life.

4

The House That Jack Built

Inequality via Category

The language of the prevailing Law and Order... is not only the
voice but also the deed of suppression. This language not only
defined and condemns the Enemy, it also creates him.

—Herbert Marcuse[1]

In this chapter, we consider how categories—those applied in
research, policy, and popular culture—are tools for the maintenance of racial
inequality. It is not a revelation that the categorization of people or things by
bureaucrats and members of the intelligentsia both is common and produces
hierarchies, imputes moralities, and distinguishes classes of people in ways that
make constructed differences seem like natural or inherent ones. Both Michel
Foucault and Herbert Marcuse devoted significant attention to this function
of naming and categorizing. We categorize human beings for research, commerce, and bureaucratic management. These categories are often racialized by
virtue of the statistical overrepresentation of some racial group in a particular category or because of media imagery and broader racial narratives. The
point, then, is not to argue that the preponderance of certain groups in certain
categories is false but rather to discuss the meaning and interpretation of such
categories and to consider the impact of choosing certain kinds of racialized
categorizations over other potential ways of categorizing people.

Moreover, I am only partly concerned with arguing that categorizations
of people are racialized, often in ways that identify people of color as morally or socially inferior and stratify those deemed "like them" in lower ranks.
That is rather obvious. More broadly, I want to pose a discussion about how
the rubrics applied to the management of categories of people operate to
entrench difference and inequality.

These categories are troubling on three distinctive fronts, all of which support the practice of inequality. First, the categories in their shorthand appli-

cations are often consistently inaccurate, either because they truncate facts or because they draw lines of distinction in incoherent or illogical ways. Thus, problems get identified incorrectly, and problematic interventions ensue.

Second, the focus on category that we find in quantitative research in particular, and in its pop cultural derivatives in policy chatter, flattens humanity in ways that are particularly dangerous, given the prevalence of racial stereotypes and the destructive narratives in our media culture. The "texts" of quantitative research get put alongside the fictional or creative nonfictional texts of popular media in our assessments of the world, dictating an interpretation of the categories that lacks human sensitivity or complexity.

Third, the manner in which categories get imagined on a structural or interpretive level (silhouettes and rubrics) sets terms for "inclusion" or "incorporation" that are based upon notions of ideal social and domestic relations that should not be given the default presumption of superiority.

To offer an example of a category that operates in these problematic ways, I want to discuss what has been termed the "crisis of fatherlessness" in the African American community.

Fatherlessness and Other Words of Exclusion

There has been a great deal of moral panic in the early years of the twenty-first century about the problem of "fatherlessness." The term "fatherless" is a provocative one because it implies not disengagement or the irresponsibility but rather complete nonexistence. The use of the term in popular media is not a case, however, of an effort to sensationalize research. Even at the level of policy, the term is used in this overdetermined way. Documents such as "Building Blocks for Father Involvement," published by the U.S. Department of Health and Human Services, use the term quite often. This representative document contains statements such as "The United States is the world's leader in fatherless families."[2] The footnote for this comment cites data, however, that detail the number of children not living in the same home as their fathers rather than children who don't know their fathers, children whose fathers have died, or children who know who their fathers are but who have not met them. Likewise, one can find the term "fatherless" applied generally to children born out of wedlock. A category like "fatherless" is quite different from that of "child living with one parent." The latter includes many children of divorce, widowing, and the like, whereas the former refers to a child born out of wedlock and has recently become a racialized term as greater attention is paid to the large number of African American children born out of wedlock. Obviously, this distinction has dramatic implications for how we "see" families with unmarried parents. It begs the question of what it means to impute nonexistence to any man who does not have a formal domestic or legal relationship to the mother of his children, particularly in a national context in which the rate of out-of-wedlock birth is highest among African Americans.

The erasure of the father in statistical reportage when the father does not have a state-recognized relationship to the child via marriage (present or past) means that the structural relation is given primacy over the substantive one. By that I mean that marriage is given greater significance than the human relationship. Evidence that African American fathers of children born out of wedlock, on average, spend more time with their children than White fathers of children born out of wedlock[3] suggests that the category "out of wedlock" may not merit all of the baggage attached to it and that the image of absent Black fathers may be far broader than is appropriate.

The argument that is developed from the discourse about fatherlessness is that fatherless children do badly. They are, according to the statistical assessments, more likely to become teen parents, drop out of school, commit suicide, be depressed, and so on.[4] In a speech during the 2008 presidential campaign, Barack Obama reiterated this "fatherless" discourse, saying:

> If we are honest with ourselves, we'll admit that what too many fathers also are is missing—missing from too many lives and too many homes. They have abandoned their responsibilities, acting like boys instead of men. And the foundations of our families are weaker because of it.
>
> You and I know how true this is in the African American community. We know that more than half of all black children live in single-parent households, a number that has doubled—doubled—since we were children. We know the statistics—that children who grow up without a father are five times more likely to live in poverty and commit crime; nine times more likely to drop out of schools; and twenty times more likely to end up in prison. They are more likely to have behavioral problems, or run away from home, or become teenage parents themselves. And the foundations of our community are weaker because of it.[5]

The problem, as I see it, with this discourse is not that it demands engaged parenting from men. That is a good thing. The problem is that the data it relies upon don't say what people think it says. If what is being measured is likelihood of dropping out of school and teenage parenting and imprisonment among kids born out of wedlock, then what is being measured is not fatherlessness but the correlates to out-of-wedlock birth. And we can go further to ask what it is about out-of-wedlock birth in the United States that leads to these outcomes, unlike in European countries, where it doesn't. Is it because out-of-wedlock birth is highly correlated with poverty in this country? Is it because our conceptions of paternal value are so highly correlated with economic factors that poor men struggle with conceiving of a useful role for themselves in the absence of economic stability?

In some ways, the conversation about fatherlessness has been a troubling inversion of the feminist critique of gender in the 1970s, in which researchers began to look at the cultural behaviors associated with masculinity and the negative impact of masculine detachment from domestic life.[6] In that moment, the concept of fatherhood was challenged and re-envisioned in relational terms. But the fatherlessness discourse today focuses not on the substantive dimensions of intimate association; rather, it sets forward as the only appropriate familial role for a father that which is found in a traditional nuclear family domestic structure. It therefore not only pathologizes Black people, who tend not to have that traditional domestic structure, but also Latino, Asian, and gay and lesbian families that frequently have different models of domestic intimate association (i.e., extended family networks, fictive kinship, multigenerational and extended co-parenting frames) and erases the progress made during the feminist movement in ideals of family life by making everything about "the man of the house" instead of cooperating, sharing responsibilities, recognizing the value of many different forms of contributing, and effective co-parenting and child rearing.

The responses to "fatherlessness" among policy analysts frequently are of two sorts. The first is remedial. Such responses include marriage-promotion initiatives and attempts to reduce the number of out-of-wedlock births by the administrative agencies associated with the welfare state, along with punitive child support policies that imprison men for arrearages (irrespective of their ability to find employment or financially care for themselves). The second is based in arguments for a retreat of policy because the problems of poor communities of color are framed as the product of fatherlessness, not inequality. Scholars like Amy Wax argue that little can be done to assist this population.[7] Those making this argument identify the high overlap between the presence of children born out of wedlock and children growing up in poverty as a causal link. Notably, President Obama, when talking about fatherlessness, consistently distinguishes himself from this perspective, arguing that there is "structural racism" that coexists with the problem of fatherlessness.

The problem with both classes of response to fatherlessness is that they generally fail to assess whether the presence in the home of nonresident fathers or the marriage of unwed co-parents would change the economic circumstances for a significant portion of children described as fatherless. Given high rates of unemployment and imprisonment among poor men of color, this is a fundamental question that should be answered before marriage is accepted as a solution to social ills. Moreover, in focusing on marriage, it diminishes the broader remedial possibilities and the importance of social networks and the sharing of resources for low-income adults. I would posit that the diminishment of tight social and extended family networks in the African American community caused by the upheavals associated with urban renewal, housing and welfare policy, and increased drug-associated crime in the mid- to late twentieth century could be identified as having a far more deleterious effect upon the lives of Black children than decreases in the number of in-wedlock births. In fact, I would argue that, rather than the common explanations offered to explain decreases in in-wedlock birth (changes in social norms wrought by the women's movement and birth control and, specific to Black people, AFDC policy that made single motherhood more advantageous than married parenthood for the very poor), we could probably find better paradigms for understanding the shift in exploding rates of imprisonment, deindustrialization, and the underground economy in the 1970s and 1980s.

The assumptions driving and following from the "fatherlessness" discourse can translate into devastating policy practices. In Solangel Maldonado's piece "Deadbroke Dads,"[8] she talks about the punitive reaction to men who fail to pay child support without adequate attention to their lack of economic opportunity. She writes, in a blogpost derived from her article "Deadbroke Dads"[9] on blackprof.com, that "Seventy percent of the child support arrears owed in 2003 was accumulated by men earning $10,000 a year or less. Over 2.5 million nonresident fathers of poor children are poor themselves. These men are not necessarily 'deadbeats'; they are 'deadbroke.'" She goes on to write:

Deadbroke Black fathers also make nonfinancial contributions—they often take care of their children in ways traditionally associated with motherhood. Because these men are often unemployed (or underemployed), they are available to take their children to school, to the doctor, and to watch them while their mothers work or run errands. Many researchers, myself included, have been surprised to learn that many "absent" Black fathers see their children not only on weekends, as divorced middle-class fathers often do, but often see them almost daily. The law does not recognize these contributions. They do not count under our current definition of child support. Maybe they should. American society is alarmed at the high percentage of absent fathers—those who have little or no contact with their children. Studies suggest that children with absent fathers are more likely than children with involved fathers to perform poorly in school, to have low self-esteem, to become pregnant at an early age, to abuse drugs, and to engage in delinquent behavior. These children also feel rejected and often blame themselves for their fathers' disappearance. . . . Many men with child support arrears, however, are compelled to hide from their children because they fear detection by child support enforcement officials and possible incarceration.[10]

Maldonado shows how the category and rubric blunt the social fabric inside. The distinction that is drawn between married and unmarried fathers assumes differences that may be inaccurate and unwarranted, and those assumed difference are used to justify a punitive accountability structure and to drive a destabilizing rather than stabilizing social policy.

Interestingly, in Barack Obama's 2008 Father's Day speech, although he singled out African American fathers in a manner that struck many as pandering to the narrative of Black failure, he fortunately resisted a simple definition of "present" fatherhood in economic or institutional terms and included a recognition of the value of interaction. Generally, however, a substantial problem with the construction of "fatherlessness" is that it draws a dividing line at a point that is nonsubstantive. If, instead, one were to draw a dividing line according to the level of parental involvement and engagement, you might have one category in which investment bankers and street corner hustlers were more likely to be found (with low levels of parental engagement) and another where teachers and unemployed stay-at-home fathers were more likely to be grouped—categories that cut across race and class lines. You also might find that, regardless of levels of paternal engagement, class and resources have a far greater impact on child outcomes than domestic arrangements, even if one sees within-class emotional differences between children who experience high levels of paternal engagement and those who don't. I have not found data that support these speculations, although I think they are likely to be true in part because of what seems to be revealed in the literature on the children of divorce: that the negative outcomes among children of divorce can be traced to the negative economic consequences of divorce when the custodial parent sees a decline in socioeconomic status and resources, the rupture in emotional attachment, and the pre- and postdivorce domestic discord.[11] This suggests that economic factors and the substantive interaction are what matters most, not the fact of being children of divorce. Moreover, middle-class children of divorce generally have good outcomes, whereas poor children suffer irrespective of family configuration. So, even if we acknowledge that high levels of healthy parental engagement are objectively superior for children's well-being, we should also recognize that the absence or presence of this engagement may not be what determines economic success.

The other problem with the fatherless discourse is that it makes invisible domestic spheres in which parental presence is emotionally destructive. There are instances in which it is a good thing for a child not to be exposed to an emotionally damaged or psychologically nonfunctional parent on a daily basis. Although we have had several decades now of growing awareness about sexual, physical, and emotional abuse within intimate relations, these are still huge social problems.[12] To focus on the formal relationship rather than the substantive one marginalizes these problems and fails to make the distinction between the "good father" and the "bad father" or the "good mother" and the "bad mother" on appropriate terms.

At the same time that we critique the discourse on fatherlessness, we should not discount the significant concerns about fathers, particularly within African American communities. Huge numbers of Black men are incarcerated, and there are literally hundreds of thousands of fathers behind bars. The absence of such large quantities of fathers, sons, brothers, and uncles from their communities and their limited opportunities for employment or for mental health treatment when they return to the community after the traumas associated with incarceration (violence, rape, bullying, isolation) create a profoundly destabilizing scenario for families and neighborhoods. Moreover, the stressors of poverty, high rates of unemployment or underemployment, unstable living situations, and exposure to community violence and the gray and underground economies create profound challenges for poor people of color.

The problem with the fatherlessness talk is not that fatherlessness isn't an issue. But it misidentifies the issue and locates the resolution in a traditional patriarchal model of head-of-household status for fathers. The cruelty of this gesture is that men who have been incarcerated, for example, have virtually no opportunities to acquire the head-of-household status without working in the illegal economy (because it is so difficult for ex-offenders to find employment) or by performing patriarchy via physical and social dominance. If the vision of fatherhood were transformed to a more expansive vision of caretaking, inclusive of everything from domestic responsibilities, to reading to children, to walking them to school, to working cooperatively with adult co-caretakers like mothers and grandparents, along with traditional forms of parenting labor like going to a job in order to provide, then there would be space for men to be seen as "good fathers" without the performance of patriarchy.

To identify the social structures that sustain poverty and encourage imprisonment has now been cast as a demonstration of bleeding-heart liberalism in the public domain. When that identification is made by African Americans, it is often further degraded as a refusal to hold Black men accountable for their behavior.

Contesting the fatherlessness talk demands more than simply pointing out the sloppiness of the term. It demands a serious consideration of the role of men in families and, in particular, of chronically unemployed or underemployed men in families. To begin with, talk in communities should not be framed around whether people "need" fathers while growing up to become good citizens and should instead be framed around how these men can and should fit into families and communities as loved and loving members and how all families, however they are constituted, can work effectively under what are often quite difficult circumstances. In order for this shift to translate to more productive policy initiatives, we must encourage policy research to extend beyond quantitative data, which in their minimalism often fail to provide information about substantive human relations, to qualitative research such as extensive surveys about relationships and values and to ethnographic research that assesses what structures of support provide necessary and sufficient conditions for effective individual and co-parenting.

Considering Other Terms

If we contrast a term like "fatherless" with another popular term in conservative research, "intact families," we can see important distinctions. The "intact family" discourse critiques both the children born out of wedlock and the children of divorce. It is a moralizing discourse for sure, in which the biological and juridically recognized relationship is presented as inherently superior. However, it does not have the same administrative social-engineering apparatus behind it, with huge initiatives and federal grants to "keep people from getting divorced." It is a discourse directed to middle-class people, in many ways policing the changing domestic arrangements in the twenty-first-century American middle class with everything from stepfamilies to transracial adoption, gay and lesbian civil unions, and single parenthood. Within this category of the nonintact family, most Black people are subsumed, and again there is a troubling slippage in which the term "intact," meaning "whole," is employed to suggest that anything but the conventional domestic partnership is one that is broken. The distinction between this and the fatherless discourse is that the logic of it does not entail a social-engineering response. Rather, self-governance is presumed. So the issue with racialized social categorization is not simply the presence of a category or the fact that a morality is associated with the category but the nature of the action we are called to take in response, whether it is personal or governmental and whether crises are attributed to the category in purely social or social and economic terms.

Both, however, are employed in an attempt to re-assert the heterosexual married-couple nuclear-family model. Alternative domestic arrangements are growing in the United States and have obviously existed throughout world history. In fact, it is clearly the case that multigenerational, extended family households are better for people who are poor because they allow for a more effective pooling of human and economic resources. While there have been some administrative allowances for those extended-family structures (kinship care in family law, broadening notions of family in public housing) they certainly haven't become accepted in popular culture as an alternative norm outside a very particular form of immigrant narrative that presumes a temporality, or a marginalization of "extra" adults (grandparents, cousins, aunts, uncles), operating as little more than a present example of a nostalgic past. In television shows like the *George Lopez Show*, or Margaret Cho's mid-1990s series *All American Girl*, "extra" adults are there, but they are an irritating and often destabilizing comic relief to the central characters as they pursue mainstream legitimacy. The ideal basic domestic silhouette remains the same. The basic domestic silhouette in popular culture dictates a set of terms for inclusion, within which certain limited forms of diversity are allowed. The prevailing idea is that the nuclear-family model must be maintained and extended family can be present if they are well-behaved, do not usurp parental authority, and are removable at will.

The terms "fatherless" and "intact family" are but two of many examples of domestic categories that have social import. Others that are incredibly worthy of deconstruction come immediately to mind. And, even as the mechanisms for the creation of these categories are subject to complex debate, they constitute decisions about how to order the world. A category like "illegal immigrant" entails a meaning quite different from "undocumented worker," both because of what is highlighted and because of the political context in which these categories are drawn. The term "illegals" has become virtually synonymous with Latinos, specifically Mexicans and Central Americans, in the twenty-first century and again misidentifies the issue as being a fundamental illegitimacy or illegality in the person, rather than a conflict about how we will address the fact that our economic order currently depends upon a substantial gray economy composed of those who work below the minimum wage with minimal access to the society's safety nets and who circulate the dollar internationally to impoverished countries with grossly unequal economic orders, while other documented residents may be perennially unemployed or underemployed.

The designation "illegal" is a politically charged term of relatively recent origin. Prior terms were "illegitimate," "ineligible," and "undesirable."[13] Joseph Nevins notes that the Immigration and Naturalization Service prohibited the term "wetback" in the 1960s and that

> the growth in the use of the term "illegal" continued into the 1990s. Although the Carter administration in the late 1970s forbade the use of the term "illegal alien" instead using terms such as "undocumented worker" or "undocumented alien" this linguistic sensitivity quickly disappeared in official circles. State authorities now almost exclusively use the term "illegal" in public and official discussions to describe unauthorized immigrants—a development replicated in public discourse as a whole.[14]

Terms are invocative. "Illegal" is one that creates a particular racial conception. Mae Ngai uses the powerful term "imported colonialism" to cogently capture the status of "illegals" who are well integrated into the domestic economy.

But the racialization of categories deemed undesirable does more than simply misidentify an issue or cast a category as inclusive of only a particular race; it goes on to define the racial group. Uncovering the discriminatory legal history of Asian and Mexican immigration, Mae Ngai also applies the designation "alien citizens" to identify the persistent construction of Asians and Latinos: "The legal racialization of these ethnic groups' national origin cast them as permanently foreign and unassimilable to the nation . . . these racial formations produced 'alien citizens'—Asian Americans and Mexican Americans born in the United States with formal U.S. citizenship but who remained alien in the eyes of the nation."[15] In many ways, this construction facilitates the ambivalent discourses about these groups as either models (of noble servitude or achievement) or threats (economic in either the low-wage or the professional/higher education spheres).

The word "criminal" as applied to those who have been convicted of crimes facilitates the creation of a boundary that makes invisible the ubiquity of illegal activity in American life.[16] It reduces criminal immorality to juridical capture or exposure, rather than a reference to the thing itself. Discussing a theory of how the category of Blackness itself has been criminalized, Michael Keith comprehends both the source of danger and the allure of these kinds of linguistic proxies: "this subject position does not refer exclusively and immutably to any empirically defined section of the population. It is an invidiously powerful categorization which connotes an imagery of 'black criminality' but achieves empirical realization in particular times and at particular places."[17] This is a much more nuanced dynamic that the cliché "there's some truth to all stereotypes." The existence of racialized categories impacts opportunity and overdetermines race as well as a subcategory of a racial group in a manner that has the potential to create a self-fulfilling prophesy. It also monoracializes multiracial dynamics. When people talk about "illegals," often absent from the discussion are the employers who seek out these workers quite deliberately and the average citizens who dine at the restaurants where undocumented workers work, who wear clothes made with sweatshop labor, who have their children cared for, their homes cleaned, and their lawns tended by undocumented people, and who benefit from cheap labor without obligation to the laborers. When people talk about crime-ridden inner cities, there is rarely discussion about the apartment owners and housing authorities that fail to keep buildings up to code or the city government that fails to keep school buildings in basic functioning order with adequate supplies, the corners filled with gray-economy entrepreneurs of bootleg media and fraudulent luxury items, and the legal but unethical gouging of payday loans providers and check-cashing fees. In both instances, there is a multiracial group of participants in the spheres of "illegality," but the terms "illegal" and "inner city" are racialized and the race attributed to them is that of the parties most vulnerable and least likely to get economic benefit from the social arrangement. Imagine, instead, if the face of illegal immigration were that of a restaurant owner or if the face of the inner city were that of the slumlord.

Terms such as "outlaw," "criminal," "inner city," and "illegal" mark the individual or place as not simply outside the protection of the law but as a threat to the social order, thus justifying prima facie discriminatory treatment. Michel Foucault understood that this sort of categorization was a means and explanation of social control, and he analyzed the growth of the term "delinquent" as such. For Foucault, the categorization of the delinquent was a method of resolving class and economic conflict by identifying not the individual criminal act as wrong but a class of individuals who in their very existence implied illegality and crime and who could easily be identified. In the United States, the designations of groups that commit crimes change, but, despite the title, they almost always become racialized terms, from "drug dealer" to "illegal alien" to "terrorist." As early as the 1960s, one finds the delinquent stereotype having racial cues. When Pilavin and Briar studied police responses in the 1960s, they noticed the police's use of interactive cues to decide whom to arrest and recognized that "These cues were so significant in determining police decisions that Blacks and those otherwise fitting the delinquent stereotype were more likely to be stopped and interrogated." Moreover, "the newer research confirms that black (and Latino) neighborhoods are more likely to be the focus of heavy police monitoring and surveillance to begin with and that black and Latino youth are more likely to be defined by police as threatening or insubordinate, more likely to be stopped more often under various pretexts, more likely to get arrested than to receive a warning, and less likely to have the charges dripped by police."[18]

Categorization, Life, and Language

Sorting is a basic human activity, but how we sort is determined to a great extent by our culture and values. Our racial history has an impact on how we sort human beings, spaces, and things. It also has an impact on what constitutes legitimate knowledge in our society. The existence of rubrics for treating categories of human beings facilitates the use of heuristics in making decisions with regard to people according to race. Rubrics in this sense can be essentially scoring tools, which tell us when someone falls into a particular category, and/or at what point action or intervention is merited to support or hinder that person. Take, for example, the criminal law enforcement context. If a person has been convicted of a crime and is at the sentencing phase, the factors that are taken into account in determining the sentence may support racial discrimination by giving mitigating value to cultural behaviors that are tied to favored group membership. Or let's take a symbolic hypothetical: imagine that a judge has learned that most teenage defendants who appear before him wearing white sneakers and blue laces become repeat offenders. When he sees a defendant in such attire, he therefore feels comfortable imposing a longer sentence than he might otherwise, imagining the clothing an indicator of some membership in an antisocial organization or reflective of some criminal ethos. But what if the relationship between attire and recidivism is one of correlation, not causation? The neighborhood where those shoes and laces are popular has a massive unemployment rate and terrible schools, and that explains the rates of recidivism. Imagine if a given defendant is more sincere than any other in his desire to avoid crime but suffers a harsher penalty by virtue of a superficial rubric. The rubric applied may get at something— but not a just assessment.

Rubrics achieve legitimacy by virtue of language, the appearance of objectivity in method of application, our sense that the categories have epistemological value, and the work of institutions that categorize individuals. The rubrics themselves may become racialized either intentionally or accidentally. We have the social sciences to thank for many of our racialized rubrics and categories (think of words like "deviant" and "sociopath"),[19] just as we have it to thank for many of the most important insights into race and racial inequality.

The work of the rubric is functional (indicating a set of actions to be taken), just as the work of the category is hermeneutic. For example, think of the category "welfare mother," and take as the rubric the process of determining whether a woman has committed welfare fraud. The category influences the application of the rubric; the language of "fraud" is criminal language but, in the context of means-tested benefits, includes things like maintaining an unreported bank account, no matter how minimal the dollar amount in the account.

The dynamic relation between category and rubric is mediated through the significations of language. The linguist Geneva Smitherman argues that "'linguistic form' both conditions and reflects 'social cognition and social behavior.'"[20] The linguistic categories that are raced are, of course, contested territory; they are shaped by communities themselves and by external forces and are never static or singular. But here we are concerned with the categories that facilitate a practice of inequality and that also shape the way life is lived within those designations. For example, the "crisis in fatherlessness" discourse places sole responsibility for social failures on Black fathers and absolves the prison-industrial complex and the ideology of patriarchy completely. Moreover, it identifies the sole appropriate intervention as one that changes the behavior of the men or the women who give birth to their children.

Racialized rubrics and categories are also institutions of a historic moment; they are a function of legitimated epistemology and practice, terms of action, not simply argument. It is this that distinguishes them among the diverse noise and perspectives in our heteroglot public sphere, as spaces through which access, power, opportunity, benefit, and detriment are distributed. They often determine who gets pruned out of the American Dream.

Additionally, their existence instructs us as to how the racial hierarchy gets re-established after the gains of the civil rights era. "Knowing," for example, that "Black people don't want to work" or that "Black men are irresponsible" actually operates as a legitimate form of knowledge alongside "data" like the disproportionate use of means-tested welfare benefits by the African American community or the high rates of incarceration and child support arrearages for African American men. The lens is not on the racial wealth gap, the development of which was supported by federal policy in the first half of the twentieth century, or on discriminatory practices in school, work, and health but rather on "information" that supports "knowledge" of Black inadequacy and failure. This epistemological framework is so smoothly embraced precisely because of our long history of relying upon it. David Theo Goldberg writes:

> Threatening to transgress or pollute the given social order necessitates its reinvention, first by conceptualizing order anew and then by (re)producing spatial confinement and separation in these modernized terms. Clearly, the main mode of social exclusion and segregation throughout the course of maturing capitalism has been brought about by, and in terms of, racialized discourse, with its classificatory systems, its order and values, and its ways of "seeing" particular bodies in their natural and social relations.[21]

Categories and rubrics may allow for immediate decision making that does not appear to be based on race but that in fact does have disparate and inequitable impact. These become conscious race discourses by virtue of the fact that our attention is drawn to the preponderance of certain ascriptive groups in particular categories and by the absence of others in particular categories. This is a distinct matter from thinly veiled bigotries, like racial coding in politics, which entails intentional manipulation of racial fears or bigotries. The racialization of categories or rubrics need not be fueled by intentional bigotry and may in fact develop from categories that were from the outset race neutral and have grown to operate as a source of racial inequality only because of the way they have been associated with a racial group. So, for example, there was a time when "welfare mother" referred to a category of persons who, it was generally agreed, merited protection and support.[22] Once African American women gained access to welfare and began disproportionately to receive welfare benefits because of their high rates of poverty, the term "welfare mother" lost its sympathetic implications and became a pejorative.[23]

Domesticity as an Arena of Categorization

As nouns rather than adjectives, our racialized categories essentialize a subset of the circumstances of a person's life. They make those circumstances stand in for a more complex evaluation of who the person is. Although the racialization of categories demonstrates something about how groups are seen and treated, we also can see something about the arenas through which we evaluate groups of people by virtue of which categories have currency. Domesticity, lawfulness, and the place one has in the economic marketplace are all arenas of common categorization. Focusing in on domesticity, it is clear that structural/spatial images are often employed to indicate the good domestic unit and to enforce a "like us" or "not like us" line of distinction. I use the term "silhouette" to describe ideas about how the domestic unit should be arranged because silhouette captures the idea of attention to the outline without necessarily attending to the texture and color of the household within. Moreover, if one meets the silhouette requirement, there might even be some greater range of choice about how one colors and textures one's life within. The two-married-adults-several-children household is the basic idealized domestic unit. This outline of a domestic structure determines insider and outsider status for domestic arrangements that impact different groups of people of color who may be "misfitted" either because the silhouette is too busy (too many children, too many adults) or because it appears to have people missing (fragmented or absent marital relationships). Even the physical landscape of the home is relevant to the concept of silhouette.

The silhouette does not merely dictate which domestic arrangements "fit" into a cultural ideal and which do not but also distinguishes between acceptable and unacceptable differences in our self-consciously hybrid culture. Deborah Chambers writes, in *Representing the Family*, that, in the twentieth century, "The modern middle class family was declared as the standard, the 'normal American family.' Lower class families, which included all non-white families and the white working classes, were treated as the exception and came to represent the prevalence of 'family disorganization.'"[24] Moreover, she describes how describing Black families as matriarchal and Latino families as hyperpatriarchal leads to images of familial disorganization. Chambers's work powerfully illustrates the silhouettes of ideal domesticity and how they are racialized. However, when she speaks about *The Cosby Show*, we have a powerful illustration of why form and substance cannot be collapsed, particularly in the complicated dynamics of post–civil rights–era race and racism. In describing the popularity of *The Cosby Show*, she writes, "The African American Cosby family is marked by a class position and by cultural capital that is notably Anglo-American within a hegemonic normalizing of middle-class and Anglo-nuclear family values. The Cosbys are upper middle class and 'cultured,' not simply in the sense of being 'educated' but educated in an Anglophone tradition. This family's cultural legitimacy is produced through their embrace of anglo-ethnic culture as an acceptable norm within their lived experiences, values and style of living." This is partly true, to the extent that the silhouette of their lives, marked by family structure, professional position, and physical space, fits within American ideals. And yet, the Cosby family was one of the most authentically culturally Black families to appear on television. From their child discipline styles to the music, art, and leisure activities they enjoyed, their speech patterns, and their relationship with and participation in the traditions of historically Black colleges, they provided access to a range of Black cultural practices and intimate associations that no other show had offered. This family, which never spoke of race, was very, very Black. The fact that few commentators seemed to notice this is likely attributable to their relatively minimal familiarity with African American culture, the fact that the Huxtables didn't name the "Blackness" of what they were doing, and the fact that the silhouette of their professional and domestic arrangements took them out of the conception of the "Black family" altogether for many, if not most, viewers. Even though I disagree with the cultural description Chambers gives of the Cosbys, I believe she captured exactly which features made the Cosbys attractive and acceptable, notwithstanding their "Blackness": upper-class status, traditional domesticity, and absolutely no talk or analysis about race, racism, or the persistence of inequality either in the Brooklyn they so poetically represented or in the nation beyond.

Chambers also argues that social science research has been highly implicated in the racialization of silhouette: "A number of prominent institutions and research centers in the United States produced a series of research projects designed to prove that familial arrangements outside the nuclear model were dysfunctional."[25] This raises a number of questions, perhaps the first of which is, given the ideological orientation of family sociology, which promotes a very specific kind of domestic arrangement, how does one use social scientific research to understand what is and isn't happening in families of color? The response this author chooses is to respect the concept of domestic choice in a manner far more sincere than that often used to pay lip service in our society. If a respect for choice is the underlying premise, then we must approach the research we see in a different fashion, looking to how we can facilitate meaningful choice given the structure of inequality that exists. This means, for example, that, rather than asking how we can get people to get married more, we should ask why, for people who wish to marry, there are such impediments to the institution, impediments that are economic and institutional in nature but that also are related to the fact that American gender culture is in flux and yet hopelessly nostalgic.

The very concept of domestic space has both racial and national symbolism and has, throughout the nation's history. In her landmark article "Manifest Domesticity," Amy Kaplan writes, of nineteenth-century letters, "In this context domestic has a double meaning that not only links the familial household to the nation but also imagines both in opposition to everything outside the geographic and conceptual border of the home. The earliest meaning of *foreign*, according to the *OED*, is 'out of doors' or 'at a distance from home.' Contemporary English speakers refer to national concerns as domestic in explicit or implicit contrast with the foreign."[26]

Kaplan goes on to argue that "Domesticity is related to the imperial project of civilizing, and the conditions of domesticity often become markers that distinguish civilization from savagery. Through the process of domestication, the home contains within itself those wild or foreign elements that must be tamed; domesticity not only monitors the borders between the civilized and the savage, but also regulates traces of the savage within itself."[27] Chambers echoes the association between this colonial-era notion of domesticity with contemporary ones: "Like politicians today, nineteenth century colonial authorities were obsessed with 'domestic instability' which was categorized and measured by the low rates of marriage and high rates of illegitimacy."[28] Without question, "domestic" minorities are often conceived of as foreign to the dominant domestic norms, and efforts to normalize them with respect to these norms have been a central element in the history of the welfare state. Moreover, the spaces of people of color have alternately been deemed alarming for posing a "threat within" to our domestic order and as somehow foreign territory (as in describing Katrina evacuees as "refugees"). At the same time, however, the welfare state, urban planning, and law enforcement have often destabilized families of color because of the intensity, frequency, and punitive consequences of their paternalistic interventions. Hence, the image of the domestic spaces of people of color as unstable becomes circular.

The role of gender in the racialization of domesticity adds further complexity. The professional groups that regulate and respond to the domestic lives of people of color are often highly populated by women: teachers, social workers, public health workers. The authority of White women as arbiters of correct forms of domesticity has historic roots in the nineteenth-century cult of true womanhood. Of course, there are the broader legislative mechanisms and political conversations that dictate policy and are male dominated, but I make the point about gender and, in particular, spheres of female influence to challenge the idea that the caring professions and a caring sensibility somehow mean that members of those professions don't or won't do damage to clients by virtue of their domestic ideologies. These professions are as implicated in practices of inequality as those that are male dominated.

With respect to the "receiving end" of practices of inequality, it is noteworthy that the blame for African American poverty has tended to be described in terms of gender, but with shifting blame over the years It was placed on women in the 1960s (the era of the Moynihan Report), on men in the 1970s (during the women's movement), on women again in the 1980s (during the conservative revolution), and on men today (as growing numbers of economically self-sufficient women of all races are having children out of wedlock). It is no accident that these discourses have tracked the gender debates in the White community. The discourse is reflective of the anxieties and preoccupations of the people who are disproportionately framing the discourse. Once again, the attention to single-parent Black households, which do not fit the silhouette of the domestic ideal, has evolved into a causal argument for Black poverty that has been widely accepted. The cultural theorist Stuart Hall describes this formulation as a self-fulfilling prophesy: "it may not be true that single parenting inevitably leads to delinquency and crime. But if everyone believes it to be so, and punishes single parents accordingly, this will have real consequences for both parents and children and will become 'true' in terms of its real effects, even if in some absolute sense it has never been conclusively proven."[29]

Some evidence suggesting this effect is found when one looks at the relationship between constructions of Black domesticity and real data over the course of the twentieth century. Much of Moynihan's argument about the decline of the Black family due to its matriarchal structure was rooted, as Chambers notes, in E. Franklin Frazier's earlier research. However, Chambers writes,

Frazier's research on three generation matriarchal black families was historically inaccurate. In fact, recent studies on nineteenth-century black families existing after the Civil War has shown that patterns of marriage, divorce, fertility and two-parent household rates were quite similar between blacks and whites.[30]

Moreover, Moynihan's report predates the "in one-generation" shift to a majority of Black children being born out of wedlock and into female-headed households. As Christopher Jencks notes, "As recently as 1960, three-quarters of African Americans were born into a family of a married couple."[31] However, the massive attention granted the Moynihan Report likely gave it power in determining how Black families were seen and saw themselves, and, if it did not create a self-fulfilling prophesy, the Report likely encouraged certain outcomes.

But one far less speculative area in which a racialized domestic rubric has powerfully controlled people is housing occupancy standards. As Ellen Pader has argued, housing occupancy "regulations derive from a combination of upper-class English ideals and outdated scientific knowledge, with concomitant moralistic and assimilationist aspirations on the part of the policy makers. Today, these social ideals still implicitly underlie much of our current urban design, affecting the ethnic, racial, and economic structure of cities, and by extension, homelessness, coercive segregation, and access to services."[32]

Pader's work distinguishes a kind of cultural difference, as seen in *The Cosby Show*, that complies with silhouette assimilability from cultural expressions of alternative models of family connectedness in domestic space. She writes:

National origin and race discrimination in housing are fairly obvious when someone is denied the opportunity to rent or purchase a home for reasons unrelated to his or her ability to pay, and the subtext is "I don't want someone of your type here," referring to color or ethnicity. But what about when the discursive text is "you're welcome here regardless of your ethnicity or race," and the subtext is, "as long as you live by my sociocultural concepts of right and proper behavior?"[33]

Latino, Asian, and African American families rely more heavily on extended-family networks and domestic structures than White Americans.[34] On one hand, then, these norms functionally attempt to exert assimilationist norms on communities of color. On the other hand, they legitimize a line of distinction between those who occupy space in one way and those who occupy space in another. Interestingly, the exclusion of immigrants from welfare benefits under the 1996 welfare reform also removed that population from certain kinds of governmental oversight. This, in some ways, might allow people to be "let alone" to make choices about their domestic arrangements (although private homeowners could enforce those norms over tenants at their discretion), perhaps a small silver lining in an inequitable cloud; irrespective of the regulatory force, the standards themselves entail judgments about how one ought to live.

Importantly, the identification of domestic arrangements with more than two people per bedroom as inferior also discourages people who may have minimal access to hard capital from developing their own forms of soft capital. I will offer a personal example to illustrate this. My maternal grandmother always offered her children the opportunity to return home if necessary. This allowed the majority of her twelve college-educated children to come home at one point or another in order to save money, to figure out new career paths, to recuperate during illness, or to transition before pursuing graduate degrees. Whereas a middle-class family might be able to offer an outlay of cash, which my grandmother could not, she was able to offer space and child care, which had significant economic value to my mother and her siblings. On any reasonable measure, my grandmother was an extraordinary parent—she kept a meticulously clean and ordered house and held high academic standards, while maintaining unbelievable sensitivity to human failings. However, her home would have failed to meet the housing occupancy standards of the U.S. Department of Housing and Urban Development, which in general, Pader notes, hover around two person per bedroom. Pader importantly notes that, while it is true that these occupancy standards are impossible given the markets for affordable housing—there simply are too many more people than rooms—the choice to sleep many to a room is not necessarily born of economic necessity but is often simply a cultural preference.

In 1998, after lobbying and litigation over occupancy standards, HUD sustained its support of the two-person-per-bedroom rule, apparently after much lobbying from apartment owners wanting to limit the number of residents in their subsidized units. The two-person rule is not logical for hygienic standards, only cultural ones. It is illustrates how cultural differentiation becomes racialized and demonized and how arbitrary norms are ascribed inherent value. The category "noncompliant" (with occupancy standards) or "unhygienic" offends fair judgment of family culture and economic necessity.

It is widely accepted that categories heighten the differences we imagine between people and mute the similarities across categories. This is one of the most powerful arguments made by those who argue for the eradication of race—as long as we identify race, we assume greater differences between people than actually exist. But racialized categories persist even without explicit mention of race. This is an instance in which we need more speech, not less. Even as we need categories in order to identify trends or problems, we must be rigorous about not reifying certain categories over all others and must sustain different methods of examination. Such multivariate analyses of the operation of race, class, gender, and culture require skepticism and demand that researchers and professionals relinquish disciplinary bigotries. Even the ideas embedded in our methods are implicated in this mix of creating racial meaning.

For example, one often hears talk about a person "becoming a statistic." That term refers to a person who has fallen into a category that is identified in quantitative research as a social failure. What I find fascinating in this term is the idea that becoming a person who "is counted" quantitatively is highly associated with being seen as a failure or marginal. This is dramatic for several reasons. "Being studied" by researchers who wish to understand negative traits (as opposed to being studied to help researchers discover health effects, for example) is disproportionately an experience of those who are poor in this country. It is also indicative of how we treat poor communities of color as monoliths and often respect and appreciate individuals from those communities only when they are seen as "different from" and "better than" (and therefore meriting more nuanced treatment than) the rest. It is not that the "statistic" has no narrative applied to him or her but rather that a judgmental narrative is often applied without distinction or attention to the individual circumstances of the "statistic." A "statistic" in this situation is just another word for belonging to a disfavored category. I would argue that, at the level of policy as well as institutional and legislative decision making, we should challenge our view of humans as "statistics" and commit to more holistic, ethnographic, and social-ecological evaluations of communities. As individuals and as community members, we should challenge the symbolic status boundaries we establish between "us" and "them" and the moralizing categories we use to mark those boundaries.

In this historic moment, we are preoccupied with who is in which categories: whether gay people will be allowed to have married nuclear families, whether Black men will marry the mothers of their children, whether undocumented workers will become citizens. We run the risk, in fixating on these categories, of missing a historic opportunity to re-evaluate the American family (in both the small and the large sense) and what makes and facilitates a healthy functional family. There would, of course, be significant disagreement about how to answer these questions, but, in pursuing them, we would be forced to look at a wider range of variables that affect life outcomes and collective well-being and, perhaps most important, to think deeply about the requirements of democracy and how to respect our fundamental human rights.

5

"I Always Feel Like Somebody's Watchin' Me"

The Racing of Privacy, Voyeurism, and Surveillance

> The freedom to form relationships in civil society . . . requires effective access to private spaces, since many such relationships can only function when protected from the scrutiny and intrusions of others.
>
> —Elizabeth Anderson

Harriet Jacobs's 1861 memoir, *Incidents in the Life of a Slave Girl*, is a remarkable text for many reasons, but perhaps the most dramatic is her recounting of the nearly seven years she spent in a small crawlspace in her grandmother's attic, hiding away from her treacherous slave master until she could be safely sent North. Jacobs writes: "I hardly expect that the reader will credit me, when I affirm that I lived in that little dismal hole, almost deprived of light and air, and with no space to move my limbs, for nearly seven years. . . . Countless were the nights that I sat late at the little loophole scarcely large enough to give me a glimpse of one twinkling star. There, I heard the patrols and slave-hunters conferring together about the capture of runaways, well knowing how rejoiced they would be to catch me."[1] The reader encounters this episode with a sense of claustrophobia, grief, perhaps even doubt. Less immediate but no less significant is its statement about privacy. Privacy in her body or home is denied the enslaved woman. Only in the attic does she find safety, albeit in a horrific fashion.

The literary critic Robert Stepto has identified a discourse around freedom in early African American literature in which achieving freedom is expressed as mobility for men and control of a domestic space for women.[2] Significantly, the elusiveness of both sorts of freedom for African Americans throughout history has been shaped by racialized conceptions of privacy and practices of surveillance. In this chapter, I argue that, while privacy has been a signature feature of American citizenship and, as Patricia Hill Collins argues, "the theme of the home as a sanctuary from outsiders and the turmoil of the public sphere creates boundaries for the biological family along lines of privacy and security,"[3] in the contemporary United States the fragile relationship people of color continue to have with the right to privacy and the persistence of intrusive and terrorizing practices of surveillance are means by which racial inequality is practiced. In 2010, Arizona passed legislation requiring law enforcement officers to stop individuals who "looked" like illegal immigrants. While ostensibly this measure was introduced to address the growing tide of undocumented residents in the states, it was readily apparent that it was a crude extension of practices of racial surveillance directed towards phenotypically Mestizo and Indian Arizona residents. And in 2009 and 2010, the Center for Constitutional Rights issued reports demonstrating the grotesque overrepresentation of Blacks and Latinos among those stopped by police in New York.[4]

Additionally, the racialized exposure of interior spaces is a feature of the practice of inequality. Although the right to privacy is a recognized constitutional right, the cultural presumption that African Americans and Latinos merit only a minimal right to privacy means that they experience disproportionate enforcement of law. This unequal surveillance means that sanctions for violation of the law are unfairly distributed.

The alienation from the right to privacy via racialized practices of surveillance is justified through racial narratives about social disorder, invasion, and moral decay. Add to this the originating conceptions of privacy as an outgrowth of property, and we can see how the (disproportionately Black and Brown) poor suffer from our class-discriminatory notions of privacy as well. Forty-five percent of people who receive Section 8 housing vouchers are African American.[5] And 48 percent of public housing is occupied by African Americans.[6] Beyond being disproportionately poor and nonhomeowners, African Americans are disproportionately occupiers of residences under some form of state oversight.

We generally talk about privacy in bourgeois terms (i.e., conversations about intrusions onto owned property and the monitoring of noteworthy financial information). At the same time, policy initiatives directed toward communities of color or poor people, who are disproportionately Black people (and often signified as Black people in political discourse and popular media), are often crafted in such a way as to presumptively intrude upon privacy in both structure and process.

By focusing on privacy, I hope to add a generally neglected dimension to the public conversation on race. In our discussions about the persistence of racial gaps, the dialogue is often framed in terms of the responsibility of the state to citizens and residents, and that is often a discussion about public benefits, public housing, and public schooling. Often, the sentiment of those hostile to efforts to address racial inequality by those means is that public benefits mean that "we" are made responsible for the care of "them" and therefore have the right to monitor "them."

Instead of focusing on the admittedly important question of public (state) responsibility, I want to identify state- or state agent–enforced exclusions from the right to privacy and state responsibility to protect the right to privacy. This extends ideas presented in my earlier work in which I argued that some of the most pernicious effects of Jim Crow were to be found in the realm of private law, specifically property and contract law, even though our historic attention to Jim Crow is almost exclusively focused on public law.[7] While the civil rights era was a period of explicit strides in public law, the gains were far less extensive in the private-law arena. And so we can see this intersection of privacy denial and racialized surveillance as a sign of the unfinished business of the struggle for racial justice.

Inequality of access to the right to privacy is also an important means by which greater penalties are imposed on African Americans and Latinos than on Whites for breaching social norms and breaking laws. If you are more likely to be watched and investigated, you are also more likely to be caught and to pay the price for social breaches. This inapposite degree of punishment for breaches of the law strikes at the heart of the social contract.

The concept of privacy can be easily divided into three aspects of human experience. First, there is privacy as a matter of space, often the home, which theoretically provides concealment from those outside its walls. Second, there is privacy as it relates to the body, a privacy against uninvited touch, viewing (under clothes), or penetration (sexual or surgical). Third, there is privacy with regard to knowledge about a person. That knowledge category is easily broken down into two dimensions: content (information about a person) and action (monitoring of mobility). The earliest conceptions of privacy in Anglo-American law—trespass, assault, and eavesdropping—indicate that that basic triad is one that has been acknowledged for some time. However, the shorthand of privacy talk has been often a simple phrase: "to be let alone."

Anticipating the Privacy Critique

Before launching into an argument on behalf of privacy rights, we must consider whether and to what extent the concept is a legitimate one. Although on an intuitive level it seems obvious that everyone would want some form of privacy, the conception of privacy in the West finds its origins in liberal philosophy, and critiques of the systemic injustices so often attendant to that philosophical framework must be considered insofar as we assert an interest in the right to privacy.

Some of the most important critiques of the right to privacy have come from feminist jurisprudence. I hope to incorporate the concerns of feminist theory into a conception of how we might articulate the demand for a more robust privacy right for people of color in the United States.

Beginning in the 1980s, feminist critics challenged the conception of privacy rights. One critique has been that the concept of privacy excludes the particularity of human relationships and all aspects of the self besides the rational, abstract, and homogeneous citizen-self from the public arena and public debate by resigning them to private space.[8] Another critique has been of the private/public dichotomy for its presumption of the protection afforded by private space. The historic association of women with private space was a means of excluding women from public discourse and commerce. In this conception, privacy rights act as a shield against potential state efforts at balancing power between men and women.[9] As Patricia Hill Collins writes, "the notion of the public sphere as a White male domain of work, politics, and leadership gains meaning primarily when juxtaposed to its private-sphere alternative—the White female domain of family, domesticity, and intimacy that houses White women and children."[10] A third critique, however closely related to the two others, has been that an emphasis on privacy encourages a neglect of responsibility to other people.[11] This critique is rooted in an interpretation of the concept of "common good" found in the republican tradition and argues that we all ought to be accountable to others for actions in both the private and the public domains.

These critiques of privacy are not useful only on a philosophical level. One can easily translate their insights into material conditions. In writing about the experience of prostitutes, Catharine MacKinnon argued, "The right to privacy is often included among civil rights. In the United States, one meaning privacy has effectively come to have is the right to dominate free of public scrutiny. The private is then defined as a place of freedom by effectively rendering consensual what women and children are forced to do out of the public eye. Prostitution is thus often referred to as occurring in private between consenting adults, as is marriage and family. The result is to extend the aura of privacy and protection from public intervention from sex to sexual abuse."[12] Women of color are both more likely to be victims of violence within the home and less likely to receive protection from that violence. And so this point is critically important for our purposes.

Critiques of the manner in which privacy rights mask domestic violence provide another context in which material reality exposes the practical dangers in private spaces.[13] In private spaces, intimate violence meted out to the subjugated members of a household—women, enslaved people, children—could and can often be carried on without a protective witness and without community or institutional acknowledgment or response.

Nevertheless, Anita Allen, a privacy expert, reflecting on the feminist critique of privacy, has argued that in fact the antiprivacy argument was largely overstated and that "The point is not to eliminate experiences of privacy but to 'socialize and democratize our conceptions of privacy.'"[14] To that end, this chapter is not merely a description of the racialized alienation from privacy but a call for the democratization of privacy to be inclusive of populations often thought to presumptively have forfeited privacy rights through "welfare dependence" or violations of social norms.[15]

Moreover, that "socialization of privacy" then must entail an attention to the needs of both collective units, like families, neighborhoods, and political/identity groups, and the individuals within those units, with an awareness that the collective unit in any community may at times be engaged in a violation of the rights of the individual therein. Or certain collective units may be overrepresented in ways that permit an intrusion upon the rights of other groups. The balance among privacy and responsibility and respect for others has to be recalibrated constantly, but this is particularly so in social contexts where racial discrimination leads to both the intrusion upon the rights of groups and also to monolithic representations of groups and to ideologies of preference for certain subcategories of groups. Hence, to advocate for privacy rights for people of color should not be interpreted to justify the potential existence of sexisms, heterosexisms, classisms, ethnocentrisms, or oppressive norms vis-à-vis individuals or subgroups within that community.

The right to privacy provides the means through which many of our notions of human respect and safe spaces for intimate and social interaction can actually exist. Collins writes that historically, "Although . . . Black civil society was policed by outsiders, it could never be totally regulated or watched to the extent of erasing all privacy. In that space of Black public-sphere privacy, resistance to the injustices created by racial segregation emerged."[16] In the 1958 case *NAACP v. Alabama*,[17] this was dramatically articulated by the recognition on the part of the Court that requiring that NAACP membership rolls be reported to the state would be an unconstitutional violation of rights. The Court stated, "We hold that the immunity from state scrutiny of membership lists which the Association claims on behalf of its members is here so related to the right of the members to pursue their lawful private interests privately and to associate freely with others in so doing as to come within the protection of the Fourteenth Amendment."[18] The juridical protection of privacy and the delimitation of the extent to which states could engage in surveillance practices in the early civil rights era provided a critical sphere in which organizing for social justice and socialization into civic culture could occur. Nonetheless, the extension of federal surveillance into monitoring activist organizations during the late civil rights era was terribly destructive to the strategic and cultural spaces so essential to social justice movement.[19]

In focusing on the intrusions upon privacy and surveillance practices in two areas common in African American life, the welfare state and criminal law enforcement, part of what I am positing is that the terms upon which formal integration[20] (both in entitlements and in society at large) has occurred have had a negative impact upon Black civil society and the extent to which it can exist as a "private" space for identity formation.[21] As well, I consider the common ground between denials of privacy for Black and Latino people, through criminal law enforcement and immigration policies, each as applied to both groups. In responding to practices of inequality vis-à-vis privacy, we are necessarily charged with asking how we might envision shoring up and, in necessary instances, rebuilding private spaces of various important sorts.

The environmental psychologist Irwin Altman argues for a conception of spatial privacy that is dynamic, one in which a person may want to sometimes be in contact with other people and other times to be alone. He argues for "building environments that are responsive and able to meet our changing privacy needs."[22] Altman describes effective privacy as the ability to regulate the boundary between the self and the environment in a normalized fashion and in relationship to a dynamic social world.[23] Such a dynamic concept of privacy is concerned not only with exclusion but also with inclusion, the terms of each, and the extent to which the individual has some control over those terms. Moreover, it also requires an engagement with what the nature of the public space is, understanding that the nature of public impacts what is desired in private space. This sense of privacy as dynamic can and should be imported to broader conceptions of privacy, as well.

In his landmark essay, "Violence and the Word,"[24] the legal scholar Robert Cover argues that legal interpretation is a matter of life and death. As he says, "legal acts signal and occasion the imposition of violence upon others." The feminist critique of privacy revealed how the legal category "private" could occasion gendered violence. Here I want to argue that the neglect of privacy as a matter of legal interpretation whereby the right is forfeited by virtue of one's "choice"[25] (and I say it in that way because that is the sort of ridiculous framework that is assumed) to be poor and Black or Brown occasions the imposition of violence as well, much of it meted out by enforcement, sanction, and neglect of the state as enacted by its agents (police, caseworkers, bureaucrats). This denial of privacy as a presumed right permits unfettered practices of surveillance, practices that provide an essential and corporeal bridge between the racial narratives described in chapter 3 and the disadvantaging practices of inequality described in chapter 2.

Surveillance and Privacy

The fact that so many surveillance studies critics have sounded the alarm bell about the loss of privacy in the contemporary surveillance society might seem to suggest that there is no particular need to distinguish people of color in a conversation about privacy rights in the United States. By this logic, one might argue that poor people of color are simply some form of miner's canary, the bird down in the mine that, with its fragile respiratory systems, is used to warn the humans of diminished air quality.[26] In that case, their experience of surveillance and privacy intrusion would simply be a sign of what is to come for all of us. Although we all should be concerned with the terms upon which surveillance practices are being extended generally, racialized practices of surveillance are significantly different from general practices of surveillance. In general, the extension of surveillance practices must be rhetorically and legally justified to the society on the basis of compelling state interests. As such, there is a balancing test that is presumed to be necessary whenever intrusions upon the civil liberties of "mainstream" members of American society (and I put "mainstream" in quotes because that category is a contingent one based upon a combination of majoritarian and political realities of the given moment) are made for the sake of what is argued to be a necessity (e.g., safety, order, security) and as such subject to a public debate. In the case of racialized surveillance there is rarely a presumption of liberty to begin with. In the surveillance practices associated with means-tested benefits, or what we popularly call "welfare," there is no balancing test demanded, nor is there one associated with immigration policies. In the context of police profiling, enough activist, judicial, and political attention has been paid to racial profiling to require that justifications be offered for practices that tend to be based on affirming racial narratives that associate groups of people with particular crimes, not as though those criminal actors are unusual in the community (which they almost always are) but rather as though they are common. As Lu-in Wang argues, "Members of targeted groups . . . suffer . . . when widespread acceptance of racial profiling leads us to regard it as normal, because that view promotes the expectation that people who look like them naturally will be watched and stopped, as well as the understanding that their rights, liberty and bodily integrity have less value than others."[27] Wang goes on to identify surveillance practices with broader denials of rights. She argues that the belief that police surveillance is natural and appropriate for certain groups "promotes the view that those groups are entitled to fewer liberties and that their rights are 'mere amenities' that may be sacrificed to protect law abiding people. Acceptance of this view results in an environment in which a pattern of discriminatory targeting seems benign, for when social understandings are so uncontested that they become invisible, the social meanings that arise from them appear natural."[28]

Moreover, there is a persistent dialogue of forfeiture of rights implicit in the conversations about Black "lawlessness" and Latino "illegality." The concept is not simply that greater policing of Black and Latino people is necessary but also that their collective behavior operates as an indicator that rights have been forfeited. The logic of the oft repeated question "why should you be upset about being racially profiled if you have done nothing wrong," I would argue, emerges only because of a conceptual subtext of group forfeiture of rights. In this view, the Black or Latino individual should expect to have to prove his rights-worthiness. As such, the distinction between anti-social and law-abiding individuals in the group is collapsed. They are all imagined as one mass group of lawless anticitizens until proven otherwise. These constructions constantly threaten to spread into other arenas and lead to further rights violation. Furthermore, they delegitimize and reduce trust in police forces within those communities.

As well, in the contemporary field of surveillance studies, which pays relatively little attention to the question of race, a greater concentration of attention is devoted to surveillance practices as they relate to knowledge about people (often distributed via cyberspace or computer database) than to issues of mobility or space. This indicates how surveillance practices in general have developed in the manner predicted and identified by Michel Foucault. However, when it comes to racial surveillance, both in the United States and abroad, contemporary technologies of surveillance have not eliminated old-fashioned forms of surveillance that are both physical and spatial. To be frisked by police[29] or airport personnel,[30] to have body cavities searched,[31] to have police kick down your door,[32] to have your refrigerator examined for adequate food by social service agency workers,[33] to be followed in retail establishments,[34] to go through a metal detector at the door of one's school,[35] to be tested for drugs during a prenatal examination[36]—all of these and more are forms of physical and spatial racialized surveillance. Although none of them are exercised solely on Black and Latino people, all of them are disproportionately and consistently exercised on Black and Latino people and in communities where large numbers of Black and Latino people live. The current experience of the fragility of privacy for a disproportionate sector of the African American community, in particular, is contiguous with earlier terrorizing practices associated with enslavement, the disciplining ideology that shaped (the often romanticized) period of radical reconstruction,[37] the violent and legal-instrumentalist backlash against reconstruction, and the Jim Crow era.[38]

I have chosen to concentrate my attention on the welfare state and policing. I've made these choices because these institutions are so prevalent in predominantly African American communities (and to a lesser but still dramatic extent in Latino communities) that, I would argue, they shape life for residents of those communities whether or not they have direct experience with these institutions. One study argues that 90 percent of African Americans will live for at least one year below the federal poverty line[39] and many of those for a number of years or an entire lifetime.[40] Moreover,

> even *within* the poverty population, blacks, Hispanics, and some Asian sub-groups experience the added challenge of residing in neighborhoods of concentrated poverty. Poor blacks and Latinos are over twice as likely to live in high-poverty neighborhoods than are poor whites. Indeed, a substantial share of poor whites reside in largely middle-class, suburban neighborhoods, while most poor blacks and Latinos dwell in much

higher-poverty, urban, racially segregated neighborhoods. Incredibly, even black and Latino households with incomes over $50,000 per year are twice as likely to live in high-poverty neighborhoods than are white households with incomes less than $20,000.[41]

Therefore, even solidly working- and middle-class Blacks often live in neighborhoods where social workers, welfare caseworkers, and police are common regulatory agents.[42] And yet theoretical discussions about African American identity and race in the post–civil rights era have disproportionately been oriented around the middle-class experience, rather than the more representative working- class and poor experience.[43] To talk about the denials of privacy rights and racialized surveillance through the landscape of poor Black communities is to identify the experience of race for residents of those communities as the central terrain upon which we should think about the operation of race and racial inequality.

While not all residents of predominantly poor or predominantly African American neighborhoods have regular encounters with the regulatory powers of public housing, welfare distribution, policing, and prison, many do, and their force is normative. For example, one study of young Black women suggests a significant knowledge of the rules of means-tested welfare benefits even among those who are not in the system.[44]

Also, an examination of these institutions provide a good space for comparison between stereotypic images of people in the ghetto, who are presumed to have regular contact with these institutions, and the literal constraints imposed on the lives of people who encounter these institutions. The dynamic relationship among schemas, stereotypes, image, narrative, and material conditions is readily explored through the discussion of these institutions. Practices of exposure and surveillance that deny privacy emerge, in part, from popular narratives of disarray and depravity in communities of color and the "need" for disciplining intervention. In the early twentieth century, Herbert Spencer, a popular eugenicist, wrote, in his book *Education: Moral, Intellectual and Physical*, that we should "Bear constantly in mind that the aim of your discipline is to produce *a self-governing being*, not a being governed *by others*."[45] In many ways, we can see that contemporary presumptions about who is self-governing and who is to be governed continue to have the eugenicist imprimatur of a distinction drawn by race.

Policing Welfare

> Privacy as a value and right is a perquisite of the privileged; it
> verges on an empty promise for those who are poor.
>
> —Patricia Ann Boling[46]

> When the state Welfare people began coming to our house, we
> would come from school sometimes and find them talking with
> our mother, asking a thousand questions. They acted and looked
> at her, and at us, and around in our house, in a way that had
> about it the feeling—at least for me—that we were not people. In
> their eyesight we were just *things*, that was all. . . . They acted as
> if they owned us, as if we were their private property. As much
> as my mother would have liked to, she couldn't keep them out.
>
> —*The Autobiography of Malcolm X*[47]

In Alice O'Connor's book *Poverty Knowledge*, she describes the professionalization of poverty research over the course of the twentieth century. Part of her project is a consideration of how race and class are treated as demographic features in the structure of "information" that is part of "poverty knowledge" but not as categories worthy of independent analysis. Such a critique lends itself to this question: what distinct knowledge is revealed if we see poverty as a feature of race rather than race as a variable in poverty? In the late twentieth century, the discourse around means-tested benefits was a highly racialized discourse. One way to read this is to say that, by racializing our conception of means-tested benefits, racial bias overdetermined a conversation that should have essentially been about poverty. Another way is to look at that discourse in order to consider how social practice is shaped by how an institution is raced and how raced institutions shape the raced lives of individuals. To that end, I share O'Connor's thought that the approach to "poverty knowledge" should change. She writes:

> a new poverty knowledge would necessarily recognize class, gender, and
> race a legitimate "units of analysis"—not simply as demographic variables
> that can be isolated and controlled for, but as dimensions of social and
> economic stratification in their own right. . . . In the new poverty knowl-
> edge, factors now treated, if at all, as mere background—history, politics,
> public and private institutions, ideology—become much more the stuff of
> direct and critical scrutiny.[48]

At the center of practices of inequality are the experiences and images of poor people of color. In "Kicking the Pigeon," the journalist Jamie Kalven recounts the story of Diane Bond, a woman who resided in the Stateway Gardens Housing Projects of the Chicago Housing Authority before the demolition of the eight-building high-rise development, which was completed in June 2007. Ms. Bond's story is distinguished because she became a plaintiff in a case against the Chicago Police Department after being continually and systematically tortured (both physically and psychologically) by a group of officers referred to as the "skullcap crew," five gang tactical officers who patrolled Stateway Gardens and terrorized it with utter impunity. These men followed her, entered her home, sexually abused her, beat her, and terrorized her with the threat of and the actual repetition of these acts. Represented by the attorney and clinical professor Craig Futterman and the University of Chicago Law School Mandel Legal Aid Clinic, Diane Bond settled with the City of Chicago for $150,000. What emerged in the context of the case, however, was statistical evidence that police officers who were consistently complained about by citizens in the City of Chicago had a less than 1 percent probability of being sanctioned.[49] As a result, there was a public outcry for the publication of the names of the officers in *Bond v. Utreras et al.*, and a group of aldermen sued for their release. Notably, the city spent millions of dollars defending the protection of those names.

Jamie Kalven writes, in his reportage of the conduct of the abusive officers:

A question persists at the center of this narrative. *Why?* . . . What possible rationale could there be for their conduct? The abuses occurred in the context of the "war on drugs." That was the pretext for raiding her building, searching her home and person, and interrogating her. But does the enforcement of drug laws, in the absence of individualized suspicion (much less a search warrant supported by probable cause), explain the abuses? Does it make sense of the senseless, sadistic conduct alleged? This is not an easy question to answer. For it demands we entertain the possibility that the abuses were an end in themselves and the drug war a vehicle to that end: the possibility that members of the Chicago Police Department terrorized Diane Bond for the perverse pleasure of it.[50]

Kalven cogently speculates that a context in which privacy denials are normative and even seen as "necessary" facilitates violent, sadistic behavior. That Ms. Bond lived in public housing and that the abuses occurred under authority of police power not only facilitated but structurally legitimated the denial of her privacy in her domestic space, her free movement, and her body. The fact that the city did not respond to citizens complaints about the "skullcap crew" likely had much to do with the fact that those who complained were overwhelmingly Black and low income.

The rules guiding the distribution of means-tested benefits also indicate that the invasion of privacy is a normative reality for those who would use the society's safety nets. Much has been written about how, until 1968, Aid to Families with Dependent Children policy, which made benefits contingent upon a mother's noncohabitation with a male partner and used routine investigation to monitor compliance with that rule, drove poor Black men out of households[51] (an empirically debatable conclusion). Another way to see this practice is as an invasion into private decision making about domestic relations. It also normalized surveillance on domestic places. Perhaps the greatest evidence of the denial of privacy rights on a philosophical level, however, can be found in the 1971 Supreme Court case *Wyman v. James*[52] (which is still good law). In that case, the Court held that welfare caseworkers might conduct warrantless searches of recipients' apartments without triggering Fourth Amendment protections so long as criminal prosecution was not threatened. This decision denied that such a practice constituted an "unwarranted invasion of personal privacy" and declared that it was in fact acceptable because of the state's interest in ensuring compliance with the program! Although home visits are no longer generally required for means-tested benefit distribution, to this day there are still widespread mechanisms through which the distribution of benefits is predicated on investigation and evaluation of the private lives of citizens.

The Personal Responsibility and Work Opportunity Reconciliation Act of 1996 (PRWORA) is the federal law that replaced AFDC with TANF (temporary aid to needy families). The program was instituted as a block grant to states, which now have a great deal of flexibility to experiment with how to execute the program. The law and its attendant programs are devoted, in multiple ways, to the control and monitor of intimate lives.

PRWORA has social engineering to reduce out-of-wedlock birth as an expressed intent. In order to receive assistance, a mother usually must disclose the name of the father of her child. This sort of practice has been declared an illegal violation of rights to privacy in other contexts. For example, in *G.P., C.M., C.H. and L.H. v. State of Florida*,[53] the Fourth Circuit federal appeals court declared unconstitutional provisions of the Florida Adoption Act that— without exception for rape or incest—required a mother who wished to put a child up for adoption and who did not know the whereabouts of the father to place newspaper ads in an effort to identify the father before parental rights could be terminated. The court identified this as an unwarranted invasion of privacy and found no compelling state interest to legitimate such an invasion. And yet, a quite similar invasion is allowed into the lives of women seeking welfare benefits. Arguably, the state interest is in making sure that the state is not providing benefits for children who are otherwise supported. However, the state might instead encourage and facilitate women on assistance to seek child support except in cases where stigma or danger makes it inappropriate. More important, the policy is rooted in an assumption that there are widespread efforts to defraud the state, assumptions born of 1980s narratives of welfare queens driving Cadillacs, a fantastic imagery to apply to a population that is overwhelmingly barely at a subsistence level of income.

Also, PRWORA requires custodial parents, usually mothers, to assign rights to child support to the state in order to receive benefits. The state thereby intervenes in the economic exchange between parents. Moreover, the requirements that mothers establish the child's paternity and assign child support establishes formal and forced contact between parents. It puts a particular hardship on those who have been victims of domestic violence. Although there is a "good cause" exemption from the requirement that mothers cooperate with the child support requirements, it is often difficult to get access to that exemption.

PRWORA's intrusive agenda manifests in a number of additional ways. It funds abstinence-only programs for states, imposing particular ideas of sexual morality. It also allows states to use their block grant funds to spend money on marriage-encouragement programs. At the same time that funds may be expended to encourage marriage, funds that might otherwise be used to provide support to needy families, states are incentivized to reduce welfare rolls and the birth of poor children with an "illegitimacy bonus" for states that reduce out-of-wedlock births and also decrease the number of abortions.

PRWORA also requires teen mothers to live at home with guardians or parents, a living arrangement that may or may not be best for all family members. More broadly, "PRWORA not only eliminates the entitlement to cash assistance, it simultaneously *toughens* the conditions on participation,"[54] and "Each state can now decide which categories of children are eligible for assistance and which are not, subject only to a requirement that families receive 'fair and equitable treatment.'"[55] The legislation is suffused with a conservative sexual morality, attempts to socially engineer the terms and outcomes of intimate association for poor people, and creates significant impediments to the use of safety nets.

This legislation also allows for waivers for specific requirements in order to carry out experimental programs intended to further the goals of benefits programs. Insofar as the federal government has a deliberate goal of reducing the number of people receiving welfare, it is understandable that waivers that reduce benefits are often approved. Such waivers are exercised at a much higher rate in states with high Black populations.[56]

One of these waivers is the imposition of family caps. A family cap is a provision whereby benefits do not increase per child after a woman has a certain number of children. States with high Black populations are much more likely to have family caps.[57] The exercise of family caps is clearly another effort at social engineering aimed at reducing the number of children born to poor mothers, premised on the narrative that poor Black women have more babies in order to get a bigger check. Notably, research does not support this narrative, but family caps—the consequence of its proliferation—have likely contributed to more children living in extreme poverty.[58]

This effort to exert control over poor people's intimate associations extends to recipients' interactions with the representative professionals. Women often report being asked questions and receiving criticism about their private lives.[59] The ideological impact of the focus on out-of-wedlock birth (the rate of which is extremely high among African Americans) may also contribute to the disparate treatment of Black women by caseworkers, who are less likely to provide them with information about employment and educational opportunities.[60]

The stringent rules for welfare receipt are enforced by way of surveillance and the imposition of sanctions for those who violate the rules. Because it is virtually impossible to feed a family on the welfare benefits provided by most states, parents must engage in activities that are in violation of rules in order to provide for their families. The imposition of sanctions elides the distinction between fraud that the average person would identify as morally illegitimate and that which is appropriate. Moreover, the states and state agents are incentivized to ignore this distinction because they are given bonuses for reducing the welfare rolls.

To identify fraud in this way further justifies intrusion into privacy because, as the logic goes, of course fraud must be rooted out. As well, when welfare recipients are victims of the violation of rules or laws, as in the case of welfare recipients who are sexually harassed by supervisors in welfare-contingent work assignments, remedies are generally impracticable, because to leave one's employment often means loss of benefits. Moreover, many women are unaware of their right to contest the imposition of sanctions or the violation of rules on the part of caseworkers and employers.

Interviews with women on welfare demonstrate that many of them experience a moral conflict over lying to the government in order to support their families and children.[61] At the same time, these same women are far more likely to be under the surveillance of child welfare agencies. On one hand, the state sets up formal rules that make mothers' protection of children fraudulent, and, on the other, mothers are consistently under suspicion for failing to protect their children. Both lead to intrusions. Although these regulations ostensibly apply without regard to color, in the early years of the twenty-first century the majority of recipients of means-tested benefits are people of color. A disproportionate number of those who have been able to successfully make their way out of welfare after the 1996 reforms have been White. Moreover, since long before welfare recipients were literally majority people of color, welfare has been conceived of as a Black institution, and therefore policy measures have been driven by racialized conceptions of who recipients are and how they must be regulated.

The Police Power and Profiling

Surveillance in the United States has always been tightly connected with race, from the patrollers and overseers during slavery to the philosophical notion that Blacks require oversight by Whites and the observational practices of racist science.[62] A practice of examination, watching, evaluation, and judgment (read punishment) constituted how the ideology of race was enacted and taught for much of our history.

Michel Foucault provided a theoretical account of how surveillance is a disciplining force when engaged in by the police power of a state. In the U.S. context, what I would term "racial surveillance" as enacted by the police power has often not been solely or even principally a disciplining force insofar as it does not necessarily have a logic attached to it, that if you do x then y will happen, so don't do x; rather, it has often been capricious and arbitrary in the dispensation of punishment. However, racial surveillance has operated to terrorize (with the threat of undue and unanticipated punishment), create hypervigilance, and identify the status of outsider. The consequence of this surveillance that ritually humiliates and terrorizes racially othered groups is a set of brutal episodes that operate as markers of inequality.

The story of police impunity in the case of Diane Bond and vis-à-vis residents of Stateway Gardens was not isolated. At the same time, the poverty of many communities of color and the lack of protection afforded by police power in those communities also allows for residents to be terrorized by those who live in the community and who are engaged in antisocial or dangerously illegal behaviors. The threat and the existence of civilian violence on the one hand terrorizes and on the other provides a narrative justification for surveillance and intrusions into the private lives of citizens on the part of the state and for the exercise of police power. Therefore, the majority of citizens in poor communities of color experienced heightened vulnerability vis-à-vis both the state and criminals. Despite the fact that in the past several decades constitutional interpretation has generally moved toward color blindness in other arenas, in the case of the state's authority to engage in surveillance persistent color consciousness has been effectively rendered acceptable, despite the fact that color is not a good proxy for criminal activity.

In *Whren v. United States* (1996), the U.S. Supreme Court asserted that "a police officer's subjective use of race in deciding to make a traffic stop will not invalidate that stop if an objectively valid reason could have supported the decision." The Court has effectively rendered racial profiling acceptable by taking the issue of race out of analysis of whether Fourth Amendment protections have been violated in police stops. The Fourth Amendment is the constitutional provision against unlawful search and seizure. As long as it was interpreted to prohibit racial profiling, the burden was on police officers to provide a race-neutral justification for stops that others claimed were motivated by discriminatory purpose or intent. In this case, the Court instead argued that claims of unconstitutional racial discrimination in police conduct should fit under a Fourteenth Amendment claim. The problem is that, in the Fourteenth Amendment context, the plaintiff has to demonstrate discriminatory impact and intent. Establishing impact is usually cost prohibitive, and demonstrating intent is virtually impossible.

Racial surveillance in policing is a multitiered practice. The first tier of racial surveillance, particularly of Black and Latino men, precedes the encounter with the police. That is to say, whether or not they are stopped, Black and Latino men are watched in far greater numbers than other sectors of the population.[63] In a study of racial profiling in traffic stops conducted in a Florida county, it was found that, while African Americans and Latinos made up about 5 percent of drivers, they accounted for more than 70 percent of those stopped.[64] There is the watching, the stopping, the detention and, sometimes, violence.

In states as varied as New York, Illinois, Florida, Maryland, West Virginia, Rhode Island, Alabama, California, and New Jersey, the practice of racial profiling in traffic stops has been documented.[65] The purported justification is often the control of drug trafficking. This excuse also is applied to explain the particularly high rates of surveillance that occur when people of color move outside communities that contain large minority populations. Jay Mee-han and Michael Ponder of Michigan's Oakland University studied Mobile Data Terminals, which are computers used by police to run license plates of drivers. Their study showed that when people of color were in predominantly White areas, then their plates were run more frequently. David A. Harris, a legal scholar, refers to these as "border stops"[66] and notes that, "Because profiling has such a strong impact on the mobility of those subjected to it—the diminished willingness of minorities to go where they feel they will get undesirable law enforcement attention—these tactics help to reinforce exist-ing segregation in housing and employment."[67]

Whether or not the consequences are that great, it is irrefutable that such behavior operates to inhibit the mobility of the surveilled sector of the popu-lation. One defense to this practice has been that higher degrees of surveil-lance are necessary for groups of people more prone to crime. In 1999, the Superintendent of the New Jersey State Police, Carl Willams, told the New-ark *Star Ledger* that "minorities perpetrated most of the drug and drug traf-ficking in his state. 'The drug problem is mostly cocaine and marijuana. It is most likely a minority group that's involved with that.'"[68] However, such logic proves circular. We cannot truly know what proportion of crimes is com-mitted by people of color because they receive such disparate degrees of law enforcement. The authors of *Whitewashing Race: The Myth of a Color Blind Society* write that "There is [a] problem with the strategy of assessing dis-crimination in the justice system by comparing rates of imprisonment with rates of arrest: it ignores the possibility that discrimination in police prac-tices strongly influences who will be arrested in the first place."[69] Or, as Har-ris notes, arrest rates simply tell you who is arrested: "In cases of consensual crimes such as drug activity and weapons offenses, arrest and incarceration rates are particularly poor measures of criminal activity. They are much bet-ter measures of law enforcement activity."[70] The rhetorical claim that the rea-son for the oversurveillance is the disproportionate level of criminal activity is unverifiable because of both the oversurveillance of some groups and the underreporting of crime.[71] According to the 2006 National Crime Victimiza-tion Survey data, approximately half of the victims of personal crime did not report the crimes to the police. This makes arrest figures unreliable indica-tors of who commits crimes overall. African Americans are more likely to be victims of personal crimes, most likely to be victimized by other Black people, and more likely to report their victimization than either Whites or Hispanics.[72] This is an important counterpoint to the popular discourse that suggests that African American communities are noncompliant with police work. But it is worth nothing that, despite these high rates of victimization and crime reporting, Black neighborhoods are more likely to be unsafe, indicating that, notwithstanding increased surveillance, police forces have not been as effective in protecting Black citizens as in protecting other groups.

Moreover, the fact that African Americans disproportionately dwell in public or subsidized housing where summary eviction for drug use or offenses[73] drives illegal activity outdoors also makes African Americans who violate the law more likely to be caught. However, the greater degree of surveillance of people of color often does not bear out higher rates of discovered criminal activity. In fact, the net result on those suspected may be lower for people of color. For example, in hit rates on planes, customs agents doing drug searches in 1998 "found drugs on the white passengers they searched at a rate of 6.7 percent. For blacks, the hit rate was lower, 6.2 percent, than it was for whites. For Latinos it was even lower, just 2.8 percent." However, 43 percent of passengers stopped were either Black or Latino.[74] This was in part a result of a generalized practice of racial surveillance operating as a stand-in for nonrace-based evaluative and investigatory tools. Once customs agents ceased using race to identify smugglers and shifted their focus to race-neutral factors, their success increased by more than 300 percent.[75] And yet, evidence like this hasn't necessarily changed the practice of racial profiling. For example, in 2009, Immigration and Customs Enforcement agents in Maryland were reported to have indiscriminately rounded up Latinos in order to meet annual arrest quotas.[76] The high-profile racial-profiling cases of the late 1990s have not had much apparent impact on the widespread national practice of racial profiling, as evinced by the comprehensiveness of the practice as detailed in the ACLU's state-by-state reporting of racial profiling in 2009.

Another common response to arguments against racial surveillance is that if someone is innocent, that person shouldn't care about being stopped and frisked or pulled over while driving. In theory, this is perhaps a rational response. But the humiliation and even terror that racial surveillance metes out is significant. We can use one or two stories out of many to provide powerful examples of this. The fate of Amadou Diallo, a Guinean immigrant who was told by police to stop, is our fear. For the danger ascribed to his presence, he was showered with forty-one bullets in the back. Or there is Oscar Grant, who was fatally shot in the back while unarmed and prostrate on an Oakland, California, train platform on New Year's Day 2009. The terror of execution without process, with no trial, no jury, no structure of evaluation, is harrowing, particularly when one does not have to violate the law, act unruly, or misbehave in order to be so punished.

While this fear is not rational, in the sense that the odds are against death, even in the worst form of racial profiling, the power and the arbitrariness of these stories do shape sentiment. The feeling is that a threatening stop could happen at any time, even given ideal compliance with the police. This is true not merely in the replication of stereotype but also in the narrative power of stories of racial exclusion or punishment.

In 1999, two troopers on the New Jersey Turnpike stopped a van carrying four young Black men. According to the troopers, the van attempted to back into them after the stop, and they responded to the perceived threat with a volley of gunshots. The van crashed into a ditch, and the four men inside were found bleeding from gunshot wounds. All of them survived, a miracle given that they claimed the officers refused to seek medical attention for them until they had pulled apart their clothes and searched the car.[77] At trial, the officers admitted that they had used racial profiling in pulling over the young men and had been ordered to do so by their superiors.[78] It appears that even though police departments are now sophisticated enough to know that they should say they arrest only when there is "reasonable suspicion," evidence suggests that crude racial profiling is still occurring. For example, in 2009 in Jackson, Tennessee, police were reported to have randomly stopped, interviewed, and photographed African Americans, without any suggestion that they were engaged in an investigation.[79] In Illinois, data collected pursuant to state legislation meant to reveal and deter racial profiling showed that "Black and Hispanic motorists are more than twice as likely to be subjected to consent searches, yet white motorists are twice as likely to be found with contraband as a result of these searches."[80] This indicates that, whereas decent criteria are being used to identify Whites who are committing crimes, Blacks and Latinos must be prepared to be assumed suspect by virtue of their race.

Police can be agents of racial authority as a result of explicit training. In a New Mexico training video intended to teach police how to isolate highway drug couriers, all the dealers in the mock traffic stops had Spanish surnames.[81] And, in a New Jersey training video, "an off screen voice tells trainees that Jamaicans dominate certain aspects of the drug trade. A picture shows a black man in informal dress and dreadlocks. The image then changes, showing a similar black man wearing a business suit with short hair. The voice admonishes trainees that they should not be fooled; these drug dealers can look like anything at all."[82] Of course, the message is that *any* sort of Black man is potentially a drug dealer. Moreover, one need not be exposed to racist police training videos to get the message that men of color pose a criminal threat. The image of Black and Latino men as criminals permeates the popular media, both news and fictional. Police, like all citizens, carry such imagery into their interactions with others. Hence, police encounters are filled with the baggage of our racial narratives.

For African Americans, the terror of the police power has a long history. It was found in slave patrols, Klan violence, vigilante lynchings, and burnings.[83] Dramatically, in the late-nineteenth-century post-emancipation era, the role of the police power was established as a kind of racial authority precisely because it did not correlate directly with the behavior of the victim.[84] And when the violence did correlate with the behavior of the victim, it was often punishment for the transgression of achieving economic or professional success.[85] Gunnar Myrdal, the author of the landmark work *An American Dilemma: The Negro Problem and Modern Democracy*, noted in the mid-twentieth century that racial surveillance and disparate treatment in criminal law enforcement were firmly established. He observed that "discrimination was the norm, and it worked in two ways. On the one hand, blacks were far more likely to be put under surveillance, arrested, and sentenced, especially in the lower courts, if their victims (or supposed victims) were white. . . . The sentences for even major crimes are ordinarily reduced when the victim is another Negro." [86] The same is true today.

Racial surveillance is an instrument of fear that also shapes national identity. Its insidiousness is that it has no bogeyman behind the curtain; it is a practice that emerges from our history, conflicts, the interests of capital, and political expediency in the nation and the world. Inculcated fears and biases motivate racial surveillance. Nowhere is the diffuse and unindividuated nature of this practice more apparent than in the fact that overpolicing is not limited to White officers but is instead systemic. Harris writes, "If both black and white officers seem to use traffic stops and searches disproportionately against blacks and other minorities, this implies that profiling is about more than the racism of a few racist whites with badges. Rather it is an institutional problem, and an institutional practice, that lies at the base of this thorny knot of difficulties."[87] The overpolicing of people of color by Black officers is even more dramatic because of the widely known episodes in which Black police officers themselves have been shot by other officers who assumed they were perpetrators.[88]

Research abounds that demonstrates the disproportionate and racially motivated surveillance of African American and Latino citizens.[89] And the more racially identifiable one is, the more vulnerable one is to being surveyed. But the question is, of what consequence is this?

Rituals of Terror and Humiliation in Racial Surveillance

The postcolonial theorist Frantz Fanon[90] and the African American intellectual W. E. B. Du Bois[91] both described the experience of existing, in part, outside oneself, that comes from being Black. The awareness of one's own flesh in a manner that is at once alienating and transcendent is a consequence of the overdetermination of the Black body in a White supremacist society. Men of color who are surveyed report that a hypervigilance develops as a tool of self-preservation. They must constantly prepare potential for a terrible episode. At best, in such episodes, surveillance is experienced as a ritual of humiliation. A man cited in Harris's book describes the emotional impact of repeated stops by saying, "Each one of those stops for me had nothing to do with breaking the law. It had to do with who I was. . . . It's almost like somebody pulls your pants down around your ankles. You're standing there in the nude, but you've got to act like nothing's happening."[92] The description of a forced consent, "acting like nothing is happening" is telling not simply for its own emotion but for its indication of what is being prepared for: one must maintain complete complicity and calm at the risk of becoming part of another narrative of excessive use of force. Being watched can kill you.

In this era of globalization, as in any moment in which movement (literal and figurative) is a defining characteristic of transformation, the metanarratives of race are often manifest in degrees of freedom of movement, and in the relation of police power to one's movement in the world. The terrorizing violence experienced by domestic men of color as part of their experience of surveillance is mirrored in the experience of immigrants of color in the practice of border policing. For Mexican immigrants, motivated by the demand for their presence in the U.S. economy and diverted by Operation Gatekeeper's vigilant protection of visible and safe zones, crossing the border in extremely dangerous mountainous regions has become more common in the twenty-first century. Operation Gatekeeper, Nevins notes, "[h]as largely failed to protect the national citizenry from the 'threat' posed by 'illegals.' Where the state has been more successful has been in creating an image of security vis-à-vis 'illegal' immigration. Today, the U.S.-Mexico boundary in high visibility or highly urbanized areas appears far more orderly than it did several years ago."[93] As a result, the image is that the "illegals" are being kept under control. However, they are just out of sight. The borders remain permeable, but now crossing them is a death trap. Our citizenry accepts this, according to Bill Ong Hing, because "Two related concepts are in play. First, the public is generally inured to police force. Second, the public is immune from it when it is invisible. In the instance of Gatekeeper, the public becomes inured to the use of police power (essentially violence) to do everything for it as long as it is not noticed."[94] The consequence has been countless deaths, an outcome well anticipated by the U.S. government. There are many whose response to this fact has been that the people assumed the risk involved by choosing to cross the border illegally. But such a response is disingenuous. Not only does the United States invite undocumented workers to participate in the economic structure; it depends upon them. Yet it opts out of offering them the basic protection of the laws and of human rights norms. It is a partial and exploitative membership, forcing consent to social rules, accepting labor, yet denying benefits, a liminal status.

Haitian immigrants' experience with racial surveillance is instructive, as well. First, the distinction between how Haitian and Cuban immigrants are treated is both political and racial. As Charles Ogletree wrote,

> Many commentators have noted the disparity between the way American immigration law treats Haitians as compared to Cubans. Illegal immigrants caught entering the United States generally are returned to their countries, but under the 1966 Cuban Readjustment Act, all Cubans who reach U.S. soil are allowed to remain. This policy has a clear racial impact when refugees from Cuba and Haiti are compared—Cuban refugees, most of whom are white, are granted citizenship, while black Haitians are repatriated. . . . As Congressman Charles B. Rangel has remarked, "[n]o one challenges the fact that any other boy who came here illegally from Haiti or the Dominican Republic, for example, would have been sent back to their home immediately. But in the Elian Gonzalez case, there was clearly a double standard, because even in our distorted dealings with Cuban refugees, the fact is Elian is an illegal alien with no legal right to be here."[95]

The surveillance of Haitians attempting to enter into the United States has been both physical and physiological. We must remember that, before it housed "enemy combatants," Guantánamo Bay was used as an HIV camp at which Haitian refugees were detained. On one hand, the treatment of Haitian refugees was abusive; on the other, the camp created the popular image of Haitian immigrants as dangerously diseased. Nowhere is a liminal status more dramatically demonstrated than there.[96] In the aftermath of 9/11, Guantánamo became a detention center again, this time for those designated as "enemy combatants," once again all people of color. In both cases, its residents were relegated to a no-man's-land. The U.S. Justice Department argued in both cases that Guantánamo lies outside the jurisdiction of the United States and is, therefore, beyond the reach of the U.S. Constitution. It is a place that was deliberately imagined as being beyond constitutional rights, under U.S. control, yet physically in Cuba. Besides the ideological force of its being a no-man's-land, it is literally outside the view of the citizenry, its dismal conditions made invisible by distance and the borders of law. The Obama administration, which initially announced plans to close Guantánamo, subsequently hesitated.

During the first term of George W. Bush's presidency, Attorney General John Ashcroft even made a claim that there was some connection between the "dangerous" Haitians and Arabs, both of whom have been housed on Guantánamo. David Joseph, a Haitian refugee who came to the United States on a boat along with two hundred other Haitians, posted bond, yet was refused release by Ashcroft, who overruled the decisions of an immigration judge and of the Board of Immigration Appeals. Ashcroft justified this act by arguing that the government had concerns about the release of undocumented Haitians without background checks because Palestinians and Pakistanis were "using Haiti as a staging point for attempted migration into the United States."

Peoples of these three "colored" nations were all imagined as national threat, and this threat was used to justify the denial of due process to people from these nations, despite the rule of law. As in the association of Haiti with AIDS, the image of "terrorist cells" is part of a discourse of pestilential threat, a risk of a dreaded conflagration that must be held back at all costs. Those costs are often the rights of people of color. And, like the ghetto harassment, the nighttime highway traffic stop, Guantánamo and border patrols are places where victims of racial surveillance and abuse (either violence or aggressive neglect) are made invisible. Most of our citizenry never has to confront what it is like to experience this humiliation.

The status of undocumented Mexicans in the United States presents some complicated issues for the study of race because of the intersections of nationalism and nativisms. Mexican immigrants make up close to 30 percent of the foreign-born population in the United States, and more than half are estimated to be here without documentation.[97] Darker-skinned Mexicans and those who do agricultural or other forms of day labor are more likely to be undocumented. To many observers, these facts might be seen to easily justify racial surveillance; if you see a particularly Mexican-looking man doing day labor, odds are good that he's "illegal." Here's the problem with such an assessment. While the suspicion that a Mexican person in the United

States is illegal might often be well founded, focusing on that fact obscures the reality that undocumented Mexicans are not unwelcome or anomalous in our society. The presence of people who do not have legal rights to be in this country is a norm in our country, and we have entire industries that operate in particular ways as a function of that presence. "Undocumented" is a firm category in our society, just like "citizen" or "permanent resident." Undocumented workers occupy a clear social role in which they are perpetually in a state of vulnerability and yet are in constant economic demand. We have one area of our social organization that presumes their presence (labor markets) and another that is ambivalent about it and therefore denies them many fundamental rights (the law). In an article titled "Mexican Immigrant Replenishment and the Continuing Significance of Ethnicity and Race,"[98] Tomás Jimenez explains how assumptions that Mexican immigration and assimilation models will follow those of European immigrants are questionable because of the ongoing arrival of new immigrants. Mexican Americans continue to be defined by and shaped by the influx of new immigrants, unlike Europeans, among whom immigration declined sharply in the 1930s and 1940s. His analysis offers useful documentation of how the presumed noncitizen or forever-foreign label applies to Mexican Americans but also reveals a deeper philosophical problem that affects many non-Black, non–American Indian people of color. Their recognition as citizens often seems to be dependent upon their dissociation from the larger ethnic or racial group. The alternative is to be suspected of being an outsider until proved otherwise.

The blurring of lines between immigration and law enforcement further establishes connections between racial surveillance of domestic citizens of color and immigrant people of color. Although immigration is well established by our constitutional law as a matter of federal jurisdiction, there are programs that hand over some immigration policing practices to local police forces. The Delegation of Immigration Authority program, conducted by the Immigration and Customs Task Force of the Department of Homeland Security and known as 287(g), allows local law enforcement officers to perform functions that usually fall within the jurisdiction of federal immigration law.[99] Although the functions are limited and the officers are usually trained, reliance upon racial profiling is heightened in this context, given that local police don't have sophisticated methods of identifying undocumented workers. Moreover, programs like these produce a chilling effect on undocumented people or people with undocumented family members who have been victims of or witnesses to crimes. And one of the few terrains upon which they are supposed to be able to rely on protection of the state is thereby weakened.

Although practices of racial profiling are framed around different "concerns" for different groups of people of color—terrorism for Middle Eastern and South Asians, immigration for Mexicans and Central Americans and Black Caribbean people, drugs for African Americans and Caribbean Latinos—they all overpolice, meaning that they are poor tools. And they all emerge out of panicked discourses about danger and threats to social order.

Stanley Cohen, a criminologist, argues that "Many large American cities are routinely described as 'ungovernable' as a result of violence, drugs, and a breakdown of policing and social services. . . . [T]his rhetoric is now taken for granted . . . the cult of national security represented by the Soviet threat has given way to a cult of personal insecurity."[100] While the cult of personal security is pitched in terms of the safety of mainstream Americans (racially coded as White), the threats to security are "multiracial." Yet, the history of this imagery on a domestic level is long. In the aftermath of slavery, much was made of the disease and decay that would befall Black communities without appropriate White supervision.[101] Likewise, as part of the cultural and economic imperialism of the late nineteenth century, nations populated by non-White people were described as lawless and decadent. The historical backdrop is useful as a lens through which to understand how the image has become self-perpetuating through many changes in nation-states and in technologies of communication. Media and politics are often vehicles for the repetition of old racial narratives in new contexts.

For the larger society, which doesn't live in communities or occupy bodies targeted by racial surveillance, it is easy to believe that all that is happening is diligent police and immigration work and not anything discriminatory. The popular racialized discourses of national intrusion and national expense speculate about terrible consequences if these communities are left to their own devices. Something must be done, the American populace is told, to prevent the decline toward which "they" may be drawing us. Nevins notes that, in the early to mid-1990s, during a period of increased fervor over the need for border patrols, Californians blamed Mexican immigrants for the state's crowded schools, air pollution, and traffic: "In this manner the environment provided a host of unflattering metaphors (such as 'pollution' and 'contamination') to attach to immigrants." Nevins, too, sees the powerful distinguishing work of this discourse, stating that "Discourse always operates in the service of particular interests or power. As such, discourse can help to construct territories or boundaries and those who belong within, the 'we' as well as the 'they' or 'other.' By establishing binary oppositions between 'us' and 'them' discourse reinforces group identity."[102] Complicating this reality is that there are real problems that must be addressed with respect to crime, with respect to how to manage immigration, with respect to terrorism. To identify racial surveillance as illegitimate, however, does not require that we deny these problems. It does require that we disallow racial categories to operate as proxies for "bad behavior."

Using a "bad behavior" justification for racial profiling and other disparate treatment on the basis of race is what Jody David Armour has termed "reasonable racism." He describes how "many may insist that their racial fears are born of a sober analysis, or at least of rough intuition of crime statistics that suggest Blacks commit a disproportionate number of violent street crimes."[103] The legitimacy of this argument is heightened for the average listener when the "reasonable racist" is a member of the law enforcement community, because the job is risky and is presumed to provide expertise in the assessment of offenders. The problem is that the "reasonable racist" then legitimizes harsh treatment of innocent people of color. Moreover, as the social psychologists Mahzarin R. Banaji and R. Bhaskar have noted, "It is a . . . hoary and fundamental principle of justice that judgments about individuals must be based on the individuals' own behavior, involving specific acts of commission and omission. Societies in which punishment was based on association . . . are regarded as barbaric by the standards of contemporary democracy."[104] Yet, their findings on the persistence of bias indicate that such group-based racial judgments are quite prevalent in the contemporary United States. This is true even in professions stereotyped as attracting more humane people than most. Like the police and welfare caseworkers, physicians and teachers who report child abuse,[105] medical workers of various stripes who suspect drug abuse,[106] child welfare workers,[107] and store personnel who suspect shoplifters,[108] are all professionals who operate in contexts in which heightened presumptions of criminality among Black people are used to justify, on both individual and collective bases, greater "investigation" in the form of surveillance and intrusions upon privacy. The problem with all sorts of citizen-professionals exercising unequal discretion in the form of surveillance is that the practice, while exacting greater penalties for misdeeds by Blacks and Latinos, is often absolved because, as Armour notes, our evaluation of what is reasonable is often merely what is "typical," and it is quite typical to hold racial bias in the contemporary United States.[109]

Racial profiling by the police is a practice that disproportionately but not exclusively impacts men and entails invasions into their physical, spatial, and knowledge-based privacy spheres. However, as the groundbreaking scholarship of law professor Dorothy Roberts has revealed, Black women and children have been targets for racial surveillance with respect to reproductive rights and child welfare. The use of long-term contraceptives and sterilization as plea-bargaining tools for Black women in criminal law, systematic drug testing for pregnant Black women in public hospitals, and the relative aggressiveness of child-removal policies for Black children demonstrate how an image of the bad Black mother works to intrude upon privacy and intimate association.[110]

On the other hand, the generalized image of the "bad Black mother" and the lower value given to Black children leads also to underresponsiveness, allowing many vulnerable children to fall through the cracks. As Roberts argues, "The National Incidence Study discovered that 75 percent of children known to be neglected in the community have not been investigated by child protective services. The state is guilty of both overintervention and under-intervention when it comes to Black families. The system haphazardly picks out a fraction of families to bludgeon, while it leaves untouched the conditions that are really most damaging to children."[111] If the mothers are generally thought to be bad, then such haphazard practice is a likely result.

Homelessness Inside and Out

In Robin West's 1987 article "Jurisprudence and Gender," she argued that women are inherently connected to other people by virtue of their reproductive bodies and social roles, while men can have "separate" identities. West resolved this distinction, however, with a call for a humanist jurisprudence that could transcend gendered experience. Critics of West's work decried it as a form of essentialist feminism, a critique also issued to other theorists of the female body like Lucie Irigaray, Catherine MacKinnon, and Martha Nussbaum. However, what these authors importantly introduced was a line of thought about how the reproductive body is itself is an arena for negotiating political and civic personage.

The seminal work for considerations of the body politic with respect to African American experience is Hortense J. Spillers's 1987 article "Mama's Baby, Papa's Maybe: An American Grammar Book." Published in the same year as West's piece, Spillers's essay avoided the dangers of essentialism by talking about what meaning is made of the Black body rather than by identifying a necessary meaning attached to it, but, like West, she pushed critical theory to engage the female body as a site of political, legal, and social meaning. Speaking of the Moynihan Report of 1965, she identified it as part "a class of symbolic paradigms that...confirm the human body as a metonymic figure for an entire repertoire of human and social arrangements."[112]

We can think of the body as a sort of home and the work that is done upon that body in reproductive and other human relationships as a communication about personhood. If the mother is defined in our culture by her relations, both social and physical, with others, then the fragility African American women experience in protecting their relationships and their children reveals a piece of how racial ideology is practiced. Dorothy Roberts is the preeminent scholar on the issue of how practices of racial surveillance in law and policy depict and destroy Black women's bodies and relationships. Relying upon the foundation she provides, I want to introduce the concept of "homelessness," both literally and figuratively, as a way to address body politics in racial surveillance.[113]

Homeless children are at the greatest risk of being removed from their parents' custody. Within a given year, approximately 22 percent are separated from their parents and put into foster or kinship care.[114] The National Center on Family Homelessness predicts that our inability to meet the need for affordable housing in the United States will dramatically increase the number of homeless families in the coming years. African Americans are hardest hit by this crisis.[115] Homelessness is already a disproportionately a Black phenomenon, with approximately 50 percent of homeless Americans being African American.[116] While welfare reform has reduced the number of people technically living below the poverty line (although the poverty line is nowhere near a living wage in most areas), it has also increased the number of people living in extreme poverty. This, too, leads to growing numbers of homeless families and children. The long-term impact of the economic crisis of the first decade of the twenty-first century will also likely impact homelessness in years to come.

Homelessness is a state of constant exposure to physical invasions of privacy, often of the most violent sort. One study found that 92 percent of homeless mothers had experienced severe physical and or sexual violence in their lives.[117] Another study found that 13 percent of homeless women reported having been raped in the preceding year, half of those at least twice.[118] Even those who find refuge in shelters are vulnerable to invasion of privacy, not simply because shelters often warehouse large numbers of people but also because they are often located in high-crime areas[119] and the homeless are easy targets because of our failure to attend to their safety in general. Notably, courts have not recognized privacy interests for homeless people in their self-created ad hoc domestic spaces.[120] And police don't require a warrant to arrest a homeless person because he or she doesn't have the protective cover of a home.[121]

Though prisons are often described as preferable to homelessness (consider the description "three hots and a cot"), prison, too, is a context in which the domestic sphere as private space is lost. In a sense, the imprisoned are without "homes" while in custody. This is a reflection not only of the absence of choice in domestic space, loss of familial connection because of distance and the cost of travel, and personal exposure in showers and dining areas, but also of the intrusion upon everything from body cavities and letters to the space of one's cell. The U.S. Supreme Court asserted in *Hudson v. Palmer*, 468 U.S. 517 (1984), that there is no right to privacy in a prison cell. Again, the prison population is disproportionately Black, with 43.9 percent of federal and state prison inmates being African American.[122] The percentage of young African American men in prison is seven times that for White men and three times that for Latino men.[123]

As many as 1.5 million children have imprisoned parents on any given day in the United States. African American children are nine times more likely and Hispanic children three times more likely than White children to have a parent in prison.[124] About 75 percent of incarcerated women are mothers, and 80 percent of incarcerated women are addicts. Half of the children of incarcerated women will not visit with their mothers while they are in prison.[125] Immigration policy creates further hardship because immigrant felons are increasingly deported, even if they have minor children who are U.S. citizens. The regulation of child visits to prison is so stringent that families feel a great deal of anxiety over the prospect of failing to comply with the requirements and being denied future visitation as a result. Noncontact visits, meaning that no touching is allowed, are common in U.S. jails. The institutional regulations that are destructive of very basic elements of human intimacy, like a child sitting on a parent's lap, are yet another arena of privacy denial. The destructive impact on relationships of these intrusions on privacy suggest that we need not neglect relationships or community and in fact might importantly facilitate them by reconsidering these rules and their negative impact.

Perhaps the most dramatic illustration of the loss of physical privacy and the absence of protection of private space in prison is found in the fact that rape in prison, of male and female inmates, by both fellow inmates and prison staff, when reported, is overwhelmingly described as occurring at night in the prisoner's cell.[126] And, although the overwhelming majority of prison sexual assaults go unreported, of those that are reported, the majority have no remedy.

If we return to the example cited earlier by Catharine MacKinnon of a prostitute, it is illustrative to note that 84 percent of women who have worked as prostitutes report current or past homelessness. There is a tight connection between the treatment of the body, the punishment of the person, and the insecurity of the home. Moreover, "women of color comprise 40 percent of those in street prostitution, 55 percent of those arrested, and 85 percent of those in jail . . . an African-American woman jailed for sex offenses will on average spend almost twice as much time in jail as a white woman."[127] Like so many other's, the "working girl's" crime is often the simple act of survival in face of the intense vulnerability caused by poverty. As in so many other arenas, the Black "working girl" is more vulnerable to the crimes of others and pays more for hers. According to Olivia Howard, whose story as a sex worker is recounted in *Listening to Olivia: Violence, Poverty and Prostitution*, "A place to stay is the biggest need for women wanting to leave prostitution. A woman wants to feel safe. . . . She needs to have a safe haven where she doesn't have to worry about paying the bills."[128] Certainly, for those women, privacy matters.

Black Thought

The 1990 exhibition "The Kitchen Table Series," by the African American fine-art photographer Carrie Mae Weems, was a narrative of photographs all centered on a Black woman sitting at her kitchen table. Others come in and out of view. But, ultimately, the tightly framed series suggested the intimate and interior life of the woman featured in every image. Weems's exhibition occurred, as the curator Dana Fris Hansen describes it, at a moment in art history in which there was a fixation on the subjugation of women under the male gaze.[129] Weems's project, however, presented a self-defined and self-reflexive Black female experience. She found inspiration for the series in the 1940s tour de force *The Sweet Flypaper of Life*, a book with verse by Langston Hughes and photographs of Harlem life by Roy Decarava.[130] In both the book and Weems's exhibition, the imagery restores a sense of intimate integrity to Black life. Weems's project engages a concept of privacy of the sort Irwin Altman imagines, one where the terms of invitation, inclusion, and exclusion exist within the artist's hands and within the hands of the woman in the photographs (Weems herself).

Privacy thought is found throughout African American art and letters.[131] Not merely does it exist as a discourse about the vulnerability of privacy (although that is certainly there); it also exists in a sense of private space at its best: precious, cherished, and embracing of both social relations and individual need. To the extent that we maintain a commitment here to try to say something generalizable, it is useful to look at African American linguistic practices as reflective of broad African American social thought about privacy.[132]

The idea here is that the prevalence and persistence of privacy talk in African American vernacular English indicates at least two things: first, that the reaction to a history in which privacy has been denied has been an ever-present concern with the maintenance of privacy and, second, that language reflects a social order around privacy that is routinely vetted, discussed, and managed within communities despite the fact that the larger social order treats the need and respect for privacy as negligible in African American communities.

All Up in My Business

The word "business" is perhaps the dominant privacy word one finds in Black English, in phrases like "all up in my business," "mind your business," "she put my business in the street," and the old-fashioned "none of your business, cutting your chinsies, keep your nose out of other folk's business" and "stay out of grown folk's business." Business is knowledge, but knowledge in the sense that it acts as a proxy for entering into an intimate terrain that requires invitation. The inappropriateness of the intrusion may be literal, in the sense of your knowing something you should not know or being in a place where you do not belong, or it may be figurative, in the sense that you are acting inappropriately with respect to another person. For example, you may know what is going on, but you'd better act like you don't.

The spatial metaphors about privacy in Black English are also often about setting boundaries about knowledge, intimacy, and appropriateness. Confrontational phrases like "Why did you call my phone?" emphasize not just that the call is unwanted but that the caller has entered into the private sphere of the called. The message is similar with "Keep my name out your mouth" as a way of lambasting gossip, "all up in my Kool-Aid" as a way of talking about both someone who gets too close and someone who wants to know too much about you or is looking too hard. As always, we should be aware that focusing on these features of language should not lead us to discount possible counternarratives of private and public space in Black language and thought. They are introduced here only to argue that it is not simply a concern imposed by our Anglo-American jurisprudential and philosophical tradition on all of us but a concept that has meaning for this community to which privacy is so frequently denied.

Survey data support this argument, as well. African Americans express significant concern about several arenas in which questions about surveillance practices have been raised. Most evidence of this can be found in their thoughts about medical research and policing. For example, African Americans express the greatest concern of any group polled about the use of medical knowledge. In a UPI-Zogby International poll about the privacy of medical records, African Americans were the most likely to express concern; 34.5 percent of Black participants gave an answer of "highly concerned." Some 30.9 percent of Hispanics in the poll also said they were "highly concerned" about the privacy of their medical records.[133] The use of DNA dragnets in criminal law enforcement provides an example of the reasons for the concern about the privacy of medical information. As Troy Duster writes

> Even when the government's actions do not constitute a search within the meaning of the Fourth Amendment, privacy concerns nevertheless arise. This is the case with so-called "DNA dragnets," in which police seek to collect samples from many individuals meeting a general description such as all black males living in a particular geographic area none of whom individually is a suspect, but one of whom may have committed the crime. DNA dragnets are ostensibly voluntary, but those from whom samples are requested may fear stigmatization or increased scrutiny if they refuse to participate.[134]

Duster alerts us that procedural problems, from lab tainting to evidence tampering, can make what is untrue appear definitive under the guise of science.[135] Suspicion of science may be an important critical stance when purported tools of objectivity are uncritically placed in fallible and subjective human hands for interpretation.

Of course, the history of racist abuse in medical research and practice, as well as the history of policing as it pertains to African Americans, means that one could read these concerns as being born of those specific histories and not broadly reflective of thoughts about privacy. But, as powerful institutional forces and institutions through which social meaning is produced, I would argue, medical and law enforcement concerns are likely central to a more general sensibility about privacy.

We can even think of the strong religious traditions of African Americans as perhaps tied to the need for an interior life that cannot be breached except perhaps in a sense of the "consent of the governed" via the moral authority of the Church. And even then, because of the Protestant theological preoccupation with the individual relationship with God, there is a private spiritual space that cannot be accessed by outsiders. On the other hand, the reported resistance of African Americans to psychotherapy and analysis might be a rejection of these professions' "interventions" into the interior space, which may have a special significance for African Americans. In a literal rendering of the perceived dangers of therapy, some states allow child welfare agencies to require a parent to relinquish parental rights before providing access to mental health services.[136]

A couple of researchers who were examining racial trauma in African American elderly people noted in their research that one of the interviewee's curtains were drawn on a sunny day, leaving the room so dark that her face was almost obscured.[137] Implicitly, the researcher tied this action to fear born of the terrorization of Black neighborhoods by violent Whites, a practice that was common well into the twentieth century. The observation was subtle and keen but perhaps even more complicated. Driving through the average working-class African American neighborhood, one finds that shades, curtains, and sheets prevent outsiders from seeing into homes. This might be a cultural practice born of fear, or it might be a cultural practice indicating people's self-definition as rights-bearing, privacy-demanding citizens. Likely, it is both and more. In either case, it is a privacy-marking gesture.

From Me to We

The concern reflected in "privacy talk" extends from the individual to families' "keep your mouth closed about family business" and even to the community, in warnings to Black public figures who are too vocally critical about Black behavior to stop "airing dirty laundry." Of course, such a discourse often collapses the diversity of communities and may be intended to suppress certain subgroups within African America. Nevertheless, this broader privacy talk is, in part, a conversation about the impact of representation. Because narratives about groups shape how individuals are treated racially, we are also concerned with the dimension of privacy that is based in "knowledge" as a form of group representation.

Discursively, it may be talked about as "airing dirty laundry," but arguably more salient is the sense that salacious interest in Black intimate partnerings or domestic relations is about an effort to intrude on privacy, to "know" something of interior lives to which one has not been invited or offered access, and the danger that that knowledge will be misconstrued, overdetermined, or punitively decontextualized. The feelings about these representations are complicated by the actual challenges faced by members of African American communities. One way to consider the intersection of representation and reality with respect to what is considered "the dirty laundry" might be to consider how the police are often conceptualized as an occupying force, rather than as protectors. Some critics of the discourse around police brutality have argued that police violence accounts for a fraction of the violence that occurs within a community and that political discourse has not been nearly as aggressive in talking about violence within the community. But, of course, these two pieces work together. When the police power operates with impunity, imposing not only killing or beatings but rituals of humiliation, sexual assault, and unresponsiveness to danger, it not only delegitimizes the authority of the police but also fails to distinguish between the victim and perpetrator, the law abider and the thug. All are cast as offenders. The antisocial forces not only have more power in that context but can properly claim a position as members of a family, rather than as intruders. This is to suggest not that communities accept the behavior of antisocial community members but rather that racial representation may alter the calculus for how best to respond to antisocial behavior and who is conceived as part of "us" versus "them."

But some dirty laundry airs itself. The violent response to the "invasion" that historically was meted out against African Americans trying to move into White neighborhoods has been perversely echoed in subsequent years in a Black-on-Black context, as disputes over territory have led to a bloodbath in many urban areas. The neighborhood as homeland, policed and protected by civilian violence, is a tragic inversion of the privacy denial and surveillance that African American historically and currently experience. This is not simply reflective of a yearning for property and the fact that we live in a violent society, although it is partly that. It is a policing of borders—imagined as private space that must be protected from those outside the walls—but also public space insofar as community members are broader than just the family. Sadly, this line of thinking ultimately serves to terrorize and limit the majority of people "who belong," as well as those who don't.

Visibility and Voyeurs

As already suggested, representations often shape public practice. Policing by police forces but also policing done by other kinds of professionals who have the power to punish exists in a dynamic relationship with the "political-industrial complex" vis-à-vis representations of people of color. Demands for punitive policies and the surveillance practices that can ensure them are coaxed from constituents via fear-mongering and the sympathetic rhetoric of responding to the concerns of the average citizen—with average citizenship constructed as White, property-owning, middle-class, nuclear-family domestic units. There is a well-established relationship between political campaigning that is dependent upon being "tough on crime" and growing incarceration rates.[138] These growing incarceration rates often aren't the product of higher rates of crime, but they consistently and disproportionately incarcerate people of color. Similarly, moral panics over immigration are frequent fodder for politicians, shaping not only their popularity but their resistance to appearing to have too much sympathy for immigrants. Even terrible spectacularized episodes of child neglect, with photographs of the dirty, abused, and dark-skinned children covering front pages, have been used for political campaigning. What we get, then, is an endless cycle of electoral political manipulation, demand, and legislative and strategic enactment and re-enactment of punishing Black and Latino people.

In fictional and semifictional media, fantastic representations of Black life are a hot market commodity, reaping financial and professional benefits for cultural entrepreneurs, politicians, entertainment media workers, and others. Often Americans don't really "see" the lives of the poor and of people of color, partly because of the infusion of these media or popular cultural representations with stereotype. One response is to argue that if we were to "see" something different, then a different social response would be elicited, particularly an eagerness to respond to inequality. The problem is that this logic seems to rest on revealing the inaccuracy of representation. In the contemporary United States, the representation of "reality" is truncated, commoditized, and fictionalized not by simple untruth but by the prevalence of spectacle. Truth is hard to define and hard to come by in the sound-byte, short-attention-span society.

Black life, in reality and fictional television and in popular music, is far more visible than the life of any other group of people of color. As J. Yolande Daniels writes, "Black space has become the site for the latent spectacle. Categorization and classification are a means by which the private is made public. The black ghetto and the Projects represent the classification and marginalization of physical space; they have been enforced through mediation and are spectacularized as pathological."[139] Daniels discusses how the racial spectacle is a seeing that collapses individual and group: "As process, the spectacle and spectator transcend the individual and collective body: they merge." In this viewpoint, the "airing dirty laundry" complaint takes on a more salient dimension. The (negative) story about a Black subject is never an individual story; it always a story about many. For those who do not "see" the physical ghetto, reality television creates theaters of the ghetto in their own spectacular version on the bare sets of talk shows or constructed domesticity like the reality programs *Flava of Love* and *I Love New York*. And, as Jeffrey Alexander says, "When citizens make judgments about who should be included in civil society and who should not . . . they draw on a systematic highly elaborated symbolic code."[140] In this instance, the identifications embedded in the symbolic code through the spectacular spheres of news and entertainment are of people in disarray, and, "If actors are passive and dependent, irrational and hysterical, excitable, passionate and unrealistic, or mad, they cannot be allowed the freedom that democracy allows. On the contrary, these persons deserve to be repressed, not only for the sake of civil society, but for their own sakes as well."[141] The truth is that visuality itself can be a tool of domination, particularly when the domination is justified through demands for the imposition of order on the "witnessed" chaos.

In discussing high-rise housing projects, David Theo Goldberg writes, "Its external visibility serves at once as a form of panoptical discipline-vigilant boundary constraints on its effects which might spill over to threaten the social fabric."[142] This interpretation (written before the systematic destruction of large-scale public housing), of course, is of a public spectacle whose meaning was dependent upon fantasy images of the interior spaces of those vertical high rises. This meaning led to repressive responses from the state. The recurring confounding theme to which we must constantly refer is that there were very real threats to life within those interiors, but the threatening and the threatened were indistinguishable in the eyes of many state agents (and others) and even could take on a cyclic relationship as victims often became victimizers as a result of trauma or in an effort to self-protect. Areas of concentrated poverty now, and high-rise housing projects then, are spaces that communicate the politics of race in the United States. As one critic writes, "architecture regulates us. . . . First, architecture can play a communicative role by expressing cultural or symbolic meanings. Second, the architecture can affect how people interact. Third, architecture can be biased and treat certain social groups or values more favorably."[143] In all three forms of architectural or landscape regulation, race is at work, not simply in creating difficult conditions for living but in communicating that the spaces where Black people live are undesirable and dangerous. Hence, the average citizen has little concern with monitoring the role of the external regulator in those communities.

"I Always Feel Like Somebody's Watchin' Me" | 121

In Hardt and Negri's *Empire,* they identify the "right of intervention" "as the right or duty of the dominant subjects of the world order to intervene in the territories of other subjects in the interest of preventing or resolving humanitarian problems, guaranteeing accords, and imposing peace." It is troubling to talk about interventions into Black communities in this way because their residents are, for the most part, not "other subjects" but U.S. citizens. The problem is that when the rules are different for different sectors of the population, you begin to find it easy to apply metaphors of national difference useful for explanation. Hence, there is talk about the "two Americas," the ease with which people turned to describing Hurricane Katrina evacuees as "refugees," and the aptness of Bloom and Kilgore's description of welfare reform practices as "colonizing" poor mothers.[144] Moreover, it suggests ways in which the citizenship distinction that is used as a shorthand for the different states of Blacks and Latinos (although this is already too simplistic, as evidenced by the growing immigrant Black population and the substantial native-born citizen Latino population) may not be as salient as we might think in terms of how people experience themselves in this country.

There is also the role of spectacle in adjudication and legislation to consider. In "Into the Blue: The Cinematic Possibility of Judgment with Passion," Alison Young considers how the translation from narrative to fantastic spectacle impacts adjudication of cases in which heterosexual men claimed that they were acting in self-defense when they murdered gay men whom they accused of making sexual advances to them. She argues compellingly that "judgment in legal texts is predicated on an aesthetics of appearance—a conversion of writing into a specular image"[145] and, of course, back into writing again. Such insight can also be applied when the image of the ghetto directly shapes social policy and clearly impacts adjudication in both criminal and family law. Bernard Harcourt argues convincingly that the broken-windows theory advanced by James Q. Wilson and his colleagues, which identified a preponderance of broken windows in a neighborhood as a sign of disorder and argued that "disorder and crime are usually inextricably linked in a kind of developmental sequence,"[146] was based on virtually no empirical evidence, yet shaped policing practices in a number of cities. The shattered windows and longstanding imagery of Black spectacles worked together to shape policy. As Harcourt writes, "Wilson's principal recommendations, other than order maintenance, included the increased use of incarceration, especially for serious and repeat offenders, more rapid trials and administration of punishment, mandatory sentencing, and reduced prosecutorial discretion over whom to charge. Wilson also advocated aggressive arrest practices as a way to lower crime."[147] The logic of controlling community space is coherent with the invasion upon individual and familial privacy. Addressing the framework that alienates African Americans and Latinos from the ability to exercise privacy rights requires more than revelation. It requires a reconstitution of the balance of power in practices of surveillance, intervention, evaluation, and judgment.

Accountability

> Accountability protects.
> —Anita Allen[148]

I am sitting in a Black hair salon in Philadelphia. It is a particularly cosmopolitan place. There are the sounds of Malinke, French, the nasal cadence of Philadelphian English, the drawl of southerners. All from the mouths of Black women variously dressed in sweatsuits, business suits, and the hijab, commonly seen in Philly's Black Muslim population. At one point, the conversation turns to uninvited visitors to one's home. One woman after another talks about how she does not answer the door—not for survey researchers, political canvassers, Jehovah's Witnesses, door-to-door fundraisers, those asking for directions. "I just don't answer it," a sixty-two-year-old in the braider's chair proclaims loudly, and then boasts that even trick-or-treaters know not to come to her door.

The conversation turns to stories of dangerous episodes in which people answered the door to strangers and paid for it with assault and then, shortly thereafter, to the idea of privacy for children. One mother of a teenager says, "My child cannot have privacy. Sure, he can be alone in his room sometimes, but I have to know what's going on with him, make sure he stays out of trouble." Others agree. The proclaimed surveillance over children is protective. The privacy described is protective. The balance between these interests is found in the concept of accountability and how one cultivates accountability in one's children, as well as protection from the outside when accountability structures seem frail. As the day goes on, I realize that in one way or another almost all of the talk is about either privacy or accountability: the child who gets into trouble when she deflects a teacher who invades her personal space, the rape of a regular client of the salon by gang members, the stop-and-frisk practice proposed by the new police chief.

When city governments propose putting surveillance cameras in public places in an effort to reduce crime, there is not the kind of public outcry against the idea from the African American community that one might expect, given that it is a population so disproportionately surveilled and incarcerated. In fact, in many instances, community residents are eager to have cameras put up to monitor streets where far too much violent crime occurs. This does not merely reflect their sense of urgency. It also indicates an investment in the apparent objectivity of the camera. Public opinion research on such surveillance shows that a majority of Black and Latino people believe that police services are inferior in Black and Latino neighborhoods. At the same time, significant numbers of African Americans identify police racial prejudice as a problem.[149]

The purported objectivity of the camera could capture misconduct (civilian and police) and "watch" that which the police fail to notice. But, as Troy Duster has warned us, we have to have a critical perspective on the purported objectivity of technologies of knowledge when applied to people of color, given that their use and interpretation always lie in the hands of subjective human beings.

The impulse for objectivity, I would argue, is a call for a means to achieve a more democratic accountability structure. The story of Diane Bond is not merely one of police brutality; it is also a tale of a brutal gang rape that occurred in a dark project corridor years ago, the kind of occurrence that can happen to anyone but to which women in communities in which the police do not act as protectors are particularly vulnerable.[150] This side of surveillance and privacy intrusion is critically important. Anita Allen takes up this kind of question by considering what should be the reasonable limits upon privacy within the state, given our responsibility to be accountable for our actions.

As she says, "Accountability norms are ties that bind. If you imagine lines drawn between each one of us and the people to whom we are accountable for personal matters, the resulting picture is a dense network of such lines—a web of accountability. The web of accountability relationships is both flexible and sticky. The web is sticky in the sense that socially determined and reinforced expectations impel us."[151]

The difficulty with talking about accountability and race is that accountability talk in American popular culture has become racialized. Those scholars, activists, and commentators who identify practices of inequality or structures of inequality that lead to racial disparities are often accused of discouraging African Americans from taking responsibility for their actions. As well, there is the argument that programs like AFDC created a culture of irresponsibility among African Americans. The discursive demand for Black accountability and responsibility implies that the average White citizen is accountable for his or her behavior, while the average Black person is not. However, as research in virtually every area shows, African Americans are consistently more likely to be held accountable for discovered transgressions than White Americans and more likely to be surveilled if they are thought to have engaged in the transgression in the first place.

At the same time, the argument that accountability does not exist in African American communities implicitly erases the presence of social order and normal social relations from Black communities, thus pathologizing Black communities out of social life. In truth, there is a high degree of conscientiousness in Black communities about how to structure accountability, given the impact of unemployment, guns, and drug dealing. But state-regulated structures of accountability as they stand now are neither ethical nor fair. We are called, then, to envision ethical surveillance practices and accountability structures that are both more humane and more fairly distributed and to require that citizens and state actors be accountable to those who are poor and Black and Brown for their transgressions and failures, as well as requiring accountability of them. Several models of how to implement these structures in policy measures exist. Those that are effective are dependent upon a participatory democratic model and include community members among those who perform the evaluations upon which accountability structures are dependent. As long as social contract theory is colloquially understood as a "love it or leave it" matter, we cannot have ethical surveillance or accountability. In truth, a robust citizenship[152] allows for citizens to engage in a dialogic relationship with the terms of the social contract on an individual and collective level, through politics, litigation, transgression, and deliberative bodies. To the extent that the ability to participate in these negotiations is limited, there is a nontrivial impact on citizenship.

One kind of institutional structure that has the possibility of reshaping accountability is the civilian review board,[153] which usually operates to oversee policing but could also be applied to child welfare agencies, state-based means-tested benefits, public hospitals, and more. If these institutions include community members and are afforded subpoena power and the right to recommend sanction and termination where appropriate, they can be an important regulatory force for agents of the police power and also for community members, because they can assist in building legitimate state-enforced norms.

This goal of reconstituting accountability also requires that the solutions pursued be guided by a model that is consequentialist, rather than simply punitive. How does one achieve the goal, we should ask, of a healthy, collaborative community in which participants cooperate and also experience their lives as safe and meaningful, rather than dangerous and fungible? The flip side of the public/political self is the terrain of the private self. The invasion of privacy becomes a narrative tool for turning Black and Brown life inside out, making claims for political rights and responsibilities that are based upon behaviors more generally hidden from view or widely misunderstood. The question we must ask, then, is not just an individuated one about whether those penalties are appropriate but also one about systematic exposure as a racial practice and what that means for experiences of citizenship.

Toni Morrison's novel *Beloved* begins with the sentence "124 was spiteful." Over the course of the novel, we learn how the home, number 124, morphs from being a domestic refuge from the reach of slavery into a prison after the central character Sethe's terrible social transgression, the murder of her child in order to protect her from slave catchers. The novel's conclusion is achieved when the interior lives of the residents of 124 can be reconciled not with the illegitimate authority of the law of slavery or Jim Crow but with the justice and healing of the surrounding community. It is there that the terms of a good privacy can be found.

6

Exceptionally Yours

*Racial Escape Hatches in the
Contemporary United States*

Given a certain set of circumstances, individual Blacks can
excel. But society is made up not just individuals, but also of
groups. The quality of the group as a whole ultimately determines the quality of the nation. A number of White men will be
suckered . . . into believing that the Black race can fit in and do
well among the White race. That is simply untrue. Some individual Blacks obviously can. But, as a whole, the race cannot.
—David Duke, "Tiger Woods, Race and Professional Sports"

I mean, you got the first mainstream African American who is
articulate and bright and clean and a nice-looking guy.
—Presidential candidate Joe Biden on Barack
Obama as a presidential candidate

Is it possible that David Duke, that avowed White supremacist, glee-
fully chuckled at (future Vice President) Joe Biden's inartful phrasing about
(future President) Barack Obama's campaign? Could he have heard it as I
did, part of a thematic in American culture in which the idea of Blackness is
dissonant to excellence and achievement and in which, in those instances in
which excellence and achievement are found in Black bodies, those individuals are cast as necessarily extraordinary and distinguished? Did Duke cheer,
believing that the truth was slipping out of Biden's liberal mouth like a greasy
chicken bone, while others (like me) felt disappointed resignation?

Like President Obama, a host of Black public figures—Muhammad Ali,
Michael Jordan, Oprah Winfrey—have been seen as symbols of the American Dream. As well, these Black public figures have been the subjects of a

particular racialized brand of American exceptionalism: Black American exceptionalism. The exportation and celebration of Black public figures as hypermodern (and, more recently, postmodern and postethnic) subjects is a two-hundred-odd-year-old American tradition. Take, for example, a figure like Frederick Douglass, who, with his extraordinary brilliance and literary and homiletic gifts, made the case for the abolition of slavery to audiences in Europe and the United States and also fueled the imaginations of his audiences as to what an African on American shores could be in an era in which the capacities of African people were generally considered to be quite minimal. In our present time, President Obama immediately began to redeem the United States to the world. After an era of violent intervention and unpunished violation of international law, he restored the world's faith in the American people by virtue of their apparent transcendence of their White-supremacist history and their appreciation of his dignity and intelligence. His Blackness mattered to the world, perhaps as much as his brilliance.

Black American exceptionalism has an essential tension embedded within. The African American figure of note and achievement is evidence for, and in some instances a sign of, the chipping away at the infrastructure of White supremacy. For this very reason, Black abolitionists and authors of slave narratives were particularly threatening to the slavocracy. And, yet, the Americanness of the subject of Black American exceptionalism predicates idealized Blackness on claims to, or actual citizenship in, the American dream. No wonder, then, that, despite the collective memory of slavery, the legacies of Jim Crow, and persistent racial inequality, generations of willing Black immigrants have followed the unwilling over the course of the twentieth century and into the twenty-first, one of them (albeit temporarily) Barack Obama's father. Black American exceptionalism sustains American mythologies of perfect democracy and unfettered possibility. It seduces believers in multiracial democracy with the aesthetics of racial equality or "color blindness." At the same time, even among those who recognize the persistence of inequality, Black American exceptionalism offers that ever-present word of the Obama presidential campaign: hope.

Black American exceptionalism, which is a term I apply to a set of public and symbolic representations of Blackness, has a related phenomenon in the practice of racial exceptionalism generally. Racial exceptionalism exists in our daily lives and doesn't depend on celebrity or international politics for its meaning. Racial exceptionalism is the practice of creating meaning out of the existence of people of color who don't fit our stereotypic or racial-narrative-based conceptions. If we look internally and focus on racial exceptionalism in the domestic arena, we see that racially exceptionalized people(s) occupy a significant role in the rendering of race and race relations in the United States of the twenty-first century. The title of this chapter riffs upon the anthropologist Carl Degler's term "mulatto escape hatch." Degler's landmark work, *Neither Black Nor White: Slavery and Race Relations in Brazil and the United States* (New York: Macmillan, 1971), identified the manner in which middle-class, mixed-race Brazilians could garner access to "White privilege," a phenomenon distinguished from the situation in the United States, with its one-drop rule of hypodescent. However, as Tanya Hernandez has noted, the United States is undergoing, in some marked ways, a Latin Americanization in its construction of race, and racial exceptionalism is a part of this development.

There tend to be two categories of response to the "exceptional." Either the person or people are seen as role models and lauded for their attainments and transcendence of the "bear" of race, or they are viewed as inauthentic, illegitimate, and threatening. These poles of thought exist both intra- and extraracially. But, if we think beyond these polemic responses, what emerges is a complex brand of racialization.

In 1903, W. E. B. Du Bois spoke of the color line as a comprehensive barrier to racial justice.[1] To the extent that the metaphor "color line" creates the sense that traversing said line is destructive of racial inequality, it is a metaphor that has lost its power. No longer can it be assumed that crossing the color line, as Rosa Parks, Claudette Colvin, and countless others did literally by challenging de jure segregation in the civil rights era, is necessarily an act of defiant protest. In the contemporary United States, crossing the borderlines created by race does not require not crossing lines as crudely drawn as those of the previous generations, nor is it necessarily politically challenging. Crossing borders into territory not generally occupied by members of one's racial group is often lauded. The fashion in which the society has become open for some people of color, like a bottleneck, means that, while some have access, most don't. While a rhetoric of open access and equality remains widespread, people of color who cross the line and gain the benefits of membership historically reserved for the dominant group gain that access through various means: access to hard and soft capital, educational opportunity, and perceived proximity to, assimilation into, and social or domestic intimacy with Whiteness and/or White people. Their traversal does not necessarily translate into any changed circumstances for the rest.

It is through this lens that we must see what Eric Lott refers to as the "new orthodoxy" of postethnicity in academic thought,[2] which emerged in works including David Hollinger's *Postethnic America: Beyond Multiculturalism*,[3]

Walter Benn Michaels's *Our America: Nativism, Modernism and Pluralism*,[4] and Stanley Crouch's *The All American Skin Game or the Decoy of Race: The Long and Short of It*.[5] The cosmopolitan idea of race advocated in this orthodoxy, while sensitive to the hybridity that infuses all American cultures, implicitly advantages those who are identified as "hybrid" or "trans/multiracial" and disadvantages those who are identified as "monoracial" (culturally or genealogically) as being somehow "behind the times" and trapped in a modernist conception of identity in post-postmodern times. While these authors provide important interrogations of the essentialization of race in political identity, they neglect to consider how the identification of people as "racial cosmopolites" is exclusionary and (upper) classed. Postethnicity, then, becomes yet another ideological terrain for stratification. It is the "exceptional" person of color who gains access to the highly valued cosmopolitan hybridity.

A State of Exception

Whereas historically assimilation was argued to be a legitimate strategy for transcending racial inequality, for a full generation now we have had a widespread (if not universal) doctrine that advocates for some degree of cultural heterogeneity. Although it is clear that a measure of cultural or social assimilation is necessary for people of color who aspire to full "incorporation" in social, political, and civic terms, such incorporation also demands that they engage in a politics of distinction. This distinction is marked vis-à-vis other people of color and is signified culturally through a rhetoric of exceptionalism. Exceptionalism is a tool for the narration of hierarchy within and between groups of people of color, and, perhaps more important, it is a tool that legitimates the practice of inequality toward those who are not in the exceptionalized group.

In this practice, Blackness operates as the ultimate signifier of monoracialism and social inferiority, and this perhaps explains the particular fascination with the Black exceptional.[6] The Black exceptional lies in the greatest contrast to the perception of his or her community. However, exceptionalism is not a phenomenon exclusive to African Americans, and we must be attentive to the distinct methods of exceptionalism that shape the diverse experiences of people of color. Exceptions may be individuals, groups (as in the image of Asian Americans as the "model minority"), or subgroups (such as Argentinians, who tend to be Whiter and more affluent than other Latinos in the United States).[7] And the means of exceptionalizing are various.

We must be careful to distinguish exceptionalism as a cultural practice from documented observations of class mobility or immobility and integration or segregation for individuals or groups. While these bodies of information often go hand in hand with narratives of exceptionalism, the practice cannot be reduced to data. Exceptionalism is a popular narrative, a cultural practice, and an interpretive frame. It shapes individual experiences and shapes how we evaluate the racial inequality that we "see" on our city streets, in our office buildings, on our television and movie screens, and in our news media.

I am therefore not making any efforts to quantify the exceptionalized. However, the category "exceptional" might lend itself to social scientific research methods through multivariate analyses of neighborhood, occupation, civic memberships, and patterns of socializing, along with public opinion survey research and ethnographies of intraracial distinctions in multiracial environments. It is my hope that this book encourages such research. For the purposes of this chapter, I am focusing on how we conceive of people of color in spaces of high achievement and what that perception says about the state of race relations. The phenomenon of exceptionalism ultimately serves to support a general stereotyping of the larger populace (especially in the case of Blacks and Latinos) and justifies that stereotyping within a social context in which racial egalitarianism is proclaimed. It accepts as normative what the federal appellate court judge and legal historian A. Leon Higginbotham described as "the precept of inferiority."[8] When the "normal state" of people of color is assumed deficiency, then the departure from that state puts one into a "state of exception." In this case, you have the terrible result that positive attributes are disproportionately ascribed to the exceptionalized and are assumed to be absent in others. It is also the case that the state of exception is marked by indeterminacy. It requires consistent validation against the potential "reversion to type." This indeterminacy and validation aren't necessarily a result of deliberate or conscious policing. It does not require external enforcement at all because it can be produced by the concept of abnormality alone, an explicitly unsettled sphere.

On Being a Role Model Minority

Exceptionalism is also a form of racial representation, and exceptionals are therefore cast as racial representatives. However, measured against the "normate" whose image follows from the precept of inferiority, the exceptional is not representative in the sense of being a "representative example" but rather is representative in a sense of "delegated authority," that is, the appropriate example of "how to be." Although in the case of exceptional groups an individual from that group may operate as a "representative example" to the group, the desired modification of the undesired other is consistently invoked in the representation. For example, a newspaper account about an individual Asian American young adult's success against the odds both supports the positive stereotyping of Asian Americans as high achieving and implicitly contrasts Asian Americans with African Americans and Latinos. Likewise, it makes invisible the significant wealth and opportunity gap that exists among Asian Americans, which is based largely on ethnicity.

Hanna Pitkin argues that representation "means the making present of something which is nevertheless not literally present,"[9] but the presence generated by the exceptional is one of contradiction, an inversion of exemplar representation. Those unexceptionals who become present in our imaginations through the counterexample of the exceptionals are then represented according to something that could be termed a trustee theory of representation. The exceptional—the better informed, the more competent and skilled, or just those "better" than others of his group—is acting in the best interest of the "group" by demonstrating model behavior or assimilability; they are good representatives, if not representative. While the constitution of "group" of which the figure is being a good representative merits deconstruction, let's set aside that problem for the moment by simply accepting that people *do* walk around with the albatross of ascriptive category about their necks, willingly or not, and, as people of color, are often either seen as representative or good representatives. Nevertheless, there are still at least two problems with the assumptions of representation. While Pitkin argues that, with respect to the substance of representation, "the represented thing or person is present in the action rather than the characteristics of the actor, or how he is regarded, or the formal arrangements which proceed or follow from the action"[10] and that therefore, in a case like this, those who aren't exceptionalized, the "unexceptionals" of a group, shouldn't be automatically suspicious of the exceptional as a figure who is seen as "different" (for example, we can reference the discussions over whether candidate Obama was "Black enough" for Black voters.) However, we also shouldn't assume that exceptionals represent the interests or thoughts of the larger group or even identify with the group. We especially should consider the question of whether the "exceptional as representative" in the case of race is interested in serving or *excluding* the constituent group. The desire to exclude may reflect a feeling of competition with constituents or other potential exceptionals, aspirations to exploit the constituent group, or simple intra- or interracial (people of color) or intercultural bigotry. Another problem is the manner in which the symbolic imagery of the exceptional representative obscures potential relevant distinctions between the representative and the represented. Actions and achievements are reified, while the significance of social origins (class, color, status) and opportunities (education, exposure) are muted. Moreover, when exceptionals are presented as model racial representatives, rarely is that image deconstructed for the legitimately divergent interests of those who are exceptionalized and those who are not[11] or the social capital exceptionals gain from their distinction and from the castigation and the calls for the reformation of the larger "undesirable" and "undeserving" category of "unexceptional" people of color.

Mutable Characteristics

Exceptionals are seen as "different," and that difference is attributed in large part to effort, conduct, and self-presentation. In antidiscrimination law, this idea of "choice" is expressed in the distinction that is drawn between mutable and immutable characteristics. Immutable characteristics, like features of the body and color, are afforded greater protection against discrimination than mutable characteristics. This was evident in the case of *Rogers v. American Airlines* 527 F. Supp. 229 (1981), in which a district court rejected the claim of Renee Rogers, an African American flight attendant who challenged the airline policy prohibiting employees from wearing cornrow braids. The court acknowledged that the hairstyle was part of her culture but concluded that, as an easily changed characteristic, it was subject to prohibition by the airline.

In providing greater protection against discrimination for immutable characteristics, the law has an assimilationist bias. This has been noted by a number of critical race theorists.[12] This bias is especially concerning now that research is showing us how mutable characteristics, such as cultural practices, styles, neighborhoods, and names, are used as proxies for race.[13] Mutable characteristics are bases upon which people can and do engage in racial discrimination that is either intended but concealed, unintended but shaped by the devaluation of the ways of being of people of color,[14] or rooted in simple unfamiliarity.

There is a problem, however, with describing the mutability question exclusively as a demand for assimilation. When we talk about a characteristic being mutable, as mentioned before, it implies choice. But many of our behaviors, habits, and tastes, the features of our habitus, are developed as a result of the contexts in which we are born and raised. And so those who are somewhat assimilated and who are therefore assumed to have certain good values or aspirations as evinced by their participation in mainstream culture might in fact merely be conducting themselves in ways to be expected because "that's how they were raised," socially and environmentally. The cultural capital of mainstream assimilation thereby gets treated as merit, rather than privilege.

Another problem with an assimilation/identity binary is that it doesn't help us answer how we should evaluate assimilationist demands and determine when they are appropriate. When I taught critical race theory in a law school, I often gave my students a hypothetical about an African American woman lawyer who works at a prestigious law firm. She's a highly competent attorney, she brings business to the firm, and she likes to wear "African-inspired" clothing to work whenever possible. The partners refuse to put her on the partnership track because her external appearance does not conform to the firm's image. Should that constitute unlawful racial discrimination? Most of my students would initially say yes and criticize the firm for being intolerant of her identity and culture. I then would ask this question: what if she had a fellow associate who was very into her Latvian heritage and wanted to wear traditional Latvian clothing to work? This almost always made them burst into laughter. Why the difference, I asked. They struggled. I posited that, because of the aesthetics of cultural nationalism in 1960s and 1970s Black activism, African clothing operates as a signifier of Black identity despite the fact that it is quite rare for African Americans to wear African clothing. When I turn the question around and ask if it is appropriate to have a corporate dress code that everyone must follow, the students overwhelmingly say yes. What they are bothered by in the original hypothetical is the sense that the aversion to the lawyer's clothing is a sign that Blackness is devalued and racial assimilation is demanded. But a better orientation is to consider which of the norms that are present in a profession or institution are reasonable and fair and how relatively accessible those norms are to differentially situated individuals.

Certain demands for professional assimilation are understandable but not universally accessible. To return to the subject of the Rogers case, chemically straightened hair is both a cultural norm and a mutable characteristic for African American women. Black female flight attendants thirty years ago and today usually have straight or straightened hair. The policy of American Airlines identified braided hair as inconsistent with the company's corporate image, notwithstanding the fact that it would be unlikely to impede professional interactions any more than racial diversity does (interracial encounters make some people uncomfortable). The hair of most African Americans is visibly and significantly different from the hair of most members of all other racial groups, regardless of how it is styled. Moreover, completely invisible in the case are questions of labor and expense. Compelled to wear her hair relaxed, Renee Rogers could not hop in and out of the shower in the morning. She likely would spend time with a curling iron in the morning or spend a night sleeping with her hair in rollers. She might not be able to fly uninterruptedly for weeks on end without visits to the hairdresser. She might not be able to travel to destinations where hair stylists for kinky, coiled hair are rare. The point is that the standard is unequally accessible, unlike (controlling for income) the requirement that someone wear a suit to work.

In bringing the case, Renee Rogers made an effort to negotiate a broader space for professional presentation based upon the reality of her hair as an immutable characteristic. This case provides an apt metaphor for the disciplining and exclusions that can occur when some colored bodies are contrasted to others and the invisible differences in access to "norms." I think the usefulness of these examples, both the hypothetical and the case, is that they offer metaphors for, as well as concrete examples of, the complex of opportunity and requirement involved in making it into the favored category of "exceptional."

Kenji Yoshino compellingly argues, in *Covering: The Hidden Assault on our Civil Rights*,[15] that access to privilege for minorities is often predicated upon their covering or masquerading critical expressions of identity. He analogizes covering to the historic practice of passing, in which genealogically and culturally identified people of color passed into Whiteness by denying their identification with their historic groups. According to Yoshino, who finds a theoretical foundation in the work of Irving Goffman, covering is distinct from passing because passing is about concealment, whereas covering is about muting. But there are important consistencies to be drawn between the two forms of assimilation. Since the days of Ellen Craft and Homer Plessy, the trope of passing as a form of racial border crossing was a double edged transgression. While there was potential for individual liberation because of the permeability of the border (Ellen Craft *could* escape from slavery by masquerading as a White man) and some broader potential for striking against racial ideology whenever someone could illustrate the instability of Whiteness (Homer Plessy argued that he was both a White man who lost the reputation of Whiteness and a man of color who was being discriminated against), individual assimilation into the category of Whiteness through passing supported the category of Whiteness itself. The same can be said for covering. Given examples of the "well-known secret" passing of a figure like the *New York Times* critic Anatole Broyard or the effective Whiteness in spite of the one-drop role that we see in someone like the singer Carly Simon, muting has a long history that reaches back into the era of passing and overlaps with it. Nevertheless, although passing was always seen as at best resistant rather than truly liberating, the success of the "covering" person of color is still often imagined as a sign of our dramatic transformation into an authentic salad-bowl culture. Yoshino alerts us that this is a mischaracterization and notes that covering entails oppressive forces on the covered. Our concern, however, cannot be limited to those who can pass or cover and the extent to which they must mute their identities. We must also be attentive to what the muting is supposed to signify about what kind of people of color have access and who has the opportunity to acquire the tools to "cover."

The Characteristics Fetish

In 1966, articles published in the *New York Times Magazine*[16] and in *U.S. News and World Report*[17] touted Asian Americans as a model minority by explicitly contrasting them to African American, specifically with respect to political activism. This representation was simplistic and divisive and policed Asian Americans by setting a terrible condition for their positive stereotype: silence about their experiences of inequality. Of course, desegregation and the expansion of immigration policies that resulted from the civil rights movement offered opportunities that had not previously existed in employment, education, and business to Asian Americans and Latinos, as well as to African Americans. And activism flowered in every marginalized community to some extent in the 1960s and 1970s. However, in the post–civil rights era, as a nation we had to figure out how to incorporate the social revolution that the civil rights movement had wrought into the mainstream American narrative. Additionally, we had to make sense of the movement away from governmental remedies for racial inequality during the 1980s, even though inequality persisted. In the midst of this, we witnessed greater access for some people of color. The composition of Wall Street, the suburbs, and universities changed. All of these transformations allowed for the emergence of clear differences between and among people formerly viewed as generally indistinguishable. Hence, a fixation grew on understanding the distinctions. What made the difference between the Blacks who "made it" and those who didn't, between Asians who became incorporated into the larger society and Blacks who did not?

People focused on these characteristics of distinction for all kinds of political purposes. For some, they provided arguments for social policy, whereas for others they were clear evidence against its usefulness. Regardless, to this day there is often a fetishizing of the "characteristics" of those capable of incorporation, particularly as inequality grows and sites of concentrated and racialized poverty proliferate. At the same time, for exceptionals, the exceptional narrative is a means by which their racialization persists despite their display of generally appreciated characteristics. So, for example, Asian Americans continue to be invoked as an exception to the inferior status of racial others among racial others, rather than simply incorporated into "Americanness," as Jewish, Italian, and Irish people have been. It is within that framework that we can understand the image of Asian Americans as "eternal foreigners," regardless of multigenerational Americanness, citizenship, or naturalization. Their economic and academic success is narrated as a kind of wonderful, though sometimes threatening, strangeness in the American fabric of racial meaning, something exceptional.

At the same time, exceptionals are deprived of a history by virtue of their identification as "first," "only," and "different." They are not placed in the context of the histories of their groups or seen as the products of their group. The characteristics of exceptionals are treated as marks of distinction, often without evidence of their distinctiveness. When we say they are hardworking, the assumption is that others are not. When we say they have "middle-class values," we assume others do not. The fetishized characteristics also can create situations in which people misidentify relevant factors in achievement. Let's illustrate this with a hypothetical. There are two cab drivers. They each have a son. One parent is an immigrant, the other native born. Despite the long hours required of a cab driver, the immigrant parent demands that the child spend three to four hours a night on academic work and oversees that work. If the child of the immigrant parent excels academically and the child of the native-born parent does not, we can easily make up a story to explain it, the gist of which would be "The native-born parent did not do enough to ensure the child's success. In contrast, the immigrant parent came with nothing and yet made sure that his child would succeed." But, mind you, we don't even know whether or not the native-born parent also did those things! And imagine that the immigrant parent has a Ph.D. in engineering from his native country, while the native-born cab driver is a high school dropout. Might not the Ph.D. know more about ensuring his child's academic success than the dropout, notwithstanding the advantages of natal citizenship? My point is not to discount the value of parental investment in school achievement or to suggest that a parent must be highly skilled to support his or her child's academic success; rather, it is to provide an illustration of how we narrate outcomes in terms of merit without engaging in rigorous comparisons of circumstances. And we apply the stock stories that are in our minds to explain what we see and therefore don't even consider that we have been less than rigorous in our assessments.

Getting the Label to Stick

One the one hand, getting the "exceptional" label to stick depends upon legitimated evidence of achievement: economic, scholastic, professional. But it also is tied to a demonstrable hybridity, which includes associations with features that are identified as "White" (whether or not they are appropriately imagined as such) in areas like language, domestic arrangements, neighborhood, taste, and style. This demand is not for complete assimilation; rather, the demands are for signs of distinction (from the "others"), signs of allegiance (to the majority), and economic success. A principal concern for how we identify the "success" of groups or individuals should be what the terms of that success are and whether we think those terms are fair or legitimate.

A quick brainstorming of Latino celebrities suggests the significance of color: Jennifer Lopez, Ricky Martin, Salma Hayek, Shakira, Jessica Alba, Christina Aguilera. Visually, Latino incorporation is imagined as highly correlated to physical Whiteness with light brushstrokes of Indianness or Blackness.[18] And, although many scholars have noted the manner in which the myth of the model minority overdetermines the experiences of certain Asian American ethnic groups whose members are far more likely to be poor than others, like the Hmong and Filipinos, disparities within Asian America are generally lost on the American public. The point is this: shorthands for signs of incorporation blunt complex realities.

For example, the high rate of interracial marriage between Asian Americans and Whites is sometimes presented as evidence that racism against Asian Americans is nonexistent.[19] It is a strange concept to think that intimate associations necessarily stand as evidence of the end of racism. No one would make the claim that intimate partnerings between men and women signal the end of sexism and patriarchy (because it is an absurd idea). Sex, love, and domesticity are integral parts of all kinds of unequal social relations, including racial ones. So, while it is clear that moving from concubinage, slave rape, and antimiscegenation statutes to state-recognized and recognizable familial relationships is an important social transformation, it is not prima facie evidence of an end to racism.[20] A better examination would look at the terms and signifiers of the intimate association. While this won't tell us anything about any particular partnering, it will tell us something about what racial meaning is made out of interracial partnering in the public imagination. So, for example, the rates of out-group marriage for Asian American women have significantly exceeded those of Asian American men. At the same time, Asian masculinity, in pornography and popular culture, has been diminished, doubted, and, I think by implication, perceived as threatening in this culture.[21] In contrast, Asian American women are often presented as docile and readily available objects of desire.[22] Given these popular images, it would seem at least premature to think of interracial relationships as a sign of diminishing racism, not because we should assume that people think of their spouses in these terms (although they might serve as the basis for initial sexual attraction) but because prevalent interracial relationships and socioeconomic success have not destabilized this imagery.

Another way to think about this is to consider how domesticity operates as a signifier of citizenship. This is particularly fruitful, I think, because of the "eternal foreigner" imagery that is often applied to Asian Americans. Perhaps the presumption of noncitizenship should be understood as having some dynamic relationship to the pattern of interracial marriage. Given that the presumption of noncitizenship is so intensely a part of both Asian and Latino racialization in the United States, the formalization of interracial intimacy through marriage and the construction of a genealogical membership in White families allows an access to Americanness that is often otherwise imaginatively and symbolically denied. I do not mean to suggest that Asian Americans and Latinos marry interracially in order to attain Whiteness; rather, I am identifying intermarriage as a particularly salient terrain on which incorporation occurs and one that symbolically excludes (i.e., Asian men, unassimilated Asian families).

In the social science literature, this is described as rates of "exogamy." Rates of exogamy are used as a proxy for becoming American for immigrant groups, and it is frequently observed that African Americans are the least likely to form exogamous unions. I think we should be wary of this line of thought for two reasons. First, it makes presumptions that interracial intimacy changes racial hierarchies, an assumption that I think can be challenged by the many examples of color-caste societies in Latin American with histories of extremely high rates of interracial intimacy. Second, it appears to collapse the goals of integration and incorporation into assimilation. If we are the heterogeneous society we proclaim to be, such collapse should not be required to transcend racial inequality. I want to make a point here of distinguishing between the political import of membership in multiracial communities, in which people of various races and ethnicities share power and participation, and the import of interracial intimacy. They may occur together, but they are quite different. One can be a member of a political community that says interracial relationships can and should operate to challenge notions of biological racism or interracial conflict, but it is not necessarily the case that interracial intimate associations will do that or put people in better positions to do that work. Moreover, given the history of race and intimate associations in the United States and abroad, there are very real dangers to that assumption.

Sexual intimacy is no harbinger of equality, as the history of sexism and patriarchy has shown us. Moreover, interracial sexual intimacy has been a signature feature of Black life since Africans first arrived on these shores. The discussion as to whether sexual relations between White men of power and their Black concubines were consensual is in many ways misleading. On one hand, it is thought, if the relationship was consensual, it suggests a love against the odds and absolves the individual man of guilt. On the other hand, it is thought, if it was coercive, it was rape, and the man is guilty. But the truth is that, whether or not the relationship was consensual, the society was guilty of creating the inequality that vested in the intimate realm by virtue of racial inequality. In some sense, the question of consent has little meaning beyond the individual story. When Essie Mae, Strom Thurmond's Black daughter, came forward, there was a sense that Thurmond was somehow being absolved by having been a decent father to her. But his parenthood did nothing to destroy the racial hierarchy represented by the terms of interracial intimacy in which a White supremacist and segregationist could be a loving father to a secret Black child.

The import of *Loving v. Virginia*, the 1969 Supreme Court case that outlawed antimiscegenation statues, is not that it celebrated interracial marriage. The import is that it gave state sanction, and therefore a host of protections and supports, to interracial partners and challenged the protective policing of Whiteness through law. So, when we look to the intersection of race, sex, and the production of children, we should not assume that, because one type of union containing people of color has been integrated into a normative framework, others necessarily follow suit. It may be that interracial unions or families, particularly if they are "assimilated" into exceptionals and read as more "White" than "other," actually have greater social access than those that are composed entirely of people of color.

It is also the case that, for Latinos and Asian Americans, when incorporation comes, it seems to come at the cost of historicocultural recognition. Think of how features of Asian and Latino cultures are imported and incorporated into the mainstream (acupuncture, green tea, salsa) as additive features to American life, which are validated by their adoption by the mainstream. And, yet, Asian American history, and the history of Latinos in the United States have a minimal public narrative. If a public claim to American identity is "heard" from Asian Americans and Latinos, it is generally acknowledged only as an additive within the discursive frame of Black American experience or in the superficial food- and consumption-based hodge-podge of pop assimilation. This "presentism" of images of Latinos and Asian Americans reflects a deep ambivalence about how these groups and their subgroups will be situated in the long run. The absence of narrative allows for ambiguity in how they will be situated. Until some consensus emerges about where "they" will fit, the public histories about them will likely remain marginal. Although this may allow greater space for incorporation for Asian Americans and Latinos than there is for African Americans because the rules of racial stratification aren't as firmly applied for them, it may also increase vulnerability to crude bigotries because people aren't socialized to avoid being aggressively racist toward non-Black people of color. Moreover, the depiction of non-Black people of color as less sensitive or angry than Blacks creates a fiction that Asians, Latinos, and American Indians don't mind racism and therefore can be subjected to it without any uproar. Additionally, those who are not exceptionalized in these groups are often identified as "foreign," and so, again, it allows Americans to avoid dealing with the claims about and against racial inequality that originate with Latinos and Asian Americans because they aren't assumed to have the rights of membership.[23] The cultural message: in order to belong, you must be complicit and assimilated. If you are resistant or unassimilated, you don't belong.

Modes of Exceptionalism

There are many points of distinction that are used to identify the exceptionalized individual and or group/subcategory among people of color, and this discussion is not exhaustive, but I want to provide a description of some common terms upon which exceptionalism occurs. The diversity of modes of exceptionalism at once gives us a glimpse into the diversity among people of color who are often lumped together and highlights the presence of intraracial inequality.

Colorism is a frequent means by which people are exceptionalized. It has roots in color caste systems that developed in the nineteenth century throughout the colonized world and the Afro-Atlantic diaspora, as well as economic privilege that developed as a result of the higher status of individuals who had genealogical relationships to upper-class Whites. That said, the assumption that the adoption of light-skin preferences within groups of people of color universally represents internalized racism has been challenged through historical discussions of aesthetics in nations like India and Japan, in which lighter skin was highly valued before European or U.S. imperialist and/or colonialist projects became part of their national history, because of the association between Whiteness and membership in the leisure or ruling classes, which did not have to work in the sun.[24] As well, there is survey research demonstrating that, while people of color might privilege light skin, they often stop short of wanting to be "white,"[25] and it is also clear that having light skin does not protect people of color from racism. Nevertheless, within the context of the United States, whatever the origins of light-skin privilege for particular populations, the association between value and lighter skin is infused with the history of U.S. race relations and the Black-White binary associations of Blackness with inferiority and Whiteness with superiority. Take, for example, the narratives from Rondilla and Spickard's book *Is Lighter Better: Skin-tone Discrimination among Asian Americans*, in which subjects describe how familial cautions against getting darkened by the sun are often threats that the person will "turn Black" and dark-skinned Asians describe other Asian Americans' assumption that they are Latino or Black (and therefore outsiders) and their practice of referring to them as such. Robin Le, a second-generation Vietnamese American woman, writes, "I grew up being taunted with the words *my dang*, which translates into English as 'black girl.'"[26] A Korean woman, Sunny Yang, says, "Ever since I could remember, my parents always encouraged my sister and me not to tan. They always said we looked like a Black person or a country bumpkin when we got dark."[27] Given that, in the histories of enslavement, colonialism, and class stratification, lighter color gets read as signaling higher class and/or caste, this colorism is, even if sometimes accidentally, inextricably linked to racialization.

Moreover, research across ethnic groups in the United States demonstrates that lighter skin leads to greater educational and professional opportunity.[28] Whatever conflicting pressures exist between the demand for physical authenticity on one hand (where people who are deemed "too light" are therefore are treated as suspect or outsiders) and the high status accorded to light skin, on the other, people apparently act, across the board, according to a value where proximity to physical Whiteness may be traded on for greater access.

Biracial identity is connected to but distinct from the exceptionalism that may be afforded by being lighter complexioned. The discursive work of biracial exceptionalism, rather than serving as a mere physical marker, is often tied to narratives of mistreatment and marginalization by both Whites and other people of color, along with arguments about having "the best of both worlds." (Interestingly, no one except virulent White supremacists ever talks about the prospect of having the worst of both worlds, although the comedian Dave Chappelle's satire has sometimes played with such concepts.) In one study of biracial (Black and White) Americans, the authors found that

> Respondents who chose "biracial" to describe their racial identity had a common set of social experiences. Many of them were middle to upper middle class, educated in private schools, raised in predominantly White neighborhoods, with predominantly White friends and relatives composing their social networks. In many of these cases, they were the only (or one of the few) non-White within their schools and communities. . . . In fact the only differences between them and their peers was the racial group membership of one of their parents. . . . In the minds of their peers, they were more like them than they were different and did not fit into their cognitive conception of "Black."[29]

As in the case of group exceptionalism, one must tread carefully with a critique of multiracial exceptionalism. The demand that we recognize the specificity of biracial experience is a legitimate one. We should not require or demand that people identify with one group or another or identify with either or both in particular ways. However, we must also deconstruct the privileged status that is often immediately accorded to multiracial people by virtue of their being genealogically "part" of some group (usually Whites) that has higher status than the other group or groups to which they belong. There is a difference between recognition of cross-cultural experiences and the use of hybridity as a status marker. Relatedly, recognition of multiracialism should not require monolithic representations of the nonmultiracially identified members of the group. To illustrate the point: the offspring of an African immigrant and a Deep South African American has as much of a "multicultural" upbringing and the prospect of having the "best of both worlds" as does the child of a White and a Black American. So, for that matter, does the child of an Argentinian American and a Dominican American. Moreover, as the saying goes, "all marriages are cross-cultural" because of the intersections of family, class, regional, ethnic, racial, educational, and occupational cultures that occur whenever people come together to raise children or forge new familial bonds. The fact that we identify racial differences as more salient than other kinds of difference has as much to do with the distribution of power and status in our society as it does with actual cultural difference or similarity.

How we think about this is further complicated in the adoption context by the fact that transnational/transracial adoptions often occur with children who are the "least desirable" within their natal national or cultural contexts, either because they are not products of traditional domestic arrangements or because they are of mixed race or belong to a racially or ethnically marginalized group in their home countries. Hence, the politics around their exodus are often infused with an inequality framework, however inapposite, on both sides. Indeed, when South Korea created more stringent restrictions on transnational adoption in response to pressure from North Korean critics, it continued to make mixed-race children readily available. When the number of transnational Latin American adoptions increased, in part in response to the decreased availability of Korean children, Indian children were overrepresented among the adoptees. Once these children arrived in the United States, however, their White parentage offered them a degree of acceptability that in many ways was not as readily afforded to their counterparts with parents of color.

Transracially adopted children go through life as visible exceptions to the presumptions and the primacy of biological relationships between parents and children. However, they do not necessarily experience their exceptional status as privilege. More often, accounts from transracially adopted kids describe feelings of displacement; they often have experiences of complete assimilation in the context of family but are presumed to be part of the unassimilated throng of their racial group when they leave their homes or neighborhoods. In *In Their Own Voices: Transracial Adoptees Tell Their Stories*, an African American woman adopted by White parents recounts, "In a class in college we were given an assignment to report on an ethnic group other than your own. I indicated that I wanted to do it on African Americans. The teacher told me no, because I was African American. I said that I didn't know anything about the African American community because I didn't live that way but the teacher didn't feel that was acceptable."[30] Although she did have an exceptional experience, she was denied recognition of that fact because of her appearance. Sandra Patton, the author of *Birthmarks: Transracial Adoption in Contemporary America*, writes, of one of her interviewees, all of whom are adults who were adopted transracially as children, "Even . . . the most white identified among them said that though most comfortable in the company of White people and most conversant in that cultural meaning system, as a person with brown skin she was typically treated like other African Americans."[31] And she writes of her interviewees generally, "Their coping mechanisms to survive the onslaught of racist attitudes, treatment, and representations they encountered involved distancing themselves from Blackness and embracing Whiteness—they largely accepted representations of African Americans as truth and posited themselves as 'exceptions' who were 'different' from other Blacks."[32]

The fact that the public face of transracial adoption has grown due to celebrity adoptions suggests that children of transracial adoption may become narratively exceptionalized in the way biracial people often have been, regardless of phenotype, because of their identification as the product of White parents. But the experiences of children of transracial adoption also reveal an important complicating feature to exceptionalism: the demand for racial authenticity or legitimacy (e.g., assimilated Blacks are still expected to be "authentic" Blacks to people of all races in order for them to act as representatives of idealized Blackness) and the simultaneous need to fortify oneself against the emotional impact of racialization, even for exceptionals.

Elite education and professional status are other ways that groups of people of color or individuals of color are distinguished from others of his or her group. However, critical masses of people of color in academic institutions or professional groups, whether the numbers are a result of a commitment to affirmative action, residential patterns, or high achievement among the group, are often seen as threatening and even illegitmate.[33] Proportion matters. And, as the literature on stereotype threat suggests, racial narratives about performance and academic legitimacy have an impact on actual performance. In David Dante Troutt's short story "The Monkey Suit,"[34] the protagonist, a young African American attorney on the partnership track, falls into a cycle of self-doubt when a first-ever but racially coded question about the quality of his writing is raised. Consistent with that literary representation, qualitative research documenting the experiences of the Black middle class reveals the surveillance that shapes how they feel they must continuously legitimate their exceptional status or find it denied.[35]

From another perspective, when exceptionalized people of color, particularly African Americans, express embarrassment about the behavior or habits of the masses of Black people, that embarrassment is shaped in part by a widespread value system in which that which is Black is assumed to be inferior and in part by a self-interested fear that that image of Blackness will overtake the exceptionalized self. While academic achievement was used historically in the African American community as a means of arguing against the ideology of racial caste, as a form of striving that had practical, spiritual, and symbolic value, the breakdown of associations between the individual achievement and the public image of the community (writ large) began as opportunity and access increased for a subcategory of African Americans. It can no longer be assumed that the achieving individual either feels a connection to the larger group or is seen as a representative of the group.

Complicating this further are diverse identities within racial groups. So, for example, African immigrants are the most highly educated immigrant population, although they don't get identified as model minorities in popular culture.[36] In fact, far more attention is paid to fraud committed by Nigerians in the United States than to Africans' high levels of professional achievement. This is a reflection of our racial politics. But I digress. The point is that there is no particular reason for a Nigerian American surgeon, for example, to be expected have a political interest in being seen as a representative of or for the African American community, except perhaps out of respect for the history of African American struggles, which led to the opening of professional and educational doors for that person, or because of her current experiences of racism. (And, in truth, affluent Asian Americans and Latinos very similarly benefited from the gains wrought by the civil rights movement and yet are not expected to have some special affinity for African Americans.) Moreover, she carries her own history and identity, and she may find it difficult or uninteresting to integrate African American history and American racialization into that identity because of her class or caste in Nigeria or because of the philosophy attendant to undergoing the enormous upheaval of immigration with emotional success. As well, if she has learned that not identifying with the African American community and instead being "exceptional" for a Black person in the United States increases her opportunity, she has a disincentive to identify with that community.

Or, take, for example, a White-skinned Mexican American college professor who teaches at an institution where the majority of Latino students are either Mestizo Mexican Americans or Puerto Ricans. If he is from a family that has been part of the elite in Mexico for generations and is genealogically Spanish, why should we expect that he wouldn't bring the distinctions of color, genealogy, and class that exist in Mexico to his interaction with brown-skinned first-generation Mexican American college students? And why wouldn't we expect that his interaction with Puerto Rican students might be shaped by the bigotries that exist in Latin America against Caribbean Latinos, especially given that these distinctions are fortified by the colorism and social hierarchies that are present in the contemporary United States?

There are growing numbers of people of color who do not culturally identify with their ascriptive groups either by choice or circumstance. These people may be legitimately seen as different from other members of their racial groups and may accept stereotypes about the members of that group that any group outsider would have; yet, they are still bound by their bodies to the American race game. Of course, there is also always the possibility that identification with the broader racial group *does* exist and is quite strong, even among those who experientially, phenotypically, and culturally differ from the majority of the group members. President Obama is a notable example of this. He is someone who, by virtue of experience and geneaology, led a life highly uncharacteristic of Black Americans and yet as an adult chose as his social network and cultural home an African American community in Chicago. Notwithstanding the media's fascination with his distinctiveness vis-à-vis other Black people, he maintained a high degree of connection to African American power brokers in Chicago and on the eastern seaboard both throughout the presidential campaign and into his presidency. Moreover, when he first traveled to Africa as president, his destination was not Kenya, his "homeland," or the politically powerful Nigeria. It was Ghana, the country of return for African Americans and a country of huge significance in the intellectual and political history of African Americans. All of that is to say that exceptional experience is not determinative of social relations. However, we should be mindful that modes of exceptionalism often reflect significant differences in experience that can lead to significant differences in perspective.

Between Exceptionalizing Oneself and Being Exceptionalized

Exceptionalism is not simply something that is externally imposed. The practice of self-exceptionalism is common. And that self-exceptionalism is not only a way for people to demand that their distinctiveness be acknowledged. It can also be a deliberate strategy to encourage an image of distinction and therefore obtain greater access. African diasporic and continental immigrants have effectively engaged in self-exceptionalism, as evinced by the research of Mary Waters,[37] deploying "cultural" difference from African

Americans in order to develop an alternative image of Blackness, one highly correlated with a broader narrative of immigrant striving.

Perhaps the most important historic precedent for the contemporary fixation on the relationship between culture and race was the internment of Japanese Americans during World War II, an action for which cultural difference, rather than the fiction of biological race, was the primary justification. Of course, the idea was that cultural assimilation was impossible, and Japanese Americans experienced enormous social pressure to destroy all external signs of Japanese or Japanese American identity. This set the stage for the idea of culture as a legitimate basis for racial suspicion and assimilation as a yardstick of loyalty and desirability.

During the internment of the Japanese, the Chinese were seen as superior. But, after the Cultural Revolution (1966–1976), the Chinese were cast as representing the "yellow peril," a role the Japanese had had recently filled. As the civil rights movement gained steam, the popular media drew distinctions between Asian Americans and African Americans, ostensibly to discourage political and social identification between them. Given that Asian Americans had been terrorized in previous generations by threats to the safety of their citizenship status, the coercive power of a positive stereotype was likely heightened. An inversion occurred; whereas once Americans had been taught that "Asians are unassimilable," they were now being told that "Asian Americans are assimilable, but Blacks refuse to assimilate." This refusal in fact was a feature of the Black Power era but was to some extent an aesthetic refusal, not a practical one, as substantial numbers of African Americans began to integrate predominantly white universities and neighborhoods for the first time.

Today, although people know culture is not inborn, we still talk about it in static terms. And so, more than a half a century later, although it is clearly mutable, culture is treated as being "in the bones." Thus, to self-exceptionalize, one must demonstrate that one belongs natally or naturally to a culture (family or social or ethnic group) that is meritorious. This poses serious a serious quandary for those who wish to reject the politics of racial inequality and yet aspire to achieve or maintain the features of economic and professional success.

When Bill Cosby caused a firestorm by indicting the Black poor for behavioral failings, he participated in a tradition of middle- and upper-class Blacks distinguishing themselves from the Black poor. This critique served to draw attention away from what might be termed the failings of the Black middle class, which, despite being a relatively advantaged group, underperforms relative to Whites at the same income level and often fails to reproduce its socioeconomic class in its children,[38] yet disproportionately benefits from affirmative action.[39] Rhetorically, Cosby and other liberal Black critics of the Black poor (as opposed to their conservative counterparts) argue implicitly for the sustainment of affirmative action in order to provide middle-class "role models" and representatives while distancing themselves from the performance gaps that exist between Blacks and Whites at every income level.

Laurence Otis Graham, author of *Our Kind of People: Inside America's Black Upper Class*,[40] brought an exceptional group—old-money Blacks—to the public's attention, using their social practices and status signifiers to identify his own brand of exceptionalism as a member of the group. Stephen Carter's mystery novels *The Emperor of Ocean Park* and *New England White* also reveal the proclivities of this elite world. In Emily Bernard's review of *New England White*, she captures the spirit of exceptionalism that suffuses this world. Witness how she describes one of the central characters, Lemaster Carlyle, a West Indian immigrant of humble origins who has risen to the position of Ivy League university president: "Lemaster achieves success in his new country by insinuating himself into an old script—as the interloper in the world of white privilege. He plays the role of the black exception; he is walking proof of progress toward diversity, yet because he is seen as unique, this exception can never really threaten the status quo. In his singularity, he is ultimately most useful in keeping white power intact."[41]

Brilliantly, Carter presents two narratives of exception with his principal characters, Lemaster and his wife, Julia, the high achieving immigrant and the old guard Black bourgeois woman. Their marriage is, more than anything else, "appropriate."

Although a good deal of the impulse toward self-exceptionalizing has been classism, it also reflects the simultaneous presence of racial anxiety and self-interest. Notably, survey research indicates that African Americans disagree with the idea that self-interested aspiration and gain is equivalent to racial progress,[42] a sentiment literarily presented in Carter's novelistic conclusion, which has the heroine retreating from her elite world into service in a poor Black community. Even among elites, there was a historic recognition of dependence upon and deep linkages (by family, civic organization, and client base) to the Black working class and the Black poor. Indeed, the Black elite's fixation on community is often a response to an anxiety about the vulnerability of the exceptional. Often one will hear educated African Americans critique a city by saying, "It doesn't have a strong Black middle class," reflecting an awareness of the vulnerability of exceptional status without community fortification. If something goes wrong, where is the network of support? Part of what enables significant upward mobility among even the poorest Asian Americans is the presence of community networks and out-of school learning experiences that are organized around ethnicity and that transcend class. Even as we see the strategic deployment of self-exceptionalizing within groups of people of color, we also see signs of persistent belief in group loyalty and linked fate.

The idea that exceptionalism challenges racism motivates many exceptionals. Asian Americans report the desire to thwart racism as a principle motivation for academic achievement,[43] a practice consistent with traditional African American conceptions of higher education as essential to realizing their aspiration for racial justice.[44] The potential for exceptional performances to effect a reduction in racial bigotry or inequality is limited without broader activism. Let's take a comparison example to illustrate this point. It is often noted that Americans are slow to elect women as governmental representatives even as we come closer to achieving broad gender equity than have many nations that have had female leaders. This indicates something about how gender works in these other nations that parallels how race works here. In a nation, the normative state of women may be one in which women are oppressed, and yet certain women achieve great prominence. The exceptional woman does not necessarily reflect the normative condition of women and may even be lauded because she exists as the counterexample. Likewise, prominent African Americans hold power and prestige at the same time as astronomical rates of imprisonment, child poverty, health disparities, and limited employment opportunity affect large numbers of African Americans. A fully equitable society is one in which there are both diversity in representation and broad access. This reality was obscured in the United States by the election of the first African American president, for good reason. Given the history of race relations in the United States and the relations between the United States in the global economy and poor countries occupied by people of color, there is symbolism in having an African American president that trickles down, notwithstanding the degree to which he is exceptionalized.

This symbolism of President Obama has the potential to alter the way people of color see themselves as members of this nation and also the way White people see African Americans in particular. But whether President Obama as representative translates to broader access for people of color depends upon at least three variables. The first relates to policy. Does he promulgate policies that ensure broader access, responding to the hopes of his most loyal constituents, African Americans and Latinos? Second, does he have a means of articulating a relationship between expanded opportunity and his ability to achieve excellence, thereby reframing debates over affirmative action, the welfare state, and other contentious racial issues, in terms of democratization of opportunity? Third, is he proffered, and accepted, as one of many, rather than one of few? Clearly, there are ways in which he will always be one of few: he went to Harvard Law School, became a senator and then president. There aren't too many Black folks in each of those categories. However, he is one of many in some ways that have the potential to shift racial narratives in useful ways.

President Obama is both exceptionalized and racialized, but his manner of deploying both is instructive. Although he is associated iconographically with Lincoln, Kennedy, and Martin Luther King, he exists within a broader tradition of Black politics. He came to politics with the blessings and support of Chicago's Black professional class, a group with a highly organized social and political network that developed within the context of Harold Washington's historic mayoralty. He is in the tradition of Adam Clayton Powell Jr., who leveraged a background in community organizing and local political maneuvering to build a notable career in Congress. He is in the tradition of Congressman Mickey Leland, who did not bear a nontraditional name but wore nontraditional attire like dashikis and kufis while serving in Congress. He is in the tradition of Douglas Wilder, governor of Virginia from 1990 to 1994, a politician who straddled the ideological divide in the midst of the culture wars. He is in the tradition of figures like Ron Brown (former secretary of commerce), Colin Powell, and Condoleezza Rice, African Americans in highly visible national offices who did not reveal any marked racial allegiance (which is seen as a positive in the mainstream) but who were instead "party" (as in political party) people.

And, in a broader sense, Barack Obama, with his elegant and accomplished nuclear family, hearkens back to the kind of civic culture and politics of respectability that were once so ubiquitous in African American life. He has not chosen an assimilationist presentation to the world; he has chosen to present Black formal culture to the world, although the world doesn't know that's what it is. He is of the Sunday morning Black men in suits and overcoats, children with greased knees and patent leather shoes memorizing Bible verses, and mothers in skirt suits who know how to put anyone in check with their eyes—that kind of Black life. At the same time, his ascendancy makes public what Black civic culture kept private for so long: he, like so many historic Black leaders, has had a deeply unconventional, unusual, conflicted, rocky, iconoclastic life on his path to prominence. He lays no claims to some inborn essentialist authentic Blackness; no, it is in the choices and commitments he has made in private and public life that he shows his color.

At the same time, Obama's critiques of Black communities are common intraracial critiques within the African American community, critiques one hears in formal institutions like churches, civic organizations, historically Black colleges, and social institutions like barbershops, restaurants, parties. Their meaning shifts, however, when they come from the president of the United States. They begin to function not as an interior voice but as an exterior one that has power to shape policy and social norms. Moreover, they have the potential to symbolically distinguish him from other Black people even as they are extremely representative of the discourse within the Black community.[45]

Even if President Obama doesn't deliberately practice a politics of distinction vis-à-vis other Black people, self-exceptionalizing through individuation has become a common part of expressing self-worth and desert among Black people in the United States. When African American people attribute the rise in the rate of incarceration or school failure among blacks to the "family" rather than the "community" or the "system" or when Black celebrities elicit sympathy by talking about how they weren't accepted by other Blacks and thus were driven to achieve and large numbers of Black people identify personal motivation as the primary determinant of life outcome,[46] it is evidence that many African Americans' ideas fit into a contemporary model in which success is tied to individual labor alone, rather than to structures of community, institutional, and social support. In contrast, before the 1980s, notions of the good life for African Americans were generally tied to community (a sense of community that sometimes was based in racial exclusion, such as racially restrictive covenants and the mob violence that often followed from the integration of neighborhoods).[47] But, in the 1980s, we witnessed a sea change in which self-interest in the private domestic sphere of family was prioritized through the discourse of "family values."[48] This, too, became racialized as poor outcomes in Black communities became highly associated with a narrative of individual fault and moral failing. But, even though exceptionals promulgate this narrative, they are also stigmatized by it, having to explicitly prove that they are "different" or suffer being seen as deficient by default.

Rethinking the "Other"

Postcolonial theorists have compellingly described the structure of race as a dialectic between the self and the other.[49] In this rubric, the other is the negation of the self, holding opposite characteristics. Where the White self is rational, the other is irrational. Where the White self is moral, the other is immoral or at least amoral.

The prevalence of the language of "the other" in virtually every academic treatment of race theory, and in many nonacademic ones, is indicative of how resonant this construct is across national and political boundaries. This is so, because so many of our racial structures are rooted in Enlightenment thought and eighteenth-century imperialism, which explicitly depended upon this construct. However, in many ways, the notion of the other is difficult to apply to a racial structure in which those that are exceptionalized may escape the binary evaluation, although they technically remain in the "other" group. Homi Bhabha, in describing colonial mimicry,[50] mined the mimetic practices of exceptionalized people of color vis-à-vis White elites to understand the subversive power of assimilationist behavior. When the racial other becomes very much like the White self, the identity of the White self is destabilized.

This analysis helps explain the history of Black American exceptionalism, as well. But today those mimetic practices have limited transgressive potential, partly because the "other" is not always "other." Think about it: is Oprah other? Colin Powell? Jennifer Lopez? Jessica Alba? As exceptions to dominant constructs of racial membership not only become more common but also become integral to the national self-concept, don't we need theory that incorporates them?

What if we were to shift our understanding to see the construction of people of color as "extreme," rather than "other"? It is not simply the opposition but the overdetermination of characteristics of the human personality that characterizes how people outside the normative framework (White, straight, middle to upper class) are seen. So, for example, although much in postcolonial theory has been attentive to the dramatic ways that people of color have been seen as primitive as opposed to civilized, we might also talk about how people of color have been seen as possessing exaggerated aspects of Western civilization. In terms of gender, for example, Black men are seen as hypermasculine, supermacho, virile, and strong, and Black women are seen as hyperfemale and fertile, with overdetermined sexual organs,[51] while Asian woman are seen as hyperfeminine. Arabs are viewed as hyperreligious,[52] and East Asian people, in this increasingly technological age, are considered hypertechnological (and described as though they are human computers).[53] In this postfeminist era, Black woman are hyperassertive; in this "sex-positive" era, Latinas are seen as hypersensual, and Latino men are hypermacho.[54] The exaggeration of aspects of social formation that are approved of allows for the possibility that these people can be tamed or assimilated, at least a few of them, but also emphasizes that their exclusions are dependent upon their own unwillingness to follow the program, rather than a vulgar bigotry executed by members of the dominant group.

The image of extremism actually can be seen in the United States as a straight trajectory from slavery to now. What has changed is that the scope of people who are imaged as tameable is wider. And, whereas extremism once had a deterministic component (for example, Frederick Douglass's brilliance was ascribed to his White ancestry,[55] but his recalcitrance with respect to racism was tied to his overly emotional Africanness), over time it has shifted to be seen as something in the blurry interstices between nature and culture. This is in part due to activist history. Resistance to the "extreme" designation was a civil rights strategy. The visual image of decent, rational, "law-abiding" (in the Augustinian sense) African Americans facing raging, out-of-control White southern mobs affected and effected changes in Americans' thinking about civil rights.[56] Likewise, the Youngers, Lorraine Hansberry's fictionalized family in *A Raisin in the Sun* (1959), which was the first play written by a Black woman to appear on Broadway, presented a respectable, tamed image that offered a contrast to the ideas of the alternately complacent and predatory Black masses that dominated in the Jim Crow era. These images had a transformative power, because the Youngers, like the students at lunch counters, were not exceptionalized. They were presented as a representative Black working-class family struggling to attain the American Dream. They, like the civil rights workers, were figures of the hope that the extremist image could be altogether expunged from the image of all Black people, not just some special few. This hope was crushed soon thereafter, influenced by various forces, including the Moynihan Report, urban uprisings, Whites' resistance to addressing racial inequality in the North, and the power of longstanding racial ideology and imagery.

Today, it is those who can be "tamed" or, to use a less charged word, "assimilated" out of the extremism who are exceptionalized. In the world of public figures, these are the Colin Powells, Barack Obamas, Oprah Winfreys. They need not have a particular political perspective, but everything about them must appear to be "in moderation." The effect of the exception is at once to ratify our egalitarianism—our nondeterministic racial order, our nonessentialism—and yet to mark a distinction. They are at the borders of race, either as model minorities or model citizens. Moreover, they are what Lindon Barrett termed "evidence of the dynamics of distinction,"[57] whereby a particular value is accorded to that which supports the border of race in the United States. Thus, the value of the exceptional ironically imprisons him on the border of inequality.

The fragile compromise over affirmative action has occurred on the terms of the embrace of exceptionalism and on the aversion to racial "extremes." In *Grutter v. Bollinger*, 539 U.S. 306 (2003), the case that upheld the University of Michigan Law School's affirmative action policy, it was remarkable how many amicae briefs came from institutions of wealth and power. The consistent theme was that we need a diverse population within the professions because we live in a diverse nation and world, and we're facing globalization. Diversity is an asset because people of color have access to or can be "representatives" to various communities at home and abroad and in many cases may offer legitimacy to the corporations, governments, or institutions they represent. However, elite institutions have been willing to adopt affirmative action in part because of the powerful socialization afforded by attending such institutions, socialization that increases the value of these people of color as representatives to other people of color (in addition to being themselves representatives of people of color). Gaertner and Dovidio argue that it is when there are alternative notions of membership in an in-group that White racial biases can be diminished, because people of color can become part of a multiracial "we."[58] This is not to suggest that racism isn't present in elite institutions but rather that their status as engines for producing the economic elite provides another basis for such membership besides race, making affirmative action nonthreatening to their mission and identity. The epistemological and social acculturation of the institution wards against the "extreme." However, commitment to affirmative action does not necessarily mean commitment to ameliorating systemic racism (although it certainly does more good than harm to such a project).

The dominant racial narratives about affirmative action are on one hand a narrative about how diversity is good and reflects our rich society and on the other hand a view of affirmative action as a disincentive to excellence: it lets in unqualified Blacks and Latinos and gives them a free ride. The former line of thought emphasizes the significance of pluralistic membership and access, while the latter wants more rigorous evaluation of the propensity to a certain kind of racial extremism, namely "laziness." However, neither side of the mainstream debate promotes widespread structural change in which the general competence of children (or adults) of color is assumed.

Grutter v. Bollinger provides evidence that our legal order supports exceptionalism. The case, in contrast to *Gratz v. Bollinger*, *Parents Involved in Community Schools v. Seattle*, and *Meredith v. Jefferson County Board of Education*, allowed the University of Michigan Law School to retain its affirmative action policy but set a standard in which considerations of race in admissions have to be part of a holistic assessment of the student. This means that the only way race may be considered is the way it is done in elite contexts where there is a limited and self-selected pool of applicants and a good deal of resources. The rare get access, the rest do not. What a long way we are from the vision of *Brown*! And so, affirmative action modestly compensates middle-class Blacks and Latinos for the discrimination they experience and leaves out virtually everyone else.

I want to return to a much earlier affirmative action case, *Regents of the University of California v. Bakke* (1978), as a means of recasting the exceptionalism presumption. In that case, the University of California medical school's program of setting aside a specific number of places for African American candidates was declared unconstitutional, although the Court did say that race could continue to be considered in public university admissions. In education, contracting, employment, and many other arenas where affirmative action was practiced, the message of *Bakke* soon became a rallying cry against "quotas." Today, even the most assertive proponents of affirmative action say they reject "quotas." The reality is that life opportunity is largely framed by experiences over which a child has little control. There is a high correlation between family wealth, school quality, enrichment experiences, and the outcomes of children. Knowing that, we see that objective measures of achievement are not the products of merit by and large but rather the products of the intersection of privilege and opportunity. Moreover, in most highly desirable arenas (competitive colleges and jobs, for example), there are far more qualified people than there are "spots." Qualification is important; evidence of hard work is important. In these environments, an individual should come with the skills and habits necessary to perform the necessary work. But imagine if an elite college school said, "We will set a base of criteria that we identify as qualifications for achievement in this environment. Once we identify everyone in the pool who meets those criteria, we will compose a class that mirrors the diversity of this nation in terms of ethnicity, race, class, geography, culture, political ideology, family size, etc." Although there would be an "art" to this process, it would also entail quantification, that is, quotas. Quotas are disturbing to privileged people of all racial groups because they have the potential to throw out the prospect of deploying privilege to self-exceptionalize and instead to allow for some random distribution of access once a certain level of achievement has occurred. But, in fact, quotas within a qualified pool are more likely to be fair and not dependent upon the deployment of privilege.

Authenticity

The counterforce to exceptionalism is the demand for racial authenticity. One way to understand this is within what John R. Hall refers to as "cultural structuralism," a framework that "recognizes heterologous markets, currencies, and grounds of legitimation of multiple kinds of cultural capital."[59] Internal tests of authenticity often find community members evaluating one another on the basis of language, geography, social behaviors, and taste. These habits and features are forms of cultural capital that are seen as signifying allegiance to and sophisticated knowledge of the group. Some of them mark one as having the features of elite members of the group, others give one the styles of the "masses," and others still may be read more generally as signifiers of "belonging."[60] This internal surveillance is partly born of histories in which racial or national domination always involved some cooptation of members of subjugated groups. Tommie Shelby appropriately points out, however, in *We Who Are Dark: The Philosophical Foundations of Black Solidarity*,[61] that these markers of authenticity are not foolproof indicators of allegiance and may even allow terrible betrayals to go unnoticed. Moreover, the suppression of and discomfort with difference intolerably prunes publics within communities of color of their rich tapestry of experiences and potential sites of intersection with other public spheres. On the other hand, to the extent that exceptionals may be used to justify bigotry against the unexceptionalized, the threat of betrayal by exceptionalized figures is real. Those who are exceptionalized, however, often experience the suspicion and trepidation of other people of color as censure for their success, on the one hand, and may experience guilt about enjoying access denied to many others, alienation, and placelessness, on the other. This occurs within groups and between groups sitting under the awkward umbrella "people of color."

So this begs the question of how we should read resistance to assimilation. There are multiple ways for it to present. There is some resistance that is rooted in a refusal to accept other norms as inherently superior to one's own, particularly in the absence of a compelling moral or ethical reason for the displacement. For some, there is the belief that assimilation will have little payoff, so the loss of cultural distinctiveness is not worth the remote benefit. There may be opposition to the culture identified with the maintenance of inequality. And there may even be antisocial behavior that gets described as authentic, what I termed in my first book "thug mimicry." The fact that we don't ordinarily distinguish these resistances from one another causes some confusion. Not all resistance to assimilation is created equal.

Not all of it is absolute rejection. But let's take up one for a moment—the sense of a cost-benefit analysis that goes along with assimilation. If we imagine that the "rules" for incorporation might one day be codified and the "state of exception" instead might count as a firm intermediate status (some critics have argued this has already occurred) or disappear altogether for those who meet the requirements of incorporation (becoming White?), there is a question as to how capacious the space for incorporation will be. Certainly, today, Asian Americans are contending with changing rules as it is quietly thought that "too many" Asian Americans meet the exceptional standard. The persistence of glass ceilings and a long history of excluding the excellent, measured against a short history of affirmative action, make many people of color suspicious as to whether assimilating into the norms of incorporation will be fruitful.

Integral to this discussion but woefully underacknowledged is the traumatic history of the assassination of African American leaders during the civil rights movement. The murder of those who philosophically advocated for broad incorporation of Blacks fueled the sense among some African Americans that if one was to achieve, it had to be as an exceptional, and this encouraged some to question the prospect of full incorporation altogether.

Prominent in the dialogue about how to improve the lot of impoverished communities is role model theory. The idea is that people should be provided with role models within their "group" to offer hope and to make real the prospect of their achievement. This theory makes sense and can be tied to the pursuit of racial justice only if the opportunity promised is real and broad. It is difficult to adequately measure how real the opportunities to transcend the circumstances of one's birth and rearing are, given the complex variables at play in an individual's life. Choices, obstacles, and opportunities always form a complicated tangle. We can say neither that opportunity does not exist as a blanket statement nor that the society is fully open. We do witness vast institutional forces as barriers to access, but we also see a history of activist traversal of unbelievable barriers set up by racist action. However, to take this line of thought to its natural conclusion means that we must be asking ourselves what broad incorporation would look like and how to pursue it. The picture is not the same for everyone, even among those advocates for racial equality.

Critical Exceptionalism and Broad Incorporation

> We didn't come for no two seats when all of us is tired.
>
> —Fannie Lou Hamer, discussing the seating of the
> Mississippi Freedom Democratic Party at the
> Democratic National Convention, 1968

The general function of the exceptions is to provide evidence that the society is open, and to substantiate our creed (even if it is not good evidence). Another function is to quell the ongoing fear that there is some deterministic meaning in race, even as we have rejected that belief on any explicit level. See, we say, it is not in the blood because we have evidence of "in group differences!" And yet the idea of in group differences still allows for David Duke to generalize about black inferiority while acknowledging some exceptions to the rule.

Exceptionalism, however, has political possibilities beyond offering self-reward and assuaging cultural anxieties if the exceptionalized figure acts to revise her role as representative. The critical race theorist Patricia J. Williams, like many in her generation of critical thinkers, has used her exceptionalism in order to argue for broad incorporation of people of color. Through narration, she employs her extraordinary intellect to animate and unsettle the precept of inferiority. We read her stories of being among the faceless "Blacks" when her exceptionalism goes unrecognized, but those stories are brought into the exceptional terrain of Ivy League law professor. She therefore disturbs Black facelessness. The kind of critiques lodged by Williams and other progressive public intellectuals of color are critical exploitations of and resistance to the manner in which *they* have been exceptionalized.

A beautiful example is found in Williams's classic story of being miscast as White when she was applying for a mortage on the telephone. She writes:

> I am not only middle class, but I match the cultural stereotype of a good white person. It is thus perhaps that the loan officer of this bank, whom I had never met in person, had checked off the box on the Fair Housing Form indicating that I was white.
>
> Race shouldn't matter, I suppose, but it seemed to in this case so I took a deep breath, I crossed out white, I checked the box marked black and sent the contract back to the bank. That will teach them to presume too much, I thought. A done deal, I assumed. Suddenly the deal came screeching to a halt. The bank wanted more money as a down payment. They

wanted me to pay more points, as certain charges are called, they wanted to raise the rate of interest. Suddenly I found myself facing great resistance and much more debt.

She is forced to confront how the ineluctable fact of her Blackness destabilizes the access that goes along with being exceptional. She's not just her, she is "them," and she's punished because she has revealed herself to be part of the "them." The language is humorous, but the implications are cutting.

> I exist in the world on my own terms surely. I am an individual and all that. But if I carry the bags of logic out with my individuality rather than my collectively imagined effect on property values as the subject of this type of irrational economic connotation then I, the charming and delightful Patricia J. Williams, become a bit like a car wash in your back yard only much worse in real price terms. I am more than a mere violation of the nice residential comforts in question. My blackness can rezone them altogether by the mere fortuity of my location.

She goes on to contemplate what it would mean to pursue invisibility and presents hiding inside her home as an imagistic symbol of passing. She asks:

> Will the presentation of myself disperse the value of my home, my ownership, my property? This is madness I am sure, as I draw the curtain like a veil across my nose. In what order of things is it rational to thus hide and skulk? It's an intolerable logic. An investment in my property compels selling of myself.[62]

Exceptionalism is a species of property. It is traded upon and whipped out to gain admission. But Williams poignantly concludes her essay by reminding us of the spiritual and social costs of that negotiation. And she challenges us to recognize the absurdity of thinking that exceptional incorporation is enough. However, we face a daunting task when we try to imagine how we might pursue broader incorporation. The discourse of exceptionalism alienates us from even believing that broad incorporation can take place for members of racial minority groups. But it is worthwhile to consider how we might rewrite the discourse.

One potential strategy as it relates to African Americans might emerge from studying, sharing, and reviving the practices of traditional African American institutions. Jim Crow–era Black schools, civic associations, and churches socialized community members into sophisticated practices and affirmations of Black excellence, striving, and citizenship. This history is submerged. If we look to contemporary state-, academy-, and corporate-sponsored expressions of Black history month, for example, they are overwhelmingly accounts of exceptional individuals, not collective excellences such as these. This is a pedagogical failing and a missed opportunity to address what Nancy Fraser refers to as "misrecognition" of groups that is basically "social subordination—in the sense of being prevented from participating as a peer in social life." She argues for a politics of "recognition" as a "politics aimed at overcoming subordination by establishing the misrecognized party as a full member of society, capable of participating on a par with the rest."[63] The exceptional has the potential to call for the recognition of the many by trading on the access afforded the few. Critical exceptionalism can and should identify membership in communities, or descent from traditions, of excellence. If we understand the tradition President Obama and many other exceptionals have relied upon, it becomes very clear he isn't nearly the first articulate and bright one we've had.

$$7$$

Black Taxes and White Wages

The Social Economy of Race

WHITE SOLDIERS: Well here comes one johnny cuckoo on a
   cold and stormy night. . . . Well what did you come for?
BLACK MAN: I came to be a soldier . . .
WHITE SOLDIERS: Well you look too black and dirty . . .
BLACK MAN: Well I'm just as good as you are, on a cold and
   stormy night . . .
   —"Johnny Cuckoo" Bessie Jones and the Sea Island Singers

The children's clap song "Johnny Cuckoo," from the Georgia Sea Islands, recounts the story of Black people who came to support the Union cause during the Civil War and whose service was rejected. Eventually, the Union Army would need Black labor in order to claim victory over the Confederacy. But, at that moment, the labor that was so highly valued so long as Blacks were chattel slaves was devalued when Blacks became free. This proved a harbinger of how race and value would be reconstituted after emancipation. Labor performed by White hands was worth more.

W. E. B. Du Bois first described the "wages of whiteness" in the late nineteenth century as the economic exchange value given to White skin. Later, this theory was extended in the work of Peggy McIntosh[1] (who developed a theory of White skin privilege), David Roediger[2] (who theorized the wages of Whiteness as a matter of nineteenth-century racialization), and Cheryl Harris[3] (who described Whiteness as property), among others. Colloquial African American talk about the "Black tax" has been extended into academic considerations of the real economic costs associated with being Black in the work of Jody David Armour,[4] Thomas Shapiro,[5] and Melvin Oliver.[6] In all of this work, Whiteness has been compellingly described as a form of capital. The economic description of race is at once metaphorical and literal, reflecting abstract concepts of human value that translate into concrete realities. From Du Bois to these more recent theories, the notion of an income deriving from Whiteness or a deficit applied to Blackness has been an important means of understanding how race, as a social construct, becomes "real" and how the "is it race or is it class" discussion about inequality in the United States often fails to account for how race produces economic conditions.[7]

In this chapter, I want to discuss the social economy of race, and by that I mean the means by which value (of real and personal property, employment, and other things) is shaped by the degree to which those things are associated with, come from, or are controlled by or proximate to a given racial group. This chapter is not a presentation of the significant wage and income gaps along racial lines. That work has been done very compellingly elsewhere. Rather, I am interested in the economic production of race itself and how that production is profoundly debilitating to any remedial efforts to address our history and present of racial inequality unless we confront it directly.

The signature social history for understanding this phenomenon is the history of the Federal Housing Authority in the mid-twentieth century. Through the practices of redlining and of subsidizing wealth creation for White Americans via mortgage policy, the FHA institutionalized the racialization of real property.[8] This practice created and sustained wealth gaps and residential segregation patterns that persist today. Moreover, it institutionalized a system of race-based valuation that would be embraced by the society as a whole, as evinced by ongoing informal real estate practices and home-buyer preferences long after the FHA policy had changed.[9]

The association of race and value, however, is contingent. The racialization of particular tasks and cultural spheres means that various things may have higher value when associated with Blackness, Whiteness, Asianness, Indianness, or Latinidad. For example, the White rapper and nanny are both likely to be treated as suspect. Nevertheless, in general, the racial stratification that we see in society is mirrored in our valuations and translates into economic consequences. There is very minimal discussion of this impact in the public arena. As Amartya Sen writes, "income inequality, on which economic analysis of inequality so often concentrates, gives a very inadequate and biased view of inequalities, even of those inequalities that can be powerfully influenced by economic policy."[10] Although more attention is currently being paid to the significant racial gaps in wealth accumulation, as discussed in Dalton Conley's *Being Black Living in the Red*,[11] which are far larger than the gaps in income, we still often fail to consider how this gap gets produced by our values and systems of value. Again, we are not concentrating here on a static picture of ongoing gaps in income, but rather considering a more complicated cyclic system of worth that has economic consequences but cannot be reduced to that which is measurable in simple economic terms.

There are also psychosocial impacts of the devaluation of racialized people. Recall the Kenneth Clarke doll study that was used to great effect in the *Brown v. Board of Education* school desegregation case, a study in which young African American children disproportionately chose the White doll over the Black. One might easily read this study as reflecting the children's ideas about which doll was more "valuable" or "worthy" in an objective sense. This study has been repeated in various ways over the years, with different populations and nuances, but the consistent result is that children in some way manifest the racial inequality and biases we live with. While we often think about things like Black dolls and children's literature in terms of esteem, and appropriately so, these things, along with Black and Hispanic History Month and Black History requirements in some school districts, should also be understood as spaces for asserting value to things associated with people of color and their our society.

Value, Merit, and Utility

The value that is placed on things, or their worth, is not simply their "use-value" in late capitalist societies. The value of many things has to do with "soft" factors that are quantifiable only to the extent that we can count human preferences. In a society with such a long history of racial injustice, it makes perfect sense that human preferences often reflect racial stratification. Expertise in valuation is not simply about an objective assessment of the usefulness of an object; it is also about a subjective calculus of what people will pay for the object and other variables that shape its appeal. The value of something may be determined by how it is evaluated in comparison to other objects and how that relationship is shaped by and impacts our social relations. As well, people will pay for familiarity, prominence, status, exclusivity, and rarity. The aversion that many people have for communities of color, for example, cannot be dismissed as only a reflection of the poverty and crime in so many of those communities. First, we have evidence that such an aversion is present regardless of the existence of any evidence that there are problems of that sort.[12] Second, poverty, like wealth, is something that is constantly reproduced. When more experienced and skilled teachers are given "plum" assignments in Whiter and more affluent districts[13] or when employers don't hire people from "that neighborhood,"[14] we have examples of preferences that sustain inequality by minimizing opportunities to develop greater human capital in communities of color.

The concept of merit, an "earned value" attributed to a person, has become highly associated with affirmative action debates and thereby highly racialized. The efforts to remedy the history of racism were rolled back in the 1980s and 1990s with a discourse framed largely around undeserved reward and the lack of "merit." The merit talk is able to evade being categorized as "racist" in the public eye because it does not depend upon racial determinism but relies on the idea of "objective assessment." The notion of objective assessment is highly flawed, however, because such objective assessment does not account for the context in which achievement is attained, which is often simply evidence of how inequality manifests in academic performance. As such, differences in achievement are too often reflective of differences in opportunity to be identified as a function of merit. Increasingly, the economic turn to discussions of inequality has devoted attention to gaps in cognitive skill or human capital.[15] These ideas neatly dovetail with the arguments of merit in affirmative action because it can be argued, that Blacks and Latinos who perform below par on measures of skill are not equipped to be in those environments and also are not deserving of aid, because there isn't the right fit in terms of skill.[16] Underlying it all is the question of worthiness as it relates to access to employment. If commentators and policymakers can convince the public and legislatures that people don't have the capacity or inclination to achieve a form of human capital, then it is easy to argue for denying them greater access to real, social, or cultural capital in education and employment.

On the other hand, Thomas Shapiro, in a thorough assessment of the privileges found in inheritance and home appreciation, shows that Whites in the United States have been accorded dramatic unearned benefits relative to African Americans,[17] benefits that have their roots in discriminatory policies and practices that were sustained, even by conservative estimates, until the late 1960s.

The evidence of the way race impacts value, or what I term the *social economy of race* ("social" because it occurs in the midst of the world of human interaction, and "economy" because I am talking about the circulation of capital), appears in the realm of real property, movable goods, and the exchange value of labor. Research on pay equity reveals that gender and race both impact salary paid for the same work and skills. Critics of this research note that it often doesn't include analyses of the quality of schools attended or length of employment. But these areas also reflect the practice of inequality. If one can show that if you control for quality of school and length of employment all disparities in compensation disappear, that doesn't mean that things are fair. That means that we have problems with unequal access to high-quality education and with the initial willingness of employers to hire White women and people of color.

The work of Devah Pager illustrates how the high value associated with Whiteness and the devaluation associated with Blackness is so dramatic for many employers that it can have a greater influence that evidence of criminality or work history.[18] Skin color also has an impact on wages and employment, demonstrating another dimension of the economic impact of the intersection of race and preference.[19] Other research supports the argument that racial preference as an independent variable shapes market opportunities for job candidates.[20] Moreover, as a codependent variable associated with neighborhood, social networks, and cultural capital, it also exerts a substantial influence. So do groups differ in their possession of such resources to a degree that might account for most of the operation of race and value? The economist William A. Darity argues that "the empirical record displays widespread evidence of a gap in treatment of members of ascriptively different groups even after controlling for productivity linked differences— evidence of raw discriminatory differentials across groups, across countries, and across time."[21] Hence, there is unequal treatment that exists notwithstanding measurable differences in skill or knowledge. That inequality is exacerbated by groups' unequal access to skills and knowledge. While access to capital of various sorts (financial, social, cultural) can minimize inequality for people of color, it is unlikely that they will completely neutralize the stigma associated with color or hair or facial features; they will likely continue to operate as competing forms of capital. The case of Asian Americans provides a telling example of the intersection of race and human capital because there is evidence that members of this group are less likely to be promoted to supervisory and upper management positions than are comparably trained Whites.[22] Even if we can attribute some of this to the large number of Asian American professionals who were not educated at American universities, we can still see the intersection of nationality and "value" as part of the social economy of race in the United States.

Given the inequitable distribution of education in this society and the manner in which social networks are impacted by race, it is certain that there is a greater aggregation of human capital among Whites in general than among Blacks or Latinos[23] (although certain subgroups, like West African immigrants, belie such a general trend—and that itself is a reflection of the terms of admission to the nation in U.S. immigration policy). A cycle of inequality is sustained by the translation of race-based ideas about value and worth into opportunity and access or the lack thereof.

The market for real property illustrates some of the most dramatic evidence of the social economy of race. As Thomas Shapiro writes, "Homeownership is by far the single most important way families accumulate wealth."[24] The presence of Black people reduces the "value" of a home because Blackness in the neighborhood reduces the desirability of a property for many homebuyers.[25] The persistence of discriminatory practices in real estate markets shows this. Maintaining the "Whiteness" of communities is of economic benefit to realtors who want to maximize their commissions and reputations. The fact that predatory lenders focused on African American communities, thus making this community especially vulnerable to the foreclosure crisis of the first decade of the twenty-first century, is further indicative of both the wealth gap and bigotry in the lending industry that leads a greater proportion of Black homebuyers to accept bad mortgages.[26]

This also indicates how the "utility" of a dollar is diminished in Black hands. Amartya Sen argues that one has to consider inequality in terms of the "individual's real opportunity to pursue her objectives" and to do this "account would have to be taken not only of the primary goods the person holds but also of the relevant personal characteristics that govern the conversion of primary goods into the person's ability to promote her ends."[27] If opportunities in the mortgage and home purchase market continue to be limited by race independent of capital and creditworthiness, then we can see specific evidence of the diminished utility of the dollar in a person's hand because he or she is a person of color. Moreover, evidence that people of color pay more for cars and are generally expected to pay more for many things,[28] all else being equal, indicates that, in our culture, individuals consistently reproduce the relationship between race and value by diminishing the utility of a dollar in colored hands. This occurs not only with major life purchases but with the mundane, as well. When a person goes shopping, the benefit of the experience will be shaped by the willingness of the staff to assist that person and to treat that person with dignity, whether the person is imagined as a valued customer or a potential thief, and the extent to which he or she is accommodated.[29] All of this is part of the value of the experience. When a customer goes to a restaurant, the courtesy and efficiency of the waitstaff are part of the value of the experience. So the exchange value in these encounters cannot be measured simply by whether the customer received a particular item for a particular price or received a particular dish; it also should be measured in the pleasure received from the exchange based upon the interactions in the process of purchasing. There is evidence to suggest that African Americans consume nonessentials more than average.[30] It would be interesting to envision a metric for evaluating whether this increased consumption might in part be motivated by an effort to achieve a higher aggregated level of pleasure in consumption, a level that perhaps is more easily achieved for Whites. It also might be interesting to assess how what is purchased among different racial groups is tied to interactive dynamics in retail establishments.[31]

Sen goes on to argue that, although income is "a crucially important means . . . its importance lies in the fact that it helps the person to do things that she values doing and to achieve states of being that she has reason to desire. The worth of incomes cannot stand separate from these other concerns, and a society that respects individual well being and freedom must take note of these concerns in making interpersonal comparisons as well as social evaluations."[32] So one level of concern for race and economics is simply the curtailment of market prospects due to racial gaps in wealth and income; another level is how race impacts one's value as a laborer and the value of the things one own; yet another level is how one's racial body shapes the exercise of economic power; and yet another level concerns how all three influence one's future prospects for gaining or losing economic power.

The Equal Employment Opportunity Commission (EEOC) and employment discrimination law are more sophisticated than virtually any other area of government and law in identifying how contemporary racial inequality is practiced. The EEOC identifies the impact of subtle bias and argues that intentional discrimination "includes not only racial animosity, but also conscious or unconscious stereotypes about the abilities, traits or performance of individuals of certain racial groups." Even comments by an interviewer such as "We're looking for a clean-cut image" or 'Because of our sophisticated upscale location, we need to look for certain 'soft skills,'" could be reflective of racial stereotyping or bias."[33] Moreover, they instruct employers not to use the social networks that sustain racial discrimination in looking for potential employees.[34] This recognition of how inequality is practiced in employment has not eliminated racism, but it does reveal that we have some institutional sophistication about race and value in employment that can create a foundation for richer discussions of the social economy of race as related to law and policy.

So far we have been talking largely about how race impacts the commoditization of human attributes or services, but it is also the case that race impacts the valuation of the entire person. Take, for example, the great premium that is paid for the healthy eggs of young, educated white women[35]—a reflection of the value of the prospect of a white child, as measured against the relative affordability of the adoption of children of color.[36] Or, we can use the phenomenon referred to as "missing White woman syndrome" to illustrate this point. This term has developed as a result of the hugely disproportionate media coverage when White women, as opposed to women of color, are missing. Several instances in the early 2000s in which White and African American women were missing at the same time crystallized this point.[37] But it is more than simply racial bias or empathy that drives this; it is the sense that certain women are "worth more." We also see disparities that reflect class or social role (for example, sex workers who are missing or victims of rape get minimal attention from police or the general public);[38] given that the ultimate threats imagined when someone is missing are death and/or horrible abuses and torture, this strikes at the very heart of our sense of fundamental human value.

Place

> if agents hold a negative stereotype about blacks they may think (correctly) that on average and all else equal, commercial loans to blacks post a greater risk of default or black residential neighborhoods are more likely to decline. But this can hardly be the end of the story. What about the possibility that race conveys this information only because agents expect it to, and then act in ways that lead to the confirmation of their expectations? What if blacks have trouble getting further extensions of credit in the face of a crisis, and so default more often? Or what if nonblack residents panic at the arrival of blacks, selling their homes too quickly and below the market value to lower income buyers, thereby promoting neighborhood decline?
>
> —Glen Loury, *The Anatomy of Racial Inequality*[39]

In *The Anatomy of Inequality*, economist Glen Loury describes the cyclic process of expectation and consequence that aids in the reproduction of the devaluation of homes owned by African Americans and the maintenance of wealth gaps. The home is the primary source of wealth for Americans, and both African Americans and Latinos are far less likely to own homes[40] and more likely to have unfavorable mortgage terms.[41] African Americans have

1/10 the average net worth of White Americans.[42] Michael K. Brown and his colleagues, in *Whitewashing Race*, describe this process as racial accumulation and disaccumulation. They describe how racial accumulation and disaccumulation occur in multiple realms, many of which are associated with "place." Although a certain degree of the experience of the social economy of race is carried with one's body, and wherever one goes, there are significant impacts that come from being in racialized places. Home value is obviously a major one, but so is the quality of care in hospitals that exist in communities that serve people of color (both the actual treatment and the surveillance and interactive dynamics), the quality of education in schools (again resources and interaction both matter), and the social networks that translate to information and opportunity.[43]

The popularity of the pejorative "ghetto" in the first decade of the twenty-first century was unquestionably a means of making an association between poor Black people and behaviors or styles that are undesirable. It associated Black people with a devalued space and affirmed that devaluation. It also codified the racialization of the word "ghetto" in the United States as Black. The ghetto is Black and is imagined as essentially chaotic, morally, aesthetically, and culturally bankrupt, dangerous, and bad. In fact, the designation "bad neighborhood" operates as a stand-in for poor and Black or Latino. Using the word "ghetto" rather than a slur for Black people avoids the racial determinism that is widely understood as "racist" and yet may be freely racist. This gets a racial "pass" in part because it is language used within the Black community to create symbolic boundaries between self and "other" lower-status Blacks. To call someone "ghetto" means not that one is necessarily poor and Black or that all who are poor and Black must fall into this category but that one has negative traits that are highly associated with the poor and Black, thus affirming a debilitating racial narrative. It also marks the ghetto as a place of shame. As the geographers Audrey Koyabayashi and Linda Peake write, "no geography is complete, no understanding of place or landscape comprehensive, without recognizing that American geography, both as a discipline and as the special expression of American life, is racialized."[44]

Although critics who challenge people in poor communities of color to reclaim their neighborhoods through clean streets and community policing programs often make good arguments in terms of self-efficacy, they neglect the reality that even with such initiatives, place still gets racialized in ways that have dramatic economic consequences. Galster, Mincy, and Tobin argue, when talking about the loss of working-class employment in Black communities, "racism is increasingly becoming 'placism'" because "racial differences in the space opportunity structure are generating racial disparities in poverty."[45] Redlining and other ongoing practices of geographical bias, as well as the policing of geographic borders, indicate of how much race and geography are proxies for each other and also produce identity.[46] As David Delaney argues, "race . . . is what it is and does what it does precisely because of how it is given spatial expression."[47] The realness of race is most apparent in the material world. The exposés provided by social justice movements, from advocates for environmental justice to urban renewal activists, have demonstrated that the devaluation of the lived environment associated with people of color and most especially African Americans not only leads to economic inequality but also has deep physiological and psychological consequences that reach into the very value of life. It is unsurprising, then, that so much violence that occurs in Black communities is over contested space. While urban violence in the 1980s revolved around drug-dealing real estate, twenty-first century violence over space seems to be more abstract, a vexed and devastating expression of longing for and destructive assertion of property. Notwithstanding the substantial impact of this violence, its agents are few compared to its victims. However, the prevalence of such violence overdetermines the representation of entire communities and creates stigma such that the victims fail to get adequate care and attention.[48]

Human Cost

The popular culture racial discourse about place is matched by a political discourse that describes certain segments of the population largely in terms of their "cost." The dismantling of welfare occurred largely through the political force of a discourse about the taxpayers being forced to "pay for" people who didn't work and their children. Undocumented workers are often described as "costing" Americans money by virtue of their use of public hospitals and attendance at public schools. Populist media hosts frequently talk about people who receive certain sorts of public assistance or who use public resources as drains upon the economy and the well-being of the nation. Even imprisoned people are described in terms of their economic cost, notwithstanding the cheap labor they, like undocumented people and low-wage workers, provide.

There's a way that racial narratives and proxies for race likely work in the imaginations of people engaging in discrimination that makes it possible for us to avoid the straightforward evidence that there are "wages of Whiteness" (and of other races, depending upon context). Without the revelation of this fact, remedial efforts appear to be nothing more than "undeserved gain" for underperforming people.

To describe human beings as a cost impacts the perception of their human value. It also rhetorically erases whatever economic contribution they are making as workers and as consumers (in terms of both circulating dollars and the payment of sales taxes). It also likely operates as justification for resistance to hiring, which in turn stifles the human productivity of people affected by such prejudices. If poor people of color are imagined as those who impose a cost upon society, rather than as contributors, then of course it is more challenging to call attention to their needs, care, and usefulness. The ultimate representation of this type of thought is found in the lack of care we show when it comes to the death of poor Black and Brown people. The infant mortality rate for African Americans was 2.3 times that for non-Hispanic Whites in 2005.[49] In 2003, the homicide death rate for young African American men was sixteen times higher than that for White men; the rate for Hispanic young men was six times higher than that for young White men, and for young Asian men it was twice the rate for young White men. The rate of HIV-related deaths among African American men in 2003 was seven times higher than the rate for white men.[50] Black women are murdered at three times the rate of White women.[51] This brief accounting of significant disparities in causes of death should be a source of enormous alarm, but because, as the spoken-word artist Ise Lyfe says so succinctly, "We don't care about Black death," it becomes almost normative in our lives.

Aesthetics and Culture

Pierre Bourdieu provided the seminal theoretical framework for understanding how culture could operate as a form of capital.[52] Given that race has some significant overlap with cultural groupings, it makes sense to presume that people of color in the United States have unequal access to the kind of cultural capital that provides economic rewards.[53] But a more complicated dynamic has emerged as we celebrate heterogeneity and consumption in the twenty-first century United States. The performance of racial paradigms has aesthetic and commodity value. Leticia Saucedo explores this in her discussion of employers' desire that Latino workers fit into a particular subservient social role.[54] This performance of status both creates market opportunities and oppresses. In the case of the popular media, reality television and hip hop music are spheres in which enormous profit is gained by African Americans acting out life in poor Black communities, places that people avoid in real life but voraciously consume in entertainment. The authenticity of these performances is complicated to evaluate. Suffice it to say, however, that they entail strategies for engaging audiences or employers by appealing to pre-existing racial narratives. In Kanye West's song "Diamonds (from Sierra Leone)," Jay Z rhymes "I'm not a businessman, I'm a business, man/Let me handle my business, damn!,"[55] identifying his own commodification even as he is a person who has harnessed the power of his brand more successfully than virtually any other rapper. There is a good deal of money made, and individual economic opportunity garnered, through the widespread consumption of the performance of race roles. The thug, the mammy, the gardener, the tragic mulatto, the Suzie Wong, the nanny, the angel, the noble savage, the angry Black—these are repeatedly bought and sold. Although these generate revenue, they also operate to implicitly thwart the recognition of people of color who don't occupy such roles. Moreover, the consumer package of the role or performance becomes overdetermined and collapses within it cultural attributes that become further devalued by virtue of their association with stereotype. The vernacular speech and styles of African Americans, Latinos, and Asian Americans are all completely legitimate cultural styles and practices. And yet, in their own ways, they are identified as inferior, deficient, or unattractively awkward, in part because of their associations with stereotypes.

The antisagging ordinances provide an excellent example of this. In the early twenty-first century, a smattering of towns developed ordinances that allowed for the issuance of fines or misdemeanors for "sagging" pants in the style popular for young hip hop aficionados.[56] Although sagging pants have cross-cultural appeal and are worn by kids of all races, they are highly associated with Blackness and criminality. It is often recounted that the style originated in prison, where young men's pants hang low because belts are not allowed in prisons for safety reasons. That narrative about the origins of sagging is employed as evidence of the moral bankruptcy of the style.

The effort to criminalize sagging, moreover, places a cost upon participating in a cultural practice that has no objective offensiveness. Although undergarments are exposed when a person's pants are sagging, they are usually only boxers, which look identical to shorts. Young women of all races and classes routinely expose more skin in far more provocative fashion. Notably, it is often African American adults who rail most vociferously against sagging, not unlike the way their parents railed against afros and skin-tight bell bottoms. And, while intergenerational conflict over style is normal, the criminalization of style is not. Antisagging discourse reflects a consistent undercurrent in American culture that hold that, to use the language of Black English, if people of color would just "act right," then they would have equal opportunity. This is not just a demand for assimilation but a cost applied to the failure to assimilate and a valuation of expressive identity.

Clothes, speech, and style are spheres in which people communicate two different kinds of information. One is about social position, actual and aspirational. The other is about personal aesthetics and commitments. To repudiate the styles associated with the poor and colored is tautological because they are already repudiated for being poor and colored. Insofar as styles are associated with them, they will be treated as inherently suspect in this society unless they become so popular that they are effectively deracialized. But far more important than a simple challenge to the aesthetic tautologies of inequality is a consideration of the communicative function of expressive culture. This is not just communication of the person who wears the clothing but the communication of the corporations that market particular clothes to particular communities. To what social position are they being ascribed by being sold certain things? How do people confirm or distinguish social roles by virtue of expressive culture? The high rates of consumerism among people of color[57] should be seen in light of the communicative power of expressive culture. The accoutrements or artifactual additions to the person may operate as efforts to distinguish oneself from the social role to which one has been ascribed. I may have a greater desire for consumer goods if I feel a greater compulsion to counternarrate my identity because my body has been devalued because of my race. Consumerism in many instances may reflect a desire for images of a kind of success that is rarely realized in social interaction, real property, or long-term economic stability.

Consumers

As previously discussed, poor Black and Brown people in this country are often depicted as taxes or costs upon the economy. But a more nuanced approach to the question of where they fit into the economy reveals a seminal economic role. This population, particularly those who receive social welfare benefits, unquestionably fits into the economy as important consumers—of goods, as well as services. There is an entire professional class that depends upon providing services to these people, and administering the provision of those services.[58] Hence, these professionals rely upon the perceived needs of this population to legitimize their compensation, and the cyclic economic structure that supports the provision of these services may actually create a disincentive to remedying the problems being addressed. John McKnight provides a powerful critique of this system in his book *The Careless Society*,[59] in which he illustrates how the professionalization of services to poor communities fuels a profound diminution in the capacity of communities to solve problems and to work collaboratively. As it stands, serving the needs of the poor has been disproportionately framed in terms of making them consumers of professional services, rather than providing stable employment and safe environs. This is not to say that social work, counseling, clinics, and the like don't serve important needs but rather to suggest that they exist within a structure where benefits accrue to those in high need but often disappear when even minimal opportunities for self-stabilizing or self-efficacy emerge. Take, for example, a young woman I know, an orphan who was adopted and raised by a now deceased grandmother. She lives with virtually no familial support. She plans to attend college and works full time but finds it extremely difficult to keep herself afloat. She explains that if she had a baby she would be able to get assistance with an apartment, food, and medical care. Or if she were an addict, she could access a host of other social services. Because she is making good choices life choices, she fails to meet the requirements for many services.

In poor communities of color, citizens and residents have little choice as to how the services are distributed, what services are provided, and, even more, how the money spent on "their behalf" is allocated. In fact, what McKnight shows is that the allocation has more to do with the structure of the service economy than with the needs of communities.[60] If this is so, then the failure of the services to address the problems is logical and doesn't indicate the cultural failures that conservatives decry as plagues within the communities. If a woman knows that it is easier to get an apartment and health care as a single woman, then why would she marry an underemployed man?[61]

These services are often described as the province of political liberals, but they have definite counterparts in traditionally conservative realms. The social historian Daryl Scott has argued that the idea of Black Americans as damaged, culturally or psychologically, provided the foundation for various arguments, from the plaintiff claims in *Brown v. Board of Education* to the culture-of-poverty theses and tough-on-crime measures.[62] The arguments about the behavioral manifestation of this damaged state and ideas about appropriate response to it vary according to one's political perspective. The difference is that, in the conservative world, "services" are more often focused on punitive responses to problems, such as calls for higher rates of imprisonment (the penitentiary has a service model even as rehabilitation is no longer at the core of its role) and the privatization of entities (e.g., jails, prison health care) that traditionally have been under the purview of the state.[63] The rise of privatization of prisons and schools is alarming because it implies that it is appropriate for the profit motive to have a role in decision making about how to prepare and protect citizens. The role of the state in shaping the civic life of its citizens should be philosophically separate from constructing rewards for individualized greed and instead should be animated by a sense of the public good. The operators of prisons and the companies that provide food, clothing, and medical care to the imprisoned receive economic benefit from the social "needs" associated with the prison-industrial complex. While the imprisoned receive less than subsistence wages for their labor, the production of wealth for those who provide goods necessary for their imprisonment is substantial. This problem is likely to worsen with increasing privatization of prisons (and schools, for that matter), because privatization completely derails the responsibility to protect citizens, instead prioritizing the profit motive. Moreover, in that context, labor is conceived of as a service (work requirements for welfare recipients or prisoners) not for the recipients of the fruits of the labor but for the laborer herself (!) because it "teaches responsibility," and therefore norms such as a living wage are considered inapplicable. In both instances, the profit comes from the persistence of the problem. One cannot help acknowledging how this echoes an old racial discourse about labor and punishment in American history, in which the control of Black, Mexican, and Chinese labor was seen as a tool for civilizing and disciplining unruly or threatening people, and the need for control was seen as persistent. Even a concept like forcing people from welfare to work, which would seem objectively good, is punitive if work is not available.

If we shift from thinking about poor Black and Brown people as consumers of service and instead see them as consumers of goods, we should also be conscious of who profits from this consumption. A class of small-business owners benefits from the limited access to consumer goods in poor communities and uses higher prices to offset higher insurance costs and the risk involved with setting up shop in economically depressed areas.[64] As in the case of the service providers, these parties are disproportionately (though by no means exclusively) other people of color, although in many instances they are of a different ethnicity from the consumers or of the same ethnicity but from a different socioeconomic class.

The economic benefits accruing to individual people of color by virtue of providing services or goods to poor people of color should make us revisit and question the idea of the "racial role model" as a tool for racial uplift because of what kind of role models one is likely to encounter in one's own community. The supposed role model might very well be the agent of one's economic exploitation or may depend upon the limited mobility or access of others in their group for his or her status. Thus, relationships between ethnic groups and socioeconomic classes within the broad category "people of color" require a more complex analysis. If the primary college-educated person of color seen in a community is a social worker who may provide help but also may be the person who removes children from homes, then the usefulness of that person as a role model is immediately suspect. When people critique the use of music stars and athletes as role models for kids in poor communities of color, we should interrogate that critique for failures to rigorously consider the alternatives. It might be psychologically easier to identify the professional athlete as the model of success than the overworked physician at the public hospital who barely has a moment to listen to your description of your ailment and may provide you with substandard treatment because of bias or lack of resources. Whom a child aspires to be is as much a product of opportunity and the clarity of the route to success (i.e. kids know how ballers become ballers) as it is of the pomp and circumstance surrounding the career.

We consume images of our desire and aspiration in American culture.

Inhibiting Remedy

A great deal of scholarship has been focused on the manner in which racial segregation fuels poverty among African Americans and Latinos.[65] The argument that often follows is that integration is essential for remedying racial inequality. It is true that concentrations of people without money will obviously have less opportunity than concentrations of people with money, but I want to challenge the integrationist resolution because of how it leads us to interpret the statement that segregation begets poverty. The unstated implication can often be for the listener that integration is good because of the moral, cultural, and social benefit of proximity to Whites, not because of the economic benefits that exist and are accorded to White spaces. Massey and Denton identify the work of racism in causing enormous gaps in wealth tied to geography, which are then translated to services. But it bears repeating that this is true because of our culture of valuation, not because of the inherent value of proximity to Whites. The reader might think this obvious, but when we consider the presumptions of value in speech, sartorial matters, style and the like that emerge, and how these presumptions of value are shaped by the devaluation of things associated with people of color, the question must be raised again. It is not the case that segregation itself creates inequality; it is the meaning and value that are attributed to the segregated spaces and the unequal distributions that go along with the racialization of spaces that produce and reproduce the existing inequality. That value translates to valuation and devaluation of homes, schools, workers, children, and more. To pursue integration is a laudable goal, but so is undoing the wages of Whiteness such that integration (and existing as a member of a minority in that integrated space) would not be so often required for increasing opportunity for people of color.

If we are honest, we understand that the national economy as it stands "needs" unemployed people because the market cannot support all the able-bodied low-skilled workers at a living wage while maintaining the high profit margins of mid- to large-size businesses and corporations. On the other hand, there is an alarmist buzz about a coming shortage of skilled and professional workers. One response to this could be to invest in educational opportunity to increase the pool of skilled workers. Another could be to devote substantial energy to ensuring that "off-the-books" employees could not continue to displace and/or undercut low-skilled workers. But, of course, when providing the necessary education or developing a commitment to ensuring a living wage is perceived as providing a benefit for those who are a drain or a cost to the society and who are therefore described in the terms of our social economy of race, the political will to pursue such initiatives will be lacking.

In response to evidence of high rates of unemployment and underemployment in the African American community and of discrimination in employment markets, people often retreat to ethnic culture to provide explanatory justifications for the social economy of race. The work ethic or domestic habits of a culture (read racial group) is admired or reviled and used to explain why certain groups are more or less attractive to employers. There are a couple of problems with such lines of thought. They allow for grotesque generalizations about quite diverse groups, and they support the concept that race may be legitimately used as a shorthand for a set of qualities while discounting other potentially salient "similarities" across individuals and groups. Finally, they justify penalizing an individual on the basis of demographic information or stereotypes about a group. This social-cost language ultimately gets in the way of the foundation of liberal thought—respect for the individual citizen.

The challenge is that the practice of inequality must be addressed both as it affects individuals and as it affects groups. Certainly, economically devastated communities need solutions that bring to them the economic benefits of the cities and nation where they exist. And individuals should not be forced to bear the burden of a devaluation of their racial group. But the dynamic between individual and group is extremely tricky in this instance. It is only in the aggregate that we can "see" the cost of race, so the idea often doesn't lend itself to the proof structure of, for example, antidiscrimination litigation in the individual instance. So it is difficult to individualize remedies; even if the injury is individual, we must have broad-based responses.

There are policies that make efforts to respond to the social economy of race as it impacts individuals and groups. The best example of the former is affirmative action. The structure is such that it restores a value (increased consideration in an applicant pool) to account for the value that has been taken away from people as a result of racial stigma and/or inequality. Affirmative action is a modest yet increasingly controversial (and, in the eyes of the Supreme Court, usually illegitimate) effort to provide an individual remedy to a broad inequality. So, for example, while Asian Americans face little stigma in the academic context, making their exclusion from affirmative action in schools (except for in underrepresented areas) perhaps somewhat logical, in professional contexts where Asian Americans often face glass ceilings or are prevented from moving into areas that don't fit ascribed racial performance, they should be candidates for affirmative action. The problem is, of course, that the discourse of affirmative action is one in which people are seen as receiving an unearned benefit, rather than just compensation. This is partly because the wages of Whiteness are not openly explained in our society. Because Whiteness is normalized, describing Whiteness as an unearned benefit is a challenging argument to make. But greater traction might be gained by using the historic frame of "the Black tax." The Black or Brown tax might describe actual circumstances as diverse as the lower value of being an A student at a subpar school, racial discrimination in the classroom, and the unequal distribution of information and resources to students on the basis of race.[66]

An example of a group effort to respond to the social economy of race is found in community development corporations. These entities, which fund community groups involved in economic development projects, are laudable for their appreciation of community resources and the goal of community-based self-determination. However, one means of evaluating their effectiveness is to measure their impact on property values. This potentially measures one aspect of the social economy of race—whether proximity to communities of color continues to have a negative a value. However, because, in many of these communities, there are low rates of home ownership, the measurement may be measuring not an impact upon the community but rather the value of the investments of the landlords, which itself may be dependent upon the soft preferences (which are often racially based) of potential residents or purchasers. One must ask who owns property, what property divides are thereby created, and whether the increase in property value creates greater cost (rent, consumer goods) rather than greater value or opportunity for residents of the community.

On the other hand, efforts to increase rates of home ownership are impacted by the problem of devaluation and predatory lending, both direct consequences of the social economy of race. The easiest way for an individual to protect against this impact is to move away from other people of color so that he gets the "value" of Whiteness. This creates greater gaps between the middle class and the working class, destabilizes neighborhoods of people of color, and decreases the stability of the working class, whose members have more difficulty "moving away" and therefore rarely see significant appreciation in the value of the homes they might purchase.

All of this to say that the social economy of race proves an enormous challenge. However, one way to begin is to address institutional norms through professional organizations of business owners, mortgage lenders, and realtors.[67] If we can diminish the degree to which their work sustains the real property-based pathways to appreciation and depreciation, we can make a serious intervention into a primary sphere of race-based economic inequality. We also need to work against what is considered "race knowledge" about certain groups among employers and assert norms of workplace interaction that thwart the racist messaging of subservience and punishment, just as we have worked to establish norms of workplace interaction that thwart traditional gender hierarchies. This can happen at the level of policy and in antidiscrimination legislation but also in media and in community-based activism.

The development of human capital within communities of color is also extremely important, particularly in light of the growing tide of globalization. The argument that the higher reserve wages of African Americans makes them vulnerable to being displaced in employment markets is accurate but runs the risk of oversimplifying the complicated terrain of race and globalization.[68] On the one hand, the fact of the mobility of immigrant populations means that their experience of a given wage might be different than it is for native-born people because of a distinct cost-benefit analysis. The twenty dollars that one can send home, where it can buy a month's worth of food or shelter, is of greater personal value than the twenty dollars one can give a baby's mother to buy one can of formula. In either case, however, the measure of the benefit is premised upon a state of inequality, global or local, and, as Douglas Massey points out, "In a global economy, people who have nothing to offer to the world market but the physical power of their own labor will do poorly, and the only way for a nation to simultaneously reduce levels of income inequality and to promote economic growth is to invest in education."[69] Hence, a primary area of focus for responding to the persistence of inequality and unequal valuation has to be investment in greater educational opportunities and broader access to skilled and professional work for poor Americans of color. This explains, in part, the importance of the movement to equalize funding for public schools as required by state constitutions and the movement in support of federal legislation requiring states to provide a quality education to all their residents. Movements like these, which democratize opportunity (a concept that will be discussed in greater detail in the conclusion), have greater prospects than simple redistributive actions because they provide a countercurrent to the practice of inequality. Just as the practice of inequality is ongoing, the undoing of that practice must be in constant motion.

As a final matter, we should examine places that are racialized as Black or Brown and yet are seen as highly "valuable" internally and externally to identify the conditions under which such communities can flourish. The places that are racialized Black but that are seen as having high value either internally or generally are highly instructive and might provide effective models. We should ask what it takes to create such an institution, which provides such a strong counternarrative to the dominant one. We might look at residential and resort communities like Oak Bluffs, Massachusetts, and Amelia Island, Florida; effectively integrated neighborhoods like Montclair, New Jersey, and Mt. Airy, Philadelphia; schools like Whitney Young in Chicago and housing projects like Villa Victoria in Boston. A cursory assessment suggests that it takes an community ethos that is internally meaningful and externally visible and a vibrant public social, political, and cultural life. There are community efforts to corral resources that translate into measurable economic benefits (i.e., for a school, having high rate of competitive college admissions; for a landed community, ownership of highly desirable land and intergenerational transfer of that land) that become a norm, rather than an individuated exception. These communities have developed organically, but they have been sustained strategically, and their models ought to be replicated through community-based policy initiatives and philanthropic efforts.

Conclusion

Remediation, or from Proof to Possibility

The dream is real, my friends. The failure to realize it is the only unreality.

—Toni Cade Bambara

Our future is ripe, outrageously rich in its possibilities. Yet unleashing the glory of that future will require a difficult labor, and some may be so frightened of its birth they will refuse to abandon their nostalgia for the womb.

—Toni Morrison

What does the promised land of racial equality look like? When will we know we have arrived? We have antidiscrimination laws on the books, a multiracial body of elected officials, and social policy. Why aren't we there yet? The legal scholar and cultural critic Derrick Bell provocatively posited that, given our historical legacy and the culture that has emerged from it, we are unlikely to ever get there. This may very well be true, but it is also true that extraordinary things have happened and keep happening in our history. The question is, how do we prepare for and precipitate them?

When Barack Obama was elected president of the United States, many pundits speculated that this was the sign that the dream had been realized. Such proclamations quieted down as the economy tanked and vitriolic outbursts against the president became common, from street corners to the halls of Congress. It was hard to deny that this response often had the sensibility of old-fashioned racism. Just as significant if not more so were the disparities that emerged in the economic meltdown, with African Americans and Latinos and Asian Americans all faring significantly worse than Whites in this moment of crisis. No, we hadn't made it to that promised land, yet.

Please accept this final chapter as a humble effort to imagine getting closer to that land, a leap of faith into an eschatology of racial equality. Of course, full equality in every arena is an extremely unlikely outcome of even the most diligent efforts to pursue racial justice. Derrick Bell's sober assessment of the permanence of racism in the American state is hard to reject as pessimism when one looks at the mechanisms of intergenerational transfer of status, an uneven playing field, and an economic order that is increasing wealth inequality with each passing generation. But we can decide whether this reality will make us impotent or rigorous. To be rigorous, we should treat equality as an intentional practice. This idea of "practice" is intentionally open-ended. In a society and world with past and present experiences of ethnic conflict and oppression, we cannot think of something like racial justice as having an end point after which we can stop thinking about it. It must be a commitment that is consistently engaged and regularly retooled to meet the needs of the moment. Who is on top and who is on bottom, who is in and who is out will shift over time, but we can sustain a commitment to being aware of the exclusions of those relegated to the figurative basements of our society and those "standing outside our gates," as it were.

The practice of racial equality can occur on multiple levels: in quotidian human interactions and decision making, in the context of families or communities, at the level of local government, in legislation and litigation, and in federal policy. All of these are significant, not simply those that occur on a grand scale. There is no greater lesson to be taken from the civil rights movement than this: ordinary people acting together can usher in global shifts. Small, deliberate, courageous, and dedicated movement can lead to big change. This notion of a practice of racial equality and freedom is inspired by the theory of democratic equality developed by Elizabeth Anderson. Anderson describes her theory of democratic equality as one that "integrates principles of distribution with the expressive demands of equal respect."[1] Civil rights activists articulated in word, song, and action a demand for democratic inclusion. This demand didn't differentiate the poverty of the tenant farmer in the Mississippi delta from the denial of her voting rights because it was obvious that these were interdependent realities of American life. A practice of racial freedom and equality would require a collective way of being and operating in good faith toward the goals of civic and political participation and fair opportunity and access for all members of our society. It would mean inclusion and embrace, rather than mere tolerance or the erasure of difference. Relying upon Anderson's theory, in which she says, "Democratic equality guarantees all law-abiding citizens effective access to the social conditions of their freedom at all times,"[2] this practice would be attentive to the means by which "freedom to" is inhibited as a result of our culture of racial inequality and committed to the destruction of those impediments.[3]

A practice of racial equality can be understood to consist of three elements: (1) democratizing opportunity, (2) shifting narratives, and (3) building capacities to work against and transcend the practice of racial inequality.

Democratizing Opportunity

Currently, many of our social institutions reproduce inequality. We reward people for being born with privileges and punish people for being born without. Efforts to redistribute benefits are decried as unfair handouts, while unearned benefits granted at birth are ignored. Part of the problem is that our notions of American freedom and democracy aren't adequately tied to envisioning democratic access to economic security, domestic and community comfort, and political participation. But they should be. I call this "democratizing opportunity," a commitment that can work against the tide of reproducing inequality.

In order for us to commit to democratizing opportunity, we must rethink the relationship between freedom and equality, understanding equality or the aspiration to equality as part of the pursuit of freedom rather than a restraint to freedom. To yoke together freedom and equality is a counterparadigm to that which is currently applied to the concept of equality in American law. Currently, the pursuit of racial equality is balanced against individual freedoms of speech, of contract, of association. In our current paradigm, whether we intervene or not in action that is discriminatory must always be measured against the freedom or rights of the perpetrator. This is because we implicitly accept a libertarian concept of freedom, that freedom is about being "left alone," rather than "being able to." This is a problematic construction and is as troubling as our (insincere) color-blind constitutionalism in our color-conscious world. What Anderson, Cornel West, and many other scholars and activists who advocate for extending democratic principles challenge us to do is to move beyond these obfuscations in order to think about the conditions under which people can live freely, with that freedom being defined in terms of ability to participate fully in society and care for oneself and one's loved ones. If we simply look at the impact of inequalities on longevity or mental health or on civic engagement, we can see that the goal of equality is a goal of moving toward "freedom" to live, be, do, and participate. This is the kind of freedom vision that was so powerfully and brilliantly expressed in the civil rights movement.

Much of this book has demonstrated how mundane and pervasive the practice of inequality is and how inadequate our methods of addressing it. We respond to egregious incidents of old-fashioned racism with protest and litigation. While litigation is important as a space for the articulation of rules, norms, values, and potentially deterrence for those who might be inclined to engage in obviously discriminatory practices, the courts should not be the place where we concentrate our desires for governmental response to the practice of inequality. Here's why: inequality is practiced in a routine manner. Litigation can and does address individuated bad acts. And that is an extremely important function. But it cannot address our collective cultural practices without substantial complementary work. Some important parts of this work can and should be done in policy and legislation. Such legislation can support the kind of meaningful self-activity that already exists.

What are some practical examples of democratizing opportunity? One real-life example is found in the Council for Opportunity in Education. Under the leadership of President Arnold Mitchem, the Council works in partnership with university-based federal Trio programs to provide access to and support in college for low-income, first-generation college students. The Council trains students not only for academic and professional success but for community leadership roles. As of 2009, it counted two million college graduates among its numbers.

Another example is found in the work of Will Allen, founder of Growing Power. Growing Power is a national nonprofit that engages urban residents in the sustainable growth of produce for their communities. Why is this an example of democratizing opportunity? Access to healthy foods at affordable prices is inequitably distributed in this society and represents a critical element in the significant health and longevity disparities in the United States. Moreover, projects like Growing Power and Sustainable South Bronx are spaces of democratic civic participation for health and well-being, created by and for people in the communities they reach.

Smaller-scale methods of democratizing opportunity can be found in community-based programs that train enrollees in computer literacy and provide financial aid form workshops, health education initiatives, and community alternative medicine clinics. In bell hooks's book *Teaching to Transgress*, she describes the democratization of opportunity in teaching as "laying the path bare." Those of us who inventory how we learned and how we know what we know, in an honest rather than a self-congratulatory way, can easily imagine democratizing opportunity by simply sharing that knowledge more broadly in public spaces, rather than hoarding it for personal benefit.

Granted, knowledge is not the same as economic resources. But it is something we can offer irrespective of the redistributive possibilities, and for no other reason than that our democratic values demand that we lay the path bare if we are to be true to those values. Also, such democratic initiatives can operate as guides for larger policy or philanthropic initiatives. The federal Trio programs that offered the possibility of attending college to millions emerged from student protests at universities. The Harlem Children's Zone, Geoffrey Canada's incredibly successful educational program in one of the poorest urban neighborhoods in the United States, captured presidential and congressional attention after more than thirty years of growth from a community-based truancy program to a community center to a school. Importantly, it began and remains a community-based program, conscientious, deliberate, and strategic, and it has brought partners into the process that must buy into its vision, rather than the reverse. What these programs share is that they are focused on community possibilities, not merely on individual attainment, by broadening knowledge, access, and participation all at once.

Shifting Narratives

> You know my soul looks back in wonder, how I got over.
> —Mahalia Jackson, "How I Got Over"

We have to tell some different stories and repeat those different stories more often. Think about how we describe different racial groups, their histories, their present. Almost immediately, we are thrown into either stereotype or invisibility, or both, for many groups. The stories we tell and integrate into our knowledge impacts how we see ourselves, how we see others around us, how we treat them, what opportunities we provide, what expectations we have. As a preliminary move, we must revisit how we narrative the civil rights movement. Expunge the sentimental and melodramatic. Recover the authentic history of strategy, social organization, the organizing of many, the mundane sacrifices, the unanswered aspirations. Perhaps from there we can revisit the real history of the American West, which includes those now nationally categorized as "Mexicans" from before the border was created. What about all the student movements that led to the expansion of curricula to include non-Europeans? What if we told the story of "how we got over" repeatedly in order to rejigger how we see people of color but also to inspire all of us to do better?

A reflection upon the history of the civil rights movement indicates how critical the shifting of narratives was to the argumentative force of the movement.[4] Activists performed democracy in voter registration drives, civil disobedience, and freedom votes when access to the legally recognized democratic institutions was denied. They peacefully demanded rights in the face of angry mobs, who then became the ugly face of lawlessness and disorder, in contrast to the protesters decency and dignity. Thus, the inconsistency between southern governance and constitutional principles was exposed.

Narrative shifting is both an internal and external process. It is both about choosing to tell a story different from the one currently dominant about racial groups and about engaging in practices that are expressive of that shifted narrative. Shifting narratives doesn't mean simply changing images on television or in books. It requires the deliberate efforts of groups of citizens to change the practice and discourse around race in order to push a cultural paradigm shift. It requires civil participation and engagement and a distinctive set of ideas about what those things are in light of the cultural and political frameworks of communities of color. This means, too, that we must shift the narrative of how to appropriately respond to the ills of the poor, colored, and marginal in our society. A charity-based, care-taking model replicates images of damage and incapacity among those communities. Instead, these communities must be agents of their own transformations and decision makers in the choices about what new narratives must emerge for defining their communities. Hence, this is imagined as both an internal and external process—one that changes internal and external perceptions, as well as internal and external practices.

Narrative shifting, at its best, is not the creation of myths but the telling of stories about groups in ways that are politically useful and true. Narrative shifting is not trotting out individual historic figures as "role models"; it is invoking tradition, history, culture, and practice that provide powerful counterexamples to bigoted narrative. From within communities, this is a practice of intentional identity formation. External to communities, it is an acknowledgment of life-worlds outside the terms of the historic constructions of race.

Imagine two different ways of telling the story of the South Bronx, one of New York's poorest and most "colored" neighborhoods. One could describe it as a place of entrenched intergenerational poverty, high rates of crime, and despair. All of this would be accurate but insufficient to capture the spirit of the community. One could also describe it as the birthplace of a groundbreaking Parent Action Committee[5] devoted to demanding better-quality schools for South Bronx children; the birthplace of one of the most popular forms of music in history, hip hop; an unusually integrated community in the United States, home to African Americans, English- and Spanish-speaking Caribbean people, and, before them, waves of European immigrants; and the birthplace of the Fashion Moda Gallery, a seminal institution in contemporary art. The way one narratives what the South Bronx is impacts both how residents and outsiders see the location and what value we place in it. The history of self-activity among those living below the poverty line in the South Bronx defies any description of those who live within as looking for a handout, and yet also requires an acknowledgment of the inequality they experience.

My favorite line of "The Internationale," the early-twentieth-century Marxist-pantheon anthem to liberation causes, is "Reason thunders in its crater," because it suggests that, with the revelation of inequality, that which is understood as reasonable is shaken up. Shifting narratives also entails changing the debate and the discourse of our public sphere. It means, for example, challenging our casual acceptance of the fact that we wake up daily with two million people in prison and millions more in poverty, groups that are highly disproportionately Black and Brown, here in the world's hegemon, which trumpets principles of democracy and freedom across the globe. A sense of urgency about why this is the case should animate our discussions about who we are as a nation and motivate action toward making us a better nation.

Narrative shifting is discursive. It is found in the literature we read, the stories we tell, the films we watch, the magazines and e-zines and blogs we read, the images we consume.[6] It also makes no sense to talk about racist images (which reproduce racial narratives) without also talking about how easy it is to capitalize (politically and economically) upon those images. There are substantial motivations out there for sustaining racial narratives. This shouldn't paralyze us but should provide an additional argument for intentionally working to shift narratives. There are professionals who have devoted much of their careers to engaging in narrative shifting: scholars, documentary and feature filmmakers, authors of fiction. Patronizing and proselytizing their work is a mode of narrative shifting.

For educators and educational administrators, best practices must include a narrative-shifting agenda vis-à-vis people of color. Just as students regularly study the epic and profound stories of Greek mythology and the triumphant history of the Revolutionary War, the stories of African civilizations in Mali and Songhay, the history of the Mexican Revolution, the valiant efforts of Native American and Japanese American soldiers in World War II, the manner in which African Americans passionately pursued education, suffrage, and property after the Civil War are wonderful resources for study. And each can provide a means of shifting how we narrate the stories of people of color, away from frames based either on degradation and exclusion or on superficial accounts of clothing and food and toward something more substantive and meaningful.

The material for narrative shifting has been produced, in literature, and scholarship, even in film, but fashioning curricula out of them must be expanded throughout K-12 education, undergraduate education, social work training, law schools, and medical schools, (such as the University of Pennsylvania's and Harvard Medical School's "social medicine" and "cultural competency" courses). The media studies movements, as well as programs in ethnic studies and narrative theory, are all useful sources of knowledge for this work. If teachers, activists, and scholars who are inclined to pursue narrative shifting participate in or develop networks (analog or virtual) to share resources, materials, syllabi, and data that support shifting narratives, that alone can have a dramatic impact on what their students and community members learn.

Narrative shifting also has the potential to precipitate significant change in the vision of how individuals can improve the world. As stated before, I advocate a revisitation of our description of the civil rights movement. Seminal texts like Charles Payne's *I've Got the Light of Freedom: The Organizing Tradition and the Mississippi Freedom Struggle* are excellent for such purposes. Recognizing that effective efforts at reducing inequality require organizing, engagement with community, and strategy, as well as improvisation, challenges the dominant charity-based model that is offered to young adults who express interest in "doing good" in the world. Charity is good, but it does not increase democratic participation, it does not reduce inequality (although it may blunt its force), and it doesn't shift perceptions about those who are receiving charity. If, instead, the model offered to these young adults took the form of an organization like the Young People's Project, they might be more likely to think of their work (professional or avocational) as devoted to a practice of equality, rather than as a one- or two-year charitable stint before pursuing their careers. The Young People's Project's mission statement is as follows: "The Mission of the Young People's Project is to use Math Literacy as a tool to develop young leaders and organizers who radically change the quality of education and life in their communities so that all children have the opportunity to reach their full human potential." In cities across the country, members are involved in grassroots efforts to teach algebra, to work for the right of return for people displaced by Hurricane Katrina, to push for federal legislation to provide quality education for all American children, and to train young people in community building. These are participatory endeavors. In contrast to this example, there are many institutions that don't embrace a democratic model even as they promote efforts to "make the world a better place." For example, we should be skeptical if a school that is created with the ambition of increasing educational outcomes young poor people of color is created with no impact from local community members and doesn't have adult people of color in positions of authority. You cannot pursue equality without sharing power. We should be appalled if a national civil rights advocacy organization seems to be concerned only with the obstacles faced by elites in communities of color. Who is at the decision-making table shapes the conversation, the action, and the values of the organization.

Building Capacities

When the Young People's Project trains youth leaders, what it is doing is building capacities. Building capacity must be distinguished from building human capital or other forms of identifiable individual capital in the form of cultural knowledge or social networks. Building capacity is not simply what individual community members know about or what they know how to do, although it includes that. Rather, it is identifiable by an increase in collective knowledge and resources that have flows within a community and that encourage collaborative problem solving.

Capacity to Work against the Practice of Inequality

How can we unlearn the practices of inequality? In other words, how do we increase our capacities not just to act without racism but to actively promote racial equality? Discourse about race is often fraught with tension, particularly in multiracial settings. Part of this is a consequence of the deep fear Americans have about being labeled racist. For this reason in particular, intraracial as well as multi- and cross-racial discussions of race are necessary. Intraracial discussions offer the possibility of productive discussions in a context where there is decreased anxiety about being misperceived, while interracial discussions offer meaningful exchanges between differently categorized people.

Increasingly, the social psychological literature supports the idea that if people are aware of patterns of discrimination, they are better able to self-correct.[7] Not talking about race is actually detrimental to the project of addressing the practice of racial inequality. This is because, in order to do so, we have to undo our acculturation. The burden of talking about race cannot fall solely on the shoulders of people of color, and being a person of color doesn't necessarily make a person an expert on how racism works. Experience is important, but research, data, and evidence are what must be relied upon to identify the practice of inequality. Dialogue, in community-based organizations, in schools and universities, in corporations, and in government, about race and racial inequality is crucial if we are to translate information into understanding and better practices. The diversity-training industry must increasingly integrate the growing body of knowledge about contemporary inequality; at the same time, diversity professionals should share the myriad examples of communities transcending historic inequalities and discuss how they were able to do so on both the individual and the collective levels. So, for example, the civil rights movement cannot be reduced to inspiring speeches and marches if our goal is to support people's antiracist capacities. It has to include a discussion of the economic and media strategies, the ongoing dialogues and disputes, the converging interests of cold war politics and justice at home, and the emotional, professional, and health costs to the activists, both because these give examples of how complex the project was and because they provide a much more accurate and nuanced image of the achievements of the movement.

One key area of building capacity and narrative shifting among White Americans must come through a process of deconstructing the image of White racism. In the early years of the Obama administration, it appeared that a shorthand for racist/nonracist was beginning to frame around "dislike Obama" and "voted for Obama." Such truncations are troubling because they scapegoat and allow for the abdication of the responsibility to self-examine. Black Americans for generations had a saying, "There is no North and South, only down South and up South," referring to the national commitment to racism. It is no surprise, then, that mainstream enthusiasm for the civil rights movement waned as it became national, rather than concentrated in the South, and began to address issues of the economic and social consequences of inequality. The notion that traditional racial animosity is a "southern thing" has been disproved by history and politics. From the nineteenth century, northern Whites exercised their class frustrations on Black people, and there is massive current evidence of inequality in the North. But the nonracist identity of the United States has been premised upon a "southern discourse" in which the most extreme examples of racist thought were applied to one region and facilitated other equally damaging, if often more genteel, racist practices elsewhere. The appeal of the southern strategy to northerners is in the identity it grants. White identity as it relates to conceiving of oneself as nonracist is largely defined by a "not that"—not southern, not working class, not Confederate flag–bearing, not descendant of slaveholders, and so on. But these divides prove false in terms of identifying a location where the impact of inequality is meted out most strongly.

Class divisions are apparent in racial attitudes, and, while it is true that poor Whites self-report more hostility to people of color than do more affluent Whites, they have less power to affect the ability of people of color to prosper. Those who are making decisions may have less animus, but the animus they do have may be much more damaging. Addressing racism requires a rejection of those paradigmatic characterizations of racism that use history or political party affiliation as a proxy for race-virtue. In fact, the question of virtue should be expunged altogether in exchange for collective work devoted to learning how to unmake our racism.

This is also a goal for those who have historically experienced or who currently experience racial, ethnic, gender, sexual-orientation, and other forms of discrimination. Being marginalized does not legitimate the exploitation of the inferior status of others, whether it be the racial animosity between native-born people of color and immigrants, or the antagonism between members of different immigrant groups who bring the ethnic conflicts of their homelands of origin with them when they come here. One should not say that racism or ethnocentrism is bad publicly (especially if one experiences it) but then, within the nest of one's community, fail to contest the proliferation of discriminatory practices or ideas. Experiencing discrimination does not absolve one of the responsibility to behave in ways consistent with the values of freedom and equality, even in the face of discrimination from some of the very people whose rights one supports.

In addition to deconstructing the narrative of racism, embracing its everyday quality, and participating in narrative shifting and knowledge acquisition, White communities should be encouraged to look at how practices within those communities support inequality and seek collective solutions. For example, if there is evidence of inequality in local public schools or of discrimination in real estate practices, in policing, or in invitations to participate in social networks, there is no more powerful constituency in action against such phenomenon than the dominant group. The challenge, even among those within that group who are opposed to inequality and unequal opportunity, is that, for the individual, the assumption of risk (in speaking out against inequality) often seems too great, given the minimal likelihood that an individual will make a substantive difference. However, if people act as members of groups, they assume far less individual risk. Imagine if a neighborhood group decided to advocate for the inclusion of affordable housing in their midst, whether rental units or property for purchase, and then devoted itself to fully integrating those new residents into the fabric of the community, not just by "including them" but by recognizing that the community had changed and grown for the better with their presence.

Often efforts to remedy the practice of inequality suffer from the lack of political will on the part of the mainstream of American citizens. To respond to this, we should support organizations that include as part of their mission demonstrating and responding to the substantial impact of unearned benefits and inheritance, as well as asymmetric opportunity structures, in ways that enable a greater portion of the population to begin to understand that we don't practice democracy when it comes to individual opportunity to self-actualize and we do have a society in which the color of one's skin plays a significant role in one's outcomes. Simply removing the deficiency assumptions that people use as explanations for inequality would go a long way in tackling practices of inequality.

On an institutional level, professional organizations and institutions of various sorts should deliberately develop best practices devoted not merely to cultural sensitivity but also to explicitly avoiding the kind of discrimination that is recognized and supported by evidence in the given field and in analogous fields. This might be narrated in terms of complying with certain principles of fairness, or it might be implemented by eliminating or minimizing the kind of discretionary decision making in which discrimination often emerges. Which of these possibilities or which other options are best depends upon the demands, needs, and requirements of the specific institution.

But in this arena, too, there are individual acts that matter. I cannot count the times in my life when I have been standing in line at a retail establishment or in line for a cab and have been overlooked, with preference given to a non-Black person behind me. But I remember vividly the times when that person has said, "No, I think she was here before me." That simple act of grace shifts the association between race and value that a second before was in play. When I was in high school, there was a teacher who was notorious for displaying hostility to African American students. One day in class, a Black young man sat with his hand raised for the entire class and was called on not once. A multiracial group of fellow students went to complain to the administration. The impact of this collective response was greater that it would have been if the student alone had complained. Again, it was a simple act, animated by a sense of fairness and an awareness of one's own privilege that not only led to a meaningful intervention by the school administration but also challenged racial stratification, at least within that one institution. Citizens are free to watch police procedure and report misconduct, to report abuses witnessed in schools and state agencies, and to challenge inequities in the institutions in which they participate. Exercising that privilege in the service of ideals of democracy, the common good, and racial fairness is a worthy practice for us all.

Building Capacities for Communities of Color

Part of what has happened in the midst of the multidecade backlash against civil rights and the rise in racial narratives about Black and Brown deficiency is that policy initiatives addressing the problems facing those communities have borrowed increasingly from the ideational framework of criminal law. They are punitively oriented. We find this with the definitions of fraud in the welfare system, child welfare agencies, and family law, discussed in chapter 5. As Dorothy Roberts so effectively argues in the child welfare context, if the same resources that are spent removing children and shuttling them from place to place were instead spent supporting families' abilities to take care of their children, a revolution could take place in child welfare. These types of initiatives serve to reproduce inequality, rather than democratize opportunity, improve civic participation, or increase productivity. The organizing principle of policy initiatives aimed at suffering communities should be figuring out and implementing that which will maximize healthful communities and equip members of those communities to transcend or, at the very least, best withstand the impact of the practices of inequality.

If I drive just a short distance from my home to the poorest sections of North Philadelphia with my sons, they look out the window and see burned-out buildings; they feel the road ragged under our wheels; they see adults without employment on the corners; they do not see bright and shiny retail establishments; they see people who have learned to mind their business on the streets; mothers rushing their children inside. They see evidence that public works, the department of housing and urban development, the school board, the business community, and their fellow city residents have all decided that North Philadelphians are undesirable. The way we fund and run schools, take care of infrastructure and development, enforce housing regulations, and police neighborhoods (through law enforcement and social service agencies) are all the result of policy decisions through which we communicate the stratification of residents. To pursue equality and freedom necessarily means that we set higher standards in all of these arenas. Local governance and the commitments of local elected and appointed officials are therefore extremely important and, fortunately, are more easily shaped by community organizing than is national governance. As Elizabeth Anderson writes, "To be capable of functioning as a citizen requires rights to political participation, such as freedom of speech and the franchise, and also effective access to the goods and relationships of civil society. This entails freedom of association, access to public spaces such as roads, parks, and public accommodations including public transportation, the postal service, and telecommunications. This also entails the social conditions of being accepted by others, such as the ability to appear in public without shame, and not being ascribed outcast status."[8] The stigmas associated with "colored places" are carried onto colored bodies and are recounted every time someone calls another "ghetto," gives a sideways glance that is motivated by racial suspicion, follows another at the mall or museum, or gives poor service at a restaurant. This treatment is not necessarily debilitating for the mistreated. However, it is a symbol of a broader culture of inequality that does debilitate in many profound ways and is no less dramatic when it occurs than the "colored" sign above a water fountain that was a symbol of a de jure structure of inequality. For all of these reasons, demonstrated investment in and valuing of communities of color is of paramount importance. Imagine if, in addition to infrastructural investments, a local government, like that of Philadelphia, decided to invest in a racial justice initiative, with programming and fora and educational initiatives in school, churches, and community centers across the city. Alone, this would have little impact. Alongside practical implementations, however, such an initiative could help fuel a collective culture in the city that would cherish the diversity of its residents and the various contributions of all the communities to the development, culture, and history of the city, as well as acknowledge areas of conflict and competition.

Elizabeth Anderson quotes Amartya Sen: "A person's capabilities consist of the sets of functionings she can achieve, given the personal, material, and social resources available to her. Capabilities measure not actually achieved functionings, but a person's freedom to achieve valued functionings. A person enjoys more freedom the greater the range of effectively accessible, significantly different opportunities she has for functioning or leading her life in ways she values most. We can understand the egalitarian aim to secure for everyone the social conditions of their freedom in terms of capabilities." And Anderson goes on to say, "Following Sen, I say that egalitarians should seek equality for all in the space of capabilities."9

Consistent with the work of Anderson and Sen, John L. McKnight and John P. Kretzmann argue that we must depart from a needs-driven and deficiency-oriented model of responding to the poor state of urban communities and instead move toward capacity-oriented models that begin with an inventory of the skills, associations, and networks of community members. They argue that this orientation does not mean that you don't look for external support but rather that a community must be organized and mobilized to capitalize upon that support. Moreover, it has the possibility of shifting how citizens view themselves and their communities.

In Kretzman and McKnight's guidebook for community rebuilding, they assert that there are significant problems with a strategy that focuses on a "community's needs, deficiencies and problems." Although that is the dominant model, it produces a series of negative images in a community, which are presented as a whole, rather than as partial truth. It also produces an awareness among community members that they must present themselves as full of problems in order to receive services, and the dependence upon external services wears away at community interdependence and problem-solving abilities, encouraging people to instead look to external experts and professionals (many of whom, as we have seen, are affected by the racial discrimination that infects our society).

Kretzman and McKnight identify three elements of the asset-based community development model. First, it is asset based and therefore starts by assessing what is present, not what is absent. Second, it is internally focused and depends upon "agenda building and problem solving capacities of local residents." Third, it is relationship driven. It is focused on building relationships within a community. Focusing on the assets of a community and shoring those up increase the likelihood that a community will be prepared to fight against unjust practices meted out to it.

There is a great deal of nostalgia in the African American community for past interreliances, community building, and sacrifice. At the same time, however, we often forget the external elements that destabilized many of these social institutions. Although integration is often cited as a reason for the breakdown of pre-desegregation Black institutions, that claim doesn't explain enough. The problem is that integration as implemented by governmental bodies was understood as the integration of physical bodies, not the integration of power and resources; therefore, locations of traditional control and employment in segregated contexts were lost. Integration could have been enacted in a more democratic fashion. Even greater destabilization was wrought by what Mindy Fullilove has named "rootshock"—the impact of widespread urban renewal and ongoing gentrification, which fray the development of community ties and stability. We can critique this history, but we also need to arm citizens to protect and nurture their communities into the future, through social organization, educational and economic development, and property ownership. The best examples of this, some of which I have cited previously, are contexts in which communities organize in their own self-interest. In some of these instances, knowledge and skills within that community have been leveraged to gain access to important funding, publicity, public support, and various resources that assist in the actualization of the vision. Capacity building includes the recognition of aspiration and the existence of meaningful access to the routes and roots. Building capacity means supporting local reinterpretations of effective norms, standards, and goals, rather than imposing doctrinal external measures. For example, marriage-promotion legislation has often been justified as a way to achieve the goal of reducing child poverty. The reasonableness of this assumption is highly questionable, but, putting that aside for the moment, in any case such legislation does nothing to facilitate conditions that make it easier to develop enduring co-parenting relationships.

The ideal of a capacity-building orientation is also supported by the work of the policy scholar Robert Lieberman, who has shown that race policy is most successful when it is shaped by a coalition of minority group members, politicians, and other interests. But the community must be equipped to be involved in such coalitions. Capacity building itself does not eradicate inequality; it arms people with the skills to be involved in that process.

In advocating for capacity building it is useful also to distinguish between troubling disparities over which people are able to exert immediate control and those that may be influenced only by more extensive and lengthy activity. Obesity, rates of HIV infection, nutritional deficiencies, parenthood without preparation, child care, and high school graduation rates are all areas in which communities can take control almost immediately, irrespective of large-scale inequality. I can hear voices in my head saying, "Condoms are expensive, healthy food is in short supply and expensive in urban areas, schools are alienating." All of this is true. But it is also true that cooperative efforts of community groups made up of people with diverse skills and who are respected in the community can actually affect these things using the principles of economies of scale, lobbying, and the locating of multiple funding sources both within and external to the community at hand. Given the remarkable resilience of so many people who live with the most dire impacts of inequality, it is not difficult to foresee that increasing the number and size of campaigns devoted to helping people deploy that resilience in the service of improving life outcomes could be quite effective.

In addition to practical measures, one primary challenge for members of struggling communities is how to approach a discussion of internal solutions. Any self-critical posture is vulnerable to being captured by the interpretive lens of racial narratives employed to disadvantage. For example, when I delivered an oral presentation about narrative shifting, a prominent conservative law professor's response was, "Right, the way for Black people to be seen differently is for them to change their behavior." This dynamic is troubling. No people are beyond critique, but how can one engage in useful self-critique when there is a normative framework of deep deficiency? How can one avoid the identification of assets being subsumed by the critical posture? On the other hand, how can one talk about the effects of inequality without those being subsumed by an impotent-victim narrative? It seems that responding to this set of challenges requires a self-consciousness about the project of narrative shifting as a mode of argument and of existence, in which the practice of being and asserting are consistent in their rejection of and resistance to racial narratives. This is what I mean: if, for example, there is a problem with young people dropping trash on the street in a Black and Latino community, and one says, "These kids are throwing trash on the street," that observation easily slides into another piece of evidence in the narrative that blames people of color for property value disaccumulation, for the physical disrepair found in their communities, for White flight. But it may very well be true that kids are throwing trash on the street and that that is a bad behavior, both for the planet and for community self-respect. If the narrative shifting is both a mode of argument and a mode of existence, and it is geared toward the goal of building capacity, the response to this problem might be rendered this way:

We as members of this community know that we are people of value. Although we may not have much in material resources, we do have self-respect. We will raise our young people to show respect for their block, their hood, their environment, and demand the same respect from the elected officials and governmental agencies that are charged with serving them as citizens. We will embark on a campaign to clean up our playgrounds, our parks, and our streets, and we will circulate petitions and organize commu-

nity meetings to draw attention to housing that is not up to code and public facilities that are in a state of disrepair. Our self-respect is intact even when the powers that be don't show us the respect we deserve, and our demands that they respond to their constituents in our community will be unrelenting.

I do not mean to naively suggest that such a campaign would necessarily be effective. Rather, I mean to offer it as an example of how to reframe a phenomenon in a manner that does not slide into destructive racial narratives but also does not reject accountability talk or self-activity where it is needed.

Here are other examples. One thing we know is that graduating from high school is a high predictor for avoiding involvement with the criminal justice system, which virtually ensures job market failure.[10] Moreover, being highly skilled as a result of training matters. So we can say that policymakers need to invest in education. But this knowledge can also be applied practically and provide a focus for community-based organizations as they seek to apply the resources they have and decide which resources they will devote energy to acquiring. We also know that delaying the birth of one's first child and being in a household with more than one income earner (whether by virtue of marriage, family relations, or friendship) protect one against the harshest effects of economic inequality. Preventive health care in the form of physical activity, a healthy diet, and timely health screenings can offer some buffer against the greatest risks of health and well-being inequality. Sharing this knowledge and finding creative means of sharing resources in order to act in ways consistent with this knowledge are activities that can occur within community-based organizations.

We also need to fund and create more programs geared toward the proliferation of "laying the path bare." In the information age, knowledge is increasingly accessible, but also perhaps more unequally distributed. How does someone learn the appropriate use of search terms? How does one know what Web sites are reliable sources for certain kinds of information? Sharing skills for acquiring and assessing the legitimacy of knowledge builds capacity because those skills can circulate freely within a community and are not dependent upon the initial sharer. The evidence that social structures can support the avoidance of even the most pernicious influences can be found in Black youth's avoidance of drug addiction, even though their communities are flooded with drugs.[11] In their zeal not to sound conservative (by believing in the prospect of transcendence and transgression), members within communities of color often fail to acknowledge and expect the kind of resilience and innovation that their members have evinced. Hence, many of the paradigms communities of color have for themselves, in terms of both academic and general knowledge, must be shifted to recognize the spirit of possibility that has animated our greatest gains.

All that said, one could be well educated and highly skilled, have the spirit of Frederick Douglass, and still be perennially underemployed and a step away from disastrous circumstances, due in large part to the practices of inequality. And, with the current policy regime, the safety net of the welfare state is not there when one meets a cruel world. Of course, law and policy and employment and educational institutions matter, but I am arguing that they should follow and support, rather than lead and dictate, in designing initiatives to build capacity, expand democracy, and reduce inequality. Who or what should they follow? They should, of course, be responsive to people, but they should also be responsive to knowledge about what works. And this is why research matters.

Translational Research for Law and Policy

Capacity building is found not only in community activism by also in research initiatives in which individuals work collaboratively to solve social problems, taking into consideration the ideas and experiences of the citizens living with those problems. It should even appear as an ethos for how we develop funding equations for social policy measures. Einstein is often quoted as saying, "Imagination is more important than knowledge." I'm not so sure if this is correct. It seems that they are both necessary for effective innovation and intervention, at least in the context of social worlds, if not in the hard sciences in which Einstein worked. Theoretically, one could frame this in terms of the philosophy of African American artistic production. (Yes, I am going back to jazz.) Improvisation relies upon the rigorous study of form and technique, because it is that knowledge that provides a foundation for experimentalism. Our equality project should take its cues from the aesthetics of improvisation. Unger and West's *The Future of American Progressivism* argues that the choice of experimentalism and innovation must be employed to support democratic participation and self-reliance. They encourage a challenge to bureaucratic norms while acknowledging the important role of government in facilitating human creativity and experimentalism. The role of policy within this context must have flexibility without blind "trying things out." As Unger and West assert, "We reject the choice between a view that would promote popular interests without reimagining and remaking institutional arrangements and a view that sees such arrangements as pieces of a take-it-or-leave-it system."[12] For this reason, I argue for the importation of the concept of translational research to policy initiatives. What is called translational research in epidemiology is called use-based research in education. Essentially what it means is research done with the goal of making meaningful interventions in the process of collecting data. So this might be something like the Boston based teacher and scholar Kim Parker's research on the intellectual development of early-adolescent Black boys, using book clubs. In the process, she was able to determine whether the clubs had an impact on the boys' academic and personal development and how much and to collect other information about their thoughts, attitudes, and experience with school. This kind of translational research can provide models of useful data to collect, useful practices to follow, and useful policies or institutions to develop. Policy ventures must be flexible enough to support the idea of translational research, to reform these ventures when things are not effective, and to continuously refine them along the way. Traditional bureaucratic operations don't easily lend themselves to this sort of modification. The word "policy" itself is often used in common parlance as a shorthand for a refusal to negotiate, as in "it is not our policy," but if we accept that there is a social ecosystem with interdependent human actors, then we have to pursue a more ethnographic and dynamic concept of policy research and practice.

The failures to adequately address static or practiced inequality are often explained as the result of a lack of political will. This is shorthand for "There is little constituent pressure or support to guide legislators to implement different kinds of programs." The political-will problem is quite real with respect to initiatives focused on reducing the inequality experienced by communities of color, especially because our democracy is increasingly influenced by wealth and global capital on the one hand and fear and intolerance on the other. Leadership for supporting translational research must come from civic-minded elected officials and community-based and civic organizations that, as constituencies, make intentional and concerted demands.

Effective translational research has to be qualitative as well as quantitative and should draw upon multiple disciplines. It has to respond to human potential and capital, rather than punish or dialogue about deprivation. An intervention into a social ecosystem can have transformative effect if it has an impact on other aspects of the system. For this reason, people talk about the enormous impact of educating women in the developing world because women are the teachers and the providers of care in so many countries. In other cases, an intervention may have a benefit for isolated individuals but have no impact on systemic problems. To identify which interventions are necessary means that one must have a different approach to the concept of remedy, one that consults with members of the community who understand its ecosystem and also undertake thoughtful ethnographic analyses of community ecosystems before engaging in an intervention.

Translational initiatives would necessarily bring a broader swath of researchers into the realm of policy, including more sociologists, psychologists, political scientists, urban planners, and environmental scientists. And, in so doing, these initiatives would require that the researchers be engaged in a rigorous process of challenging norms, assumptions, and values tied to the practice of inequality as they choose which questions to ask and what quality of services to provide in their research. So the intervention has to be experimental, practical, and epistemological. We have to challenge what we "know" and what constitutes good or useful knowledge about race and inequality.

How might translational research work in law? The years following the *Brown v. Board* opinion saw many efforts across the country on a state-by-state, county-by-county, and city-by–city basis, to implement integration. Districts were given discretion about how to desegregate their schools. Imagine if, today, judges were to give states or municipalities within states (for matters related to state constitutional law) latitude in implementing equality provisions if and only if there were clear and explicit assessments and corrections for the duration of the implementation period. In *Grutter v. Bollinger*, the Supreme Court opinion that upheld the University of Michigan Law School's race-conscious affirmative action plan, Michigan based its defense on evidence of the effectiveness of its program in diversifying the bar and on the substantial positive outcomes associated with that transformation. If policy measures are researched with built-in reasonable translational expectations and a good model for implementing them, courts ought to be patient with such efforts because they are consistent with our visions of freedom, equality, and democracy, writ broadly, even if sometimes they challenge libertarian ideas of freedom.

Voluntary Association

In the 1990s, an important dialogue emerged within the field of African American studies, the field in which I work, about the meaning of race. It had been agreed that race was a social construct, yet a human reality. But the question remained about the meaning and uses of racial identity. In many ways, the struggle regarding this question revealed how the work of African American political and social organizations, which had and have various missions and ideologies and functions in the work of fighting against racism and nurturing African American communities, could be brought into current philosophical debates in the field. To even engage the question of political purpose or social identity is a more expansive effort than is part of traditional humanistic academic inquiry. Although in our media-saturated culture we are encouraged to think that Black people constitute a loosely organized monolith standing behind several popular public figures and a small number of civic organizations, this conversation among intellectuals continues to usher in some new ways of thinking about identity around race that is more sophisticated and compelling than racial essentialism or a simplistic politics of racial obligation.[13] I say that I am Black American; that is my racial identity. But my racial politics, the values, the hopes, the suspicions, while refracted through my experience as a Black woman, are far more nuanced and specific than an ascriptive category. Even more important, they are not determined by my experiences as a member of a particular category. I do not have to think a particular way because I have had a particular racialized experience. Clarence Thomas and Condoleezza Rice are excellent examples of this reality. While they are often easily dismissed as sellouts to the African American community, I prefer to use them as examples of how important interpretation is to identity.[14] The reason I think differently from them is not that I follow some script of how Black people are supposed to think and they do not. It is that I believe that history and current evidence support the approach to racial justice and humanity I have written about in this book, while their beliefs and actions contravene racial justice goals. Far more impactful than the fact of my Blackness is how I interpret my experiences, how I have learned from the examples of the communities I have belonged to, and the knowledge I garner from others. To merely identify with an ascriptive group and not to do the more rigorous work of thinking about what that ascriptive identity means or even to merely identify with a political party without having a more nuanced body of positions means that one doesn't tailor a rich social and intellectual life around issues of great import. Eddie Glaude's seminal text *In a Shade of Blue: Pragmatism and the Politics of Black America* presents an argument for fashioning deliberative spaces within Black communities that allow for this interpretive work to be pursued in the context of community and with the goal of addressing social challenges. This model is appropriate for all communities working against practices of inequality. Their task requires the commitment not just of time and values but also of space and institutional structures. As such, voluntary association takes on increased significance.

The voluntary associations (with a group or set of ideas and theories) that one embraces as a person who has both rights (human, constitutional) and responsibilities (to family, community, nation, world) are of greater import for one's ability to be productive in the goal of practicing equality and democracy than anything else. This requires deliberate self-consideration as a social and political being.

To act with regard to specific issues that matter requires that one think through one's values and priorities and find partners in pursuing one's goals. One can say, "I believe there should be good schools for inner-city kids," but to go the step further and be deliberate about one's role in pursuing that belief, one must have a theory about public education, a perspective on privatization, and a belief about who the necessary stakeholders are, what makes a good school, and what the responsibilities of a state to its citizens are regarding education. Too often this kind of thought is dismissed as "critiques without solutions," but, in truth, it is only through critical thought that visionaries emerge. Although not every action one takes will be devoted to the ideal vision, one's critical faculties with respect to the decisions one does make will be strengthened by the undergirding set of values, *and* if one chooses to practice one's voluntary association in a political or civic organization context, one has a chance of making increasingly more effective interventions through collective action.

In order for voluntary associations to have the greatest positive impact on civic and political life, we must use them as vehicles to increase civic equity. We must use democracy to counteract the manner in which wealth facilitates the overrepresentation of the few in political life. We have to increase the quality of basic education and access to care and avenues for self-help and self-stabilizing so that the greatest number of people can move past first-order survival concerns. At the same time, those of us who are so inclined must model lives of voluntary association, especially for the millions of people born since the 1970s who may have virtually no experience with substantive voluntary association, either in the social justice movement or in regular civic or religious institutional participation.

And this is a good time for changes to occur. The United States has had decreased international legitimacy in the wake of the wars in Iraq and Afghanistan and domestic nightmares like the treatment of citizens and residents after Hurricane Katrina; yet, after the example of a remarkable groundswell of engagement on the part of young people during President Obama's 2008 presidential campaign, it seemed Americans were interested in rehabilitating and perhaps even changing their image. We, and the world, know that we have work to do if we want to retain/regain our legitimacy in the world and our stability at home. It is insufficient to say that "we need a social justice movement." Instead, we must focus on the conditions for the creation of people prepared to engage in social justice movements around the issues of the practice of racial (and other forms of) unjust inequality. What I am talking about is in large part inclusive of a civics (self-) education that takes place in the context of community. In that process, there are at least three critical things we should be thinking about:

1. Interest convergence as a political practice—how shared or complementary interests between communities and institutions can be identified and nurtured to increase the possibility of coalition and cooperative work across and within diverse racial groups.
2. Knowledge convergence between outsider and insider communities. This requires sharing knowledge in ways that recognize the skills and capacities of people within marginalized communities, assist those outside those communities in understanding that people within them are smart, competent, and capable, and offer professional, educational, and other quality-of-life-shaping access to people within those communities.
3. Networks of interdependence that are supported by institutions as well as by social policy. This is important both intra- and interracially. Working against deep currents of individualism that are expressed as selfishness rather than self-expression is a necessary part of any movement to improve civic and political life in the midst of our consumer culture.

There is one huge barrier that has yet to be discussed and that strikes at the center of these goals. The barrier that keeps so many people from making efforts to pursue various forms of justice is the deep self-interest that characterizes this era of what might be termed "commodity citizenship." A market-based notion of social membership that identifies value and "the good life" through things and material acquisition means that conceptions of the common good drop out of civic engagement. Although the common good as a model of civic engagement has a much broader reach than the specific issue of racial equality and freedom, it is a fundamental element to any social justice movement and to the development of a broader class of citizens who find racial equality and freedom integral to their life's work. We need to renew pedagogical work in schools, colleges, universities, and community-based organizations about the nature of citizenship and identify a commitment to the common good as a principal feature of citizenship.

And, while we want to work with our current communities, we also must devote energy to the cultivation of better values in a younger generation, raising them to have the capacities to practice equality and to withstand the inequality that will likely persist. This is a pedagogical challenge for parents, teachers, school administrators, universities, and community-based organizations. To punctuate this observation, let's take a quote from the sociologist Alan Wolfe: "to view boundaries as invariably created by 'their' power over 'us' is to denigrate the capacity of people to change the definitions of the boundaries around them. For every boundary that is ascribed, others can be achieved."[15]

This quotation is just as true as the fact that the practice of inequality is a significant impediment to human thriving and democracy. In order to reconcile these two observations, one must understand the goals of building our capacities to practice equality and to withstand the practices of inequality as nurturing a kind of transformative resilience. Resilience can keep our humanity intact when the world around us threatens to pervert it. Practices of resilience are already part of every cultural tradition in this nation and certainly are part of every history of undoing historic injustice. I conclude this book, remembering the skepticism with which I was confronted so many times when I shared my ideas for this project. But my measure of possibility is not present claims to impotence; it is historic examples of resilience and then transcendence. There is no humbler root found than that of the descendant of slaves, no greater possibility than going from chattel to citizen, no stronger motivation than the legacy of those who made that transformation real. As James Baldwin once said, "There is never time in the future in which we will work out our salvation. The challenge is in the moment; the time is always now."

As Coltrane taught us, it is time to take some Giant Steps.

Notes

PREFACE

1. This double entendre refers to both Baldwin's *The Fire Next Time* and Hurricane Katrina.

INTRODUCTION

1. There were originally nine, ranging in age from thirteen to nineteen.

2. See Reynolds Farley, "Civil Rights and the Status of Black Americans," in *Race, Poverty and Domestic Policy,* ed. C. Michael Henry and James Tobin (New Haven: Yale University Press, 2004), for a discussion of how this became normalized in the second half of the twentieth century.

3. Leonard Pitts Jr., "A History of Rope and Shape," *Houston Chronicle*, October 15, 2007, Star section, 4.

4. This is perhaps the optimistic flip side of Gandy's observation that the "preference within cultural studies for models which assume complex and contradictory influences results in an almost hostile avoidance of the linear causal assumptions that are bound into . . . sophisticated multivariate statistical models." Oscar Gandy, *Communication and Race* (New York: Oxford University Press 1998), 11.

5. "Bricoleur" is a term used in literary theory and anthropology to refer to a person who creates something out of found objects, or whatever is available, and implies a combination of improvisation and resourcefulness on those engaged in "bricolage."

6. Ulf Hannerz, *Cultural Complexity: Studies in the Social Organization of Meaning* (New York: Columbia University Press, 1992).

7. In an ABC News/Lifetime television poll taken October 13–19, 1999, one-third of Whites believed that Blacks experience little to no racism.

8. Stephen Thernstrom and Abigail Thernstrom, *America in Black and White: One Nation Indivisible* (New York: Simon and Schuster, 1997), 500.

9. Michael K. Brown et al., *Whitewashing Race: The Myth of a Color Blind Society* (Berkeley: University of California Press, 2003), 40, citing a University of Chicago National Opinion Research Center poll.

10. Tanya K. Hernandez, "Multiracial Matrix: The Role of Race Ideology in the Enforcement of Anti-Discrimination Laws, a United States-Latin America Comparison," *Cornell Law Review* 87 (2002): 1093–1176.

11. See, for example, the story of Amanda America Dickson, a woman born into slavery whose White master/father "passed" her into Whiteness with the knowledge of the surrounding community. Kent Anderson Leslie, *Woman of Color, Daughter of Privilege: Amanda America Dickson 1849–1893* (Athens: University of Georgia Press, 1996).

12. See, for example, Mary Frances Berry, "Judging Morality: Sexual Behavior and Legal Consequences in the Late 19th Century South," *The Journal of American History* 78, no. 3: 835–856.

13. See, for example, Bliss Broyard's discussion of who knew about the Creole ancestry of her father, the critic Anatole Broyard, in *One Drop: My Father's Hidden Life—A Story of Race and Family Secrets* (New York: Little Brown, 2007).

14. For example, see the contrast between Justice Harlan's dissent in *Plessy v. Ferguson*, in which he describes the practice of Chinese Americans riding in train cars reserved for Whites (with quite a bit of nativist racism) and the opinion in *Gong Lum v. Rice* (1927), in which the Supreme Court declared it constitutional for Mississippi to require Chinese children to attend "colored" schools.

CHAPTER 1

1. Howard Winant, "Difference and Inequality: Postmodern Racial Politics in the United States," in *Racism, the City and the State*, ed. Malcolm Cross and Michael Keith (New York: Routledge, 1993), 110.

2. See Victor M. H. Borden, Pamela C. Brown, and Amy K. Garver, "The Top 100: Interpreting The Data," *Diverse Issues in Higher Education* 23 (June 2006): 36–39, and "African Americans Continue to Flock to Graduate and Professional Schools," *Journal of Blacks in Higher Education* 40 (Summer 2003): 10–11.

3. See John R. Logan, "Who Are the Other African Americans? Contemporary African and Caribbean Immigrants in the U.S," in *Other African Americans: Contemporary African and Caribbean Families in the United States*, ed. Yoku Shaw-Taylor and Steven Tuch (Boulder, CO: Rowman and Littlefield, 2007), and see Joy L. Lei, "(Op)posing Representations: Disentangling the Model Minority and the Foreigner" (paper presented at the annual meeting of the American Educational Research Association, San Diego, CA, April 13–17, 1998).

4. See, for example, Douglass Massey and Nancy Denton, *American Apartheid: Segregation and the Making of the Underclass* (Cambridge, MA: Harvard University Press, 1998), and Andrew Hacker, *Two Nations: Black and White, Separate Hostile and Unequal* (New York: Scribner, 1992).

5. For a discussion, see Donald R. Kinder and Lynn Sanders, *Divided by Color: Racial Politics and Democratic Ideals* (Chicago: University of Chicago Press, 1997).

6. See Margaret Chon and Donna E. Arzt, "Walking While Muslim," *Law and Contemporary Problems* 68, no. 215 (Spring 2005): 215–254.

7. For a disc-transcript of this series see CNN, "*Out in the Open: Racism in America*," December 19, 2006. Available for download at http://transcripts.cnn.com/TRAN-SCRIPTS/0612/19/pzn.01.html.

8. Among this diverse group are the social scientists Andrew Hacker, Joe Feagin, Thomas Shapiro, and Douglass Massey.

9. John McWhorter makes this argument in *Losing the Race: Self- Sabotage in Black America* (New York: Harper Perennial, 2001).

10. See Howard Schuman et al., *Racial Attitudes in America: Trends and Interpretations*, rev. ed. (Cambridge, MA: Harvard University Press, 2005).

11. *Washington v. Davis*, 426 U.S. 229, 241 (1976), was the first expression of the intent standard, followed by *Village of Arlington Heights v. Metropolitan Housing Dev. Corp.*, 429 U.S. 252 (1977). For a more comprehensive discussion of the development of the intent standard, see Michael Selmi, "Proving Intentional Discrimination: The Reality of Supreme Court Rhetoric," *Georgetown Law Journal* 86 (1997): 279.

12. See "America in Black and White: Jasper, Texas" with Ted Koppel. The town hall meeting, presented by the ABC News show *Nightline* and P.O.V./American Documentary, took place January 23, 2003, and was a dramatic illustration of this point from the perspective of White Americans who are invested in defending the image of their town, where a Black man was brutally murdered by Whites expressing racist sentiments and ideas.

13. Winant, "Difference and Inequality: Postmodern Racial Politics in the United States," 114.

14. See Kristen Myers, *Racetalk: Racism Hiding in Plain Sight* (New York: Rowman and Littlefield, 2005).

15. Phillip Atiba Goff, Jennifer Eberhardt, and Matthew C. Jackson, "Not Yet Human: Implicit Knowledge, Historical Dehumanization and Contemporary Consequences," *Journal of Personality and Social Psychology* 94, no. 2 (2008): 292–306.

16. Stereotype threat is a theory primarily developed by Irwin Katz and taken up by the social psychologists Claude Steele and Joshua Aronson. Steele's work, with which I am most familiar among the research on stereotype threats, demonstrates that when people's social identities are tied to negative or positive stereotypes, then people often under- or overperform in confirmation of those stereotypes. Numerous studies by Steele and others have been conducted to support this theory. These include the following: C. M. Steele, "Stereotyping and Its Threat Are Real," *American Psychologist* 53 (1998): 680–681; C. M. Steele and J. Aronson, "Stereotype Threat and the Intellectual Test Performance of African-Americans," *Journal of Personality and Social Psychology* 69 (1995): 797–811; C. M. Steele, S. J. Spencer, and J. Aronson, "Contending with Images of One's Group: The Psychology of Stereotype and Social Identity Threat," in *Advances in Experimental Social Psychology*, ed. M. Zanna (San Diego: Academic Press, 2002); L. Roberson et al., "Stereotype Threat and Feedback Seeking in the Workplace," *Journal of Vocational Behavior* 62 (2003): 176–188.

17. Richard J. Herrnstein and Charles Murray, *The Bell Curve: Intelligence and Class Structure in America* (New York: Free Press, 1994).

18. Helen Nugent, "Black People Less Intelligent Scientist Claims," *Sunday Times Online (London)*, October 17, 2007. Available at http://www.timesonline.co.uk/tol/news/uk/article2677098.ece.

19. For a discussion of the history of the concept of a genetic predisposition to antisocial behavior, see Jay Joseph, "Is Crime in the Genes: A Critical Review of Twin and Adoption Studies of Criminal and Antisocial Behavior," in his *The Gene Illusion: Genetic Research in Psychiatry and Psychology under the Microscope* (New York: Algora, 2004).

20. John B. McConahay and Joseph C. Hough Jr., "Symbolic Racism," *Journal of Social Issues* 32 (1976): 23–39; J. B. McConahay, "Modern Racism, Ambivalence, and the Modern Racism Scale," in *Prejudice, Discrimination, and Racism*, ed. J. F. Dovidio and S. L. Gaertner (Orlando, FL: Academic Press, 1986), 91–125.

21. T. F. Pettigrew and R. W. Meertens, "Subtle and Blatant Prejudice in Western Europe," *European Journal of Social Psychology* 25 (1995): 57–75.

22. J. Sidanius, F. Pratto, and L. Bobo, "Racism, Conservatism, Affirmative Action and Intellectual Sophistication: A Matter of Principled Conservatism or Group Dominance?" *Journal of Personality and Social Psychology* 70 (1996): 476–490.

23. For a many-decades-old example of this, see Daniel Katz and Kenneth Braly, "Racial Stereotypes of One Hundred College Students," *Journal of Abnormal and Social Psychology* 28 (1933): 280–290.

24. David O. Sears and Donald R. Kinder, "Racial Tensions and Voting in Los Angeles," in *Los Angeles: Viability and Prospects for Metropolitan Leadership*, ed. W. Z. Hirsch (New York: Praeger, 1971); see D. Kinder and D. Sears, "Prejudice and Politics: Symbolic Racism versus Racial Threats to the Good Life," *Journal of Personality and Social Psychology* 40 (1981): 414–431.

25. McConahay, "Modern Racism, Ambivalence, and the Modern Racism Scale," 91–125.

26. Pettigrew and Meertens, "Subtle and Blatant Prejudice in Western Europe," 57–75.

27. Kinder and Sanders, *Divided by Color: Racial Politics and Democratic Ideals*.

28. I. Katz, J. Wackenhut, and R. G. Hass, "Racial Ambivalence, Value Duality, and Behavior," in *Prejudice, Discrimination, and Racism*, ed. J. F. Dovidio and S. L. Gaertner (Orlando, FL: Academic Press, 1986), 35–59.

29. Larence Bobo, James Kluegel, and Ryan Smith, "Laissez Faire Racism: The Crystallization of a Kinder, Gentler, Anti-Black Ideology," in *Racial Attitudes in the 1990s*, ed. Steven A. Tuch and Jack Martin (Westport, CT: Praeger, 1997), 15–42.

30. S. L. Gaertner and J. F. Dovidio, "The Aversive Form of Racism," in *Prejudice, Discrimination, and Racism*, ed. J. F. Dovidio and S. L. Gaertner (Orlando, FL: Academic Press, 1986).

31. See for example Alan D. Freeman, *Legitimizing Discrimination through Anti-Discrimination Law: A Critical Review of Supreme Court Doctine in Antidiscrimination Law*, ed. Christopher McCrudden (Aldershot: Dartmouth, 1991).

32. For an extended and compelling discussion of this problem, see John L. Jackson, *Real Black: Adventures in Racial Sincerity* (Chicago: University of Chicago Press, 2005).

33. M. R.Banaji and R. Bhaskar, "Implicit Stereotypes and Memory: The Bounded Rationality of Social Beliefs," in *Memory, Brain, and Belief*, ed. D. L. Schacter and E. Scarry (Cambridge, MA: Harvard University Press, 2000), 139–175.

34. James Gordon Meek, "Extremist Militias See Resurgence under Obama's Tenure," *New York Daily News*, August 13, 2009, 28.

35. According to Kinder and Sanders, "a new form of prejudice has come to prominence, one that is preoccupied with matters of moral character, informed by the virtues associated with traditions of individualism." Kinder and Sanders, *Divided by Color: Racial Politics and Democratic Ideals*, 105–106.

36. Glenn Lowry, *The Anatomy of Racial Inequality* (Cambridge, MA: Harvard University Press, 2002), 26. Although I think Lowry makes a fundamental point here, I do not accept the entire analysis in this book. Lowry rightly critiques the behavioralist racism

narrative, yet does concur with the notion of the Black underclass as poorly behaved; he ascribes that behavior to inequality and advocates for what I would term an ethic of care response. I take exception to that piece of his work as collapsing poverty with behavior in a manner that the work of the social science ethnographers like Mitch Duneier and Elijah Anderson directly challenges. What Lowry's work adds that is critical, though, is an understanding of the dynamic process of the production and reproduction of inequality.

CHAPTER 2

1. Kwame Anthony Appiah and Amy Gutmann, *Color Conscious: The Political Morality of Race* (Princeton: Princeton University Press, 1998), 78.

2. The obvious exception to this is that it is taboo to compliment Whites. When positive stereotyping of Whites occurs, it is within coded language: "suburban," "middle class," "All-American," "heartland." This taboo developed because, for so long, explicit celebrations of Whiteness were tied to brutal forms of racism.

3. Hence Philomena Essed's aptly titled and landmark work *Understanding Everyday Racism: An Interdisciplinary Theory* (Thousand Oaks, CA: Sage, 1991).

4. Patricia Hill Collins, *Black Feminist Thought: Knowledge Consciousness and Empowerment* (Boston: Unwin Hyman, 1990), 221–238.

5. See Angelo Ancheta, *Race, Rights and the Asian American Experience* (New Brunswick, NJ: Rutgers University Press, 1995), for a discussion of this dynamic vis-à-vis Asian Americans.

6. *The Tyra Banks Show*, with guest Nicole Richie, September 12, 2006, The CW Network.

7. Carol Channing discusses her father's ethnicity in her memoir, *Just Lucky I Guess* (New York: Simon and Schuster, 2002), 8.

8. Bliss Broyard, "Secret Memory," *Elle*, September 2007, 582.

9. Ibid., 582.

10. Tanya K. Hernandez, "Multiracial Matrix: The Role of Race Ideology in the Enforcement of Anti-Discrimination Laws, a United States-Latin America Comparison," *Cornell Law Review* 87 (2002): 1093–1176.

11. Patricia Hill Collins, *From Black Power to Hip Hop* (Philadelphia: Temple University Press, 2006), 6–7.

12. Charles R. Lawrence III, "The ID, the Ego, and Equal Protection: Reckoning with Unconscious Racism," *Stanford Law Review* 39 (1987): 317–388 at 317, 330.

13. Jerry Kang, "Trojan Horses of Race," *Harvard Law Review* 118 (2005): 1489–1522.

14. See also Leonard Baynes, "Making the Case for a Compelling Governmental Interest and Re-Establishing FCC Affirmative Action in Programs for Broadcast Licensing," *Rutgers Law Review* 57 (2004): 235.

15. See, e.g., John F. Dovidio et al., "On the Nature of Prejudice: Automatic and Controlled Processes," *Journal of Experimental Social Psychology* 33 (1997): 510–540 at 510, 516, 517. This study demonstrated time differentials in subjects' ability to classify positive or negative words after receiving subliminal flashes of Black and White faces.

16. See B. Keith Payne, "Prejudice and Perception: The Role of Automatic and Controlled Processes in Misperceiving a Weapon," *Journal of Personality and Social Psychology* 81 (2001): 181–192 at 181; Joshua Correll et al., "The Police Officer's Dilemma: Using

Ethnicity to Disambiguate Potentially Threatening Individuals," *Journal of Personality and Social Psychology* 83 (2002): 1314–1329 at 1314, 1315, 1317.

17. Project Implicit is a project conducted at Harvard University (Web site is www. implicit.harvard.edu) that collects and allows for online evaluation of Implicit Association Tests, some of which measure and reveal racial biases. Research conducted by the Project has shown that a significant percentage of African Americans show bias toward African American visual images. Also see A. G. Greenwald and M. R. Banaji, "Implicit Social Cognition: Attitudes, Self-Esteem, and Stereotypes," *Psychological Review* 102, no. 1 (1995): 4–27.

18. Ulf Hannerz, *Cultural Complexity: Studies in the Social Organization of Meaning* (New York: Columbia University Press, 1992), 27.

19. Marx argued that consciousness, like language, was created by the conditions in which we live. See Karl Marx, *The German Ideology* 1845 (first published Moscow, 1932). Later Marxist theorists like Antonio Gramsci revised the absolute determinism of this idea and considered the possibility of consciousness resistant to the social order created by capitalist societies. These thinkers allowed for ideas rooted in Marxist theory to be applied to liberation struggles in a wide variety of social and political contexts.

20. David Theo Goldberg, "Racial Knowledge," in *Theories of Race and Racism: A Reader*, ed. Les Back and John Solomos (New York: Routledge, 2000), 168.

21. Jennifer Hochschild, "When Do People Not Protest Unfairness?: The Case of Skin Color Discrimination," *Social Research* 73, no. 3 (2006): 473–498; also see E. Uhlmann, N. Dasgupta, A. G. Greenwald, A. Elgueta, and J. Swanson, "Skin Color Based Subgroup Prejudice among Hispanics in the United States and Latin America," *Social Cognition* 20 (2002): 197–224, for strong evidence of color preferences among Hispanics.

22. See Dorothy Roberts, *Shattered Bonds: The Color of Child Welfare* (New York: Basic Books, 2002).

23. See Julie Landsman, "Confronting the Racism of Low Expectations," *Educational Leadership* 62, no. 3 (2004): 28–32; Sherry Marx, *Reaching the Invisible: Confronting Passing Racism in Teacher Education* (New York: Routledge, 2006). For a thorough understanding of the impact of teacher expectations, see Rhona Weinstein, *Reaching Higher: The Power of Expectations in Schooling* (Cambridge, MA: Harvard University Press, 2004).

24. Robert Bullard et al., "Toxic Wastes and Race at Twenty:1987–2007 Grassroots Struggles to Dismantle Environmental Racism in the United States," report prepared for the United Church of Christ Justice and Witness Ministries, March 2007.

25. See Mark Nord et al., United States Department of Agriculture Economic Research Service Economic Research Report No. 29, "Household Food Security in the United States," 2005.

26. See Valerie A. Rawlston and William E. Spriggs, "Pay Equity 2000: Are We There Yet?" SRR-02-2001, National Urban League Institute for Opportunity and Equality, Washington, DC, April 2001. See also Barbara Kilbourne, Paula England, and Kurt Beron, "Effects of Individual, Occupational, and Industrial Characteristics on Earnings: Intersections of Race and Gender," *Social Forces* 72, no. 4 (1994): 1149–1176. For an overview, see Deborah M. Figart, "Pay Equity and Race/Ethnicity: An Annotated Bibliography," National Committee on Pay Equity, Hyattsville, MD, October 2001.

27. David J. Maume Jr., "Glass Ceilings and Glass Escalators: Occupational Segregation and Race and Sex Differences in Managerial Promotions," *Work and Occupations* 26, no. 4 (1999): 483–509.

28. See John. Milton Yinger, *Closed Doors Opportunities Lost: The Continuing Costs of Housing Discrimination* (New York: Russell Sage, 1995). Also see Kedamai Fisseha and Nicholas Yannuzzi, "Linguistic Profiling: Pilot Studies on Restaurants, Car Dealerships and Apartment Rentals," unpublished article, January 12, 2007.

29. See Ira Katznelson, *When Affirmative Action Was White: An Untold History of Racial Inequality in Twentieth Century America* (New York: Norton, 2005).

30. *Unequal Treatment: Confronting Racial and Ethnic Disparities in Health Care* (report for the Institute of Medicine of the National Academies, Washington, DC, March 20, 2002).

31. David Cole, "Policing Race and Class," in his *No Equal Justice: Race and Class in the American Criminal Justice System* (New York: New Press, 2000).

32. Ibid.

33. David Cole, "Judgment and Discrimination," in his *No Equal Justice: Race and Class in the American Criminal Justice System* (New York: New Press, 2000).

34. David Cole, "The Color of Punishment," in his *No Equal Justice: Race and Class in the American Criminal Justice System* (New York: New Press, 2000).

35. I. V. Blair, C. M. Judd, and K. M. Chapleau, "The Influence of Afrocentric Facial Features in Criminal Sentencing," *Psychological Science*, 15 (2004): 674–679; I. V. Blair, C. M. Judd, and J. L. Fallman, "The Automaticity of Race and Afrocentric Facial Features in Social Judgments," *Journal of Personality and Social Psychology* 87, no.6 (2004): 763–778.

36. Jeff Manza and Christopher Uggen, *Locked Out: Felon Disenfranchisement and American Democracy* (New York: Oxford University Press, 2006), and Jamie Fellner and Marc Mauer, "Losing the Vote: The Impact of Felony Disenfranchisement Laws in the United States," Human Rights Watch and The Sentencing Project, Washington, DC, 1998.

37. Ryan S. King, "Disparity by Geography: The War on Drugs in America's Cities," The Sentencing Project Report, May 2008, http://sentencingproject.org/detail/publication.cfm?publication_id=186.

38. See Dorothy Roberts, *Shattered Bonds: The Color of Child Welfare* (New York: Basic Books, 2002).

39. The reason is racial disparities in the application of public nuisance laws.

40. See generally Herman Gray, *Watching Race: Television and the Struggle for "Blackness"* (Minneapolis: University of Minnesota Press, 1995).

41. See the quantitative analysis of marketplace discrimination in Ian Ayres, *Pervasive Prejudice: Unconventional Evidence of Race and Gender Discrimination* (Chicago: University of Chicago Press, 2001).

42. Ian Ayres et al., "To Insure Prejudice: Racial Disparities in Taxicab Tipping," *Yale Law Journal* 114 (2005): 1613–1674.

43. Anne-Marie G. Harris, "Shopping While Black: Applying 42 U.S.C. § 1981 to Cases of Consumer Racial Profiling," *Boston College Third World Law Journal* 23 (Winter 2003): 1–55.

44. While language-based discrimination is unconstitutional, as it is highly correlated with discrimination based on national origin, employers can justify discriminatory practices on the basis of language if the employee's accent or language "materially interferes" with job performance. However, since the burden of proof lies with claimants, victims of discrimination based upon their accent face an uphill battle in pursuing a remedy. Employers are, on the other hand, allowed to discriminate against employees for wearing hairstyles, like dreadlocks and afros, that are easiest to maintain for those with naturally coily or tightly curled hair because these styles are considered mutable characteristics.

Eric Bryant Rhodes, *Stories Employers Tell: Race, Skill and Hiring in America* (New York: Russell Sage, 2001), cites employers' distaste for African American language and communication styles.

45. See Lawrence Bobo and Vincent L. Hutchings, "Perceptions of Racial Group Competition: Extending Blumer's Theory of Group Position to a Multiracial Social Context," *American Sociological Review* 61, no. 6 (1996): 951–972. Also see Kang, "Trojan Horses of Race," 1534, citing research showing strong dominant-group favoritism among minority-group members.

46. Lawrence D. Bobo, "Prejudice as Group Position: Microfoundations of a Sociological Approach to Racism and Race Relations," *Journal of Social Issues* 55, no. 3 (1999): 445–472.

47. Ibid., 445–472, 446, 449, 454, 456.

48. Ibid.

49. J. F. Dovidio and S. L. Gaertner, "Aversive Racism in Selection Decisions: 1989 and 1999," *Psychological Science* 11 (2000): 315–319.

50. S. L. Gaertner and J. F. Dovidio, *Reducing Ingroup Bias: The Common Ingroup Identity Model* (Philadelphia: Psychology Press, 2000).

51. The Washington v. Davis and Arlington Heights opinions both held open the possibility that discriminatory intent could be inferred from the totality of circumstances, including disparate impact, although not defined by it.

52. Although Title VII currently has a rational relationship test as a justification for disparate impact, one can imagine that this will not always be the case, so it is useful to consider the possibility of merely requiring race neutrality for justifications.

53. See Sears and Kinder's symbolic racism theory, in which symbolic racism reflects Whites' moral codes about how to organize society, rather than beliefs that satisfy personal interests. It focuses on Blacks as group, rather than on individual Blacks. D. Kinder and D. Sears, "Prejudice and Politics: Symbolic Racism versus Racial Threats to the Good Life," *Journal of Personality and Social Psychology*, 40 (1981): 414–431.

54. Gaertner and Dovidio argue that social conservatives' racial bias is cruder, that it proclaims egalitarian standards and yet rigidly demand a particular kind of bootstraps activity on the part of the most resource-poor segments of society. But this model also supports a constitutional interpretation that fails to address racial discrimination. Moreover, the conservative shift to an intent standard for measuring racial discrimination is a kind of bootstraps model itself: "If you want us to acknowledge mistreatment, you must do the hard work to show it."

55. This also might help explain the difficulty of coalition politics among groups of different people of color. There is an interest in fueling racist practices against others if there is a competitive sense of group position that motivates race based decision making.

56. Symbolic boundary theorists trace the manner in which people form identities and maintain stratifications based upon distinctions drawn on the basis of race, class, ethnicity, and culture.

57. Aversive racism is a theory developed by Gaertner and Dovidio that describes the racism that results in the conflict between White Americans egalitarian values and learned negative attitudes toward people of color.

58. See generally *Unequal Treatment: Confronting Racial and Ethnic Disparities in Health Care* (report for Institute of Medicine of the National Academies, Washington, DC, March 20, 2002).

CHAPTER 3

1. Mark Turner, *The Literary Mind* (New York: Oxford University Press, 1996), v.

2. Ellen Spolsky, *Gaps in Nature: Literary Interpretation and the Modular Mind* (Albany: State University of New York Press, 1993), 192.

3. Roland Barthes, *Rustle of Language*, trans. Richard Howard. (New York: Hill and Wang, 1986), 278.

4. N. Dasgupta and A. G. Greenwald, "On the Malleability of Automatic Attitudes: Combating Automatic Prejudice with Images of Admired and Disliked Individuals," *Journal of Personality and Social Psychology* 81 (2001): 800–814.

5. The Committee of 100's 2001 (New York) report "American Attitudes toward Chinese Americans and Asian Americans" identified simultaneous positive stereotyping of and significant racial animus toward Asian Americans.

6. Roger C. Schank and Tamara R. Berman, "The Pervasive Role of Stories in Knowledge and Action," in *Narrative Impact: Social and Cognitive Foundations*, ed. Timothy C. Brock (Mahwah, NJ: Lawrence Erlbaum, 2002), 287.

7. Jeffrey J. Strange, "How Fictional Tales Wag Real-World Beliefs," in *Narrative Impact: Social and Cognitive Foundations*, ed. Timothy C. Brock (Mahwah, NJ: Lawrence Erlbaum, 2002), 276.

8. Schank and Berman, "The Pervasive Role of Stories in Knowledge and Action," 292.

9. Ibid.

10. *The Oprah Winfrey Show*, "Chappelle Show: Dave's Moral Dilemma," February 3, 2006.

11. Herman Gray, *Watching Race: Television and the Struggle for Blackness* (Minneapolis: University of Minnesota Press, 2004), xiv.

12. Ibid., xvii.

13. Jimmie Reeves, "Re-Covering Racism: Crack Mothers, Reaganism and the Network News," in *Living Color: Race and Television in the United States*, ed. Sasha Torres (Durham, NC: Duke University Press, 1998), 100.

14. Martin Gilens, "Public Misperceptions of Race and Poverty in Race, Poverty and Domestic Policy," *Public Opinion Quarterly* 60, no. 4: 513–535. Reprinted in *Social Science Research*, 2nd ed., ed. Turner C. Lomand (Los Angeles: Pyrczak, 1998), 340.

15. Ibid., 352.

16. Ibid.

17. See Patricia Hill Collins, *Black Feminist Thought: Knowledge, Consciousness and the Politics of Empowerment* (New York: Routledge, 2000); William W. Fisher, "Ideology and Imagery in the Law of Slavery," *Chicago-Kent Law Review* 68 (1993): 1051. A revised and expanded version was published in *Slavery and the Law*, ed. Paul Finkelman (Boulder: Madison House 1997), 43–85. For a reference to these representations in film, see Donald Bogle, *Toms, Coons, Mulattoes, Mammies and Bucks: An Interpretive History of Blacks in American Films* (London: Continuum International, 2001).

18. In 1965, Daniel Patrick Moynihan released his famous (or infamous) report decrying the pathological domestic behaviors of the Black poor: D. P. Moynihan, *The Negro Family: The Case for National Action* (Washington, DC: U.S. Department of Labor, 1965).

19. Horton, a Black man, was convicted of first-degree murder in 1974 for murdering a gas station attendant and was sentenced to life in prison. Horton was given ten furloughs

under the Massachusetts furlough program. On his last one, in June 1986, Horton raped a White woman and stabbed her fiancé in Maryland.

20. Howard Winant, *The New Politics of Race* (Minneapolis: University of Minnesota Press, 2004), 62.

21. Eduardo Bonilla-Silva, "The Linguistics of Color-Blind Racism or How to Talk Nasty about Blacks without Sounding Racist," *Critical Sociology* 28, no. 1–2 (2002): 41–64, provides an analysis of thinly veiled racial coding among Midwestern college students and residents of the metropolitan Detroit area.

22. See Donald R. Kinder and Lynn M. Sanders, "Frames and Campaigns," in *Divided by Color: Racial Politics and American Ideals*, ed. Donald R. Kinder and Lynn M. Sanders (Chicago: University of Chicago Press, 1996).

23. "Responsibility" is, of course, both a racially coded and a race-neutral word. It leaves open room for "upstanding" Black citizens who also rail against the "irresponsibility" of those in the inner city to identify with the Clinton message even if they implicitly or by association were collapsed into its negative imagery.

24. Monte Piliawsky, "The Clinton Administration and African Americans," in *The Politics of Race*, ed. Theodore Rueter (Armonk,NY: M. E. Sharpe, 1995), 398, 399.

25. Adam D. Young, "Lubbock Judge's Charged Postings Draw Crowd of Supporters, Critics," *Lubbock Avalanche-Journal*, August 21, 2009, State and Regional News section, 1.

26. *Unequal Treatment: Confronting Racial and Ethnic Disparities in Health Care*, report for the Institute of Medicine, Washington, DC, March 20, 2002, 162; M. Van Ryn, "Research on the Provider Contribution to Race/ethnicity Disparities in Medical Care," *Medical Care* 40, no. 1 (2002): 1140–1151; M. van Ryn and J. Burke, "The Effect of Patient Race and Socioeconomic Status on Physicians' Perceptions of Patients," *Social Science and Medicine* 50 (2000): 813–828.

27. *Unequal Treatment*, 163, 164.

28. *Unequal Treatment*, 173.

29. *Unequal Treatment*, 170.

30. Marianne Bertrand and Sendhil Mullainathan, "Are Emily and Greg More Employable Than Lakisha and Jamal? A Field Experiment on Labor Market Discrimination," Massachusetts Institute of Technology Department of Economics Working Paper 03-22.

31. Ibid., 7.

32. Ibid., 3.

33. Ibid.

34. Ibid., 21.

35. Ibid.

36. Ibid., 16.

37. Ibid., 18.

38. David N. Figlio, "Names, Expectations and the Black-White Test Score Gap," National Bureau of Economic Research Working Paper 11195.

39. Ibid., 18.

40. Ibid., 19.

41. Ibid., 21.

42. Roland G. Fryer and Steven D. Levitt, "The Causes and Consequences of Distinctively Black Names," *Quarterly Journal of Economics* 69, no. 3: 767–805.

43. They do not, however, control for class in order to distinguish between distinctively Black names.

44. It is also important to remember that a large proportion of the names given to African American children are also common among White and Asian American children.

45. Katherine Neckerman and Joleen Kirschenmann, "Hiring Strategies, Racial Bias and Inner City Workers," *Social Problems* 38, no. 4 (1991): 801–815; Philip Moss and Chris Tilly, "Why Black Men Are Doing Worse in the Labor Market: A Review of Supply Side and Demand Side Explanations," working paper, New York: Social Science Research Council Committee on the Urban Underclass, 1991; Philip Kasinitz and Jan Rosenberg, "Missing the Connection: Social Isolation and Employment on the Brooklyn Waterfront," working paper, Michael Harrington Center for Democratic Values and Social Change, Queens College, City University of New York, 1994.

46. Karolyn Tyson and William Darity Jr., "It's Not 'a Black Thing':Understanding the Burden of Acting White and Other Dilemmas of High Achievement," *American Sociological Review* 70 (August 2005): 582–605. See also Douglas B. Downeyand James W. Ainsworth-Darnell, "The Search for Oppositional Culture among Black Students," *American Sociological Review* 67 (2002): 156–164; James W. Ainsworth-Darnell and Douglas B. Downey, "Assessing the Oppositional Culture Explanation for Racial/Ethnic Differences in School Performance." *American Sociological Review* 63 (1998): 536–553; Grace Kao, Marta Tienda, and Barbara Schneider, "Racial and Ethnic Variation in Academic Performance." *Research in Sociology of Education and Socialization* 11 (1996): 263–297. In Roland Fryer and Paul Torelli's research, where they do find some symbolic meaning attached to the "acting White" accusation, it is not necessarily correlated to grades but rather related to behaviors. Accusations about "acting White" are more salient in public schools and schools in which fewer than 20 percent of the students are Black and are nonexistent among Blacks in predominantly Black schools or those who attend private schools. Schools with more interracial contact have an acting-White coefficient twice as large as that for more segregated schools and seven times as large for Black males). Other models we consider, such as self-sabotage among Black youth or the presence of an oppositional culture identity, all contradict the data in important way." Roland Fryer and Paul Torelli, "An Empirical Analysis of Acting White," National Bureau of Economic Research Working Papers Series 11334, 6–7. Hence, the issue may be that multiracial and racially stratified schools create an association between Whiteness and high achievement that students are picking upon, rather than creating.

47. See, for example, films like *Dangerous Minds*, *Lean on Me*, and *Freedom Writers*.

48. See James D. Anderson, "Black Rural Communities and the Struggle for Education during the Age of Booker T. Washington, 1877–1915,". *Peabody Journal of Education* 67, no. 4 (1992): 46–62, and James D. Anderson, *The Education of Blacks in the South, 1860-1935* (Chapel Hill: University of North Carolina Press,1988).

49. See Liz Bowie, "Students Voice Concern on Funding," Baltimore Sun, April 6, 2004, available at http://www.baltimoresun.com/news/education/bal-md.student-s06apr06,0,3435746.story, recounting student protestors' claims that state officials and Baltimore's superintendent of schools had failed to comply with a court order requiring the Baltimore city schools to provide $2,000 more per pupil per year. Also see Laura Loh, "City Students Lie Down in Protest over State's Lack of School Funding," *Baltimore Sun*, December 8, 2004, available at http://articles.baltimoresun.com/2004-12-08/news/0412080279_1_school-funding-city-schools-students.

CHAPTER 4

1. Herbert Marcuse, *An Essay on Liberation* (Boston: Beacon Press, 1969), 74.

2. "Building Blocks for Father Involvement," U.S. Department of Health and Human Services Administration for Children and Families (June 2004), 10.

3. Solangel Maldonado, "Deadbeat or Deadbroke: Redefining Child Support for Poor Fathers," *University of California Davis Law Review* 39, no. 3 (1994): 991–1007.

4. Carol W. Metzler et al., "The Social Context for Risky Sexual Behavior among Adolescents," *Journal of Behavioral Medicine* 17 (1994): 419–438; Deane Scott Berman, "Risk Factors Leading to Adolescent Substance Abuse," *Adolescence* 30 (1995): 201–206; David A. Brent et al., "Post-traumatic Stress Disorder in Peers of Adolescent Suicide Victims: Predisposing Factors and Phenomenology," *Journal of the American Academy of Child and Adolescent Psychiatry* 34 (1995): 209–215.

5. June 19, 2008, Apostolic Church of God, Chicago, Illinois.

6. See Rosemary Radford Ruther, "Patriarchy and the Men's Movement: Part of the Problem or Part of the Solution?" in *Women Respond to the Men's Movement*, ed. K. L. Hagan (San Francisco: Pandora, 1992), for such critiques of masculinity and patriarchy in light of their revitalization under the banner of the 1990s "Men's Movement."

7. Amy L. Wax, "Engines of Inequality: Class, Race, and Family Structure," *Family Law Quarterly* 41 (2007): 567.

8. Maldonado, "Deadbeat or Deadbroke," 995–1007.

9. Ibid.

10. Blackprof.com, December 2006. (The site is no longer available.)

11. See S. M. Stanley and F. D. Fincham, "The Effects of Divorce on Children," *Couples Research and Therapy Newsletter* (AABT-SIG) 8, no. 1 (2002): 7–10, for a useful overview of some of this literature.

12. See P. Tjaden and N. Thoennes, "Extent, Nature, and Consequences of Intimate Partner Violence: Findings from the National Violence against Women Survey," Publication No. NCJ 181867 (Washington, DC: U.S. Department of Justice, 2000). This report estimates that there are 4.8 million acts of intimate partner violence each year in the United States. Also see "Caring for Your Baby and Young Child: Birth to Age 5," American Academy of Pediatrics, May 2005, Washington, D.C, which reports that more than 2.5 million cases of child abuse are reported each year and that most of abuse takes place inside the home.

13. Cited in Joseph Nevins, *Operation Gatekeeper: The Rise of the "Illegal Alien" and the Making of the U.S.-Mexico Boundary* (New York: Routledge, 2002), 96.

14. Ibid., 112.

15. Mae Ngai, *Impossible Subjects: Illegal Aliens and the Making of Modern America* (Princeton: Princeton University Press, 2004), 8.

16. So, for example, in 2003, fewer than half of reported rape cases and fewer than 25 percent of larceny and burglary were cleared. Federal Bureau of Investigation Department of Justice Uniform Crime Reports "Crime in the United States 2003" , Section III. Reports available at http://www.fbi.gov/ucr.

17. Michael Keith, "From Punishment to Discipline: Racism, Racialization and the Policing of Social Control," in *Racism, the City and the State*, ed. Malcolm Cross and Michael Keith (New York: Routledge 1993), 200.

18. Michael K. Brown et al., *Whitewashing Race: The Myth of a Color Blind Society* (Berkeley: University of California Press, 2003), 150.

19. Although these are not universally racialized categories, behaviors that are talked about in racialized ways get treated as deviant and sociopathic in ways that could just as easily be explained as understandable responses to inequality or trauma.

20. Philip Brian Harper, *Are We Not Men? Masculine Anxiety and the Problem of African American Identity* (New York: Oxford University Press, 1996), 60.

21. David Theo Goldberg, "Polluting the Body Politic: Racist Discourse and Urban Location," in *Racism, the City and the State*, ed. Malcolm Cross and Michael Keith (New York: Routledge, 1993), 46.

22. See Joanne L. Goodwin, *Gender and the Politics of Welfare Reform: Mother's Pensions in Chicago 1911–1929* (Chicago: University of Chicago Press, 1997).

23. Policy initiatives and documents like the Moynihan Report played a role in the racialization of that term and many others. I want to illustrate, however, that the use of quantitative methods at the foundation of the racialization of such categories has to be carefully considered. Certainly it means something when there is a preponderance of people of color in a category; it indicates something that is going on in our society, but it also acquires a second meaning that is related to our racial beliefs and biases and that shapes how we choose to respond to the initial problem.

24. Deborah Chambers, *Representing the Family* (Thousand Oaks, CA: Sage Press, 2001), 51.

25. Ibid., 141.

26. Amy Kaplan, "Manifest Domesticity," *American Literature* 70, no. 3 (1998): 581–606 at 581.

27. Ibid., 582.

28. Chambers, *Representing the Family*, 37.

29. Ibid., 27.

30. Ibid., 56.

31. Christopher Jencks, "Is the American Underclass Growing," in *Urban Underclass*, ed. Christopher Jencks and Paul E. Peterson (Washington, DC: Brookings Institution, 1991), 86, Table 14. Cited in Maggie Gallagher, The Abolition of Marriage (Washington, DC: Regnery, 1996), 117: "In 1960, 23 percent of black children were born to unwed mothers." Moynihan's report was published only five years later, when approximately 25 percent of Black children were born out of wedlock.

32. Ellen Pader, "Housing Occupancy Standards: Inscribing Ethnicity and Family Relations on the Land," *Journal of Architectural and Planning Research* 19, no. 4 (Winter 2002): 300.

33. Ibid., 302.

34. See Natalia A. Sarkisian, "Kin Support in Black and White: Structure, Culture, and Extended Family Ties" (Ph.D. diss., University of Massachusetts, Amherst). See also Natalia Sarkisian and Mariana Gerena, "Extended Family Integration among Latinos/as and Euro Americans: Cultural and Structural Determinants of Ethnic Differences" (paper presented at the annual meeting of the American Sociological Association, Philadelphia, PA, August 12, 2005); Lin Zhan, *Asian Americans: Vulnerable Populations, Model Interventions and Clarifying Agendas* (Sudbury, MA: Jones and Bartlett, 2003), 8.

CHAPTER 5

1. Linda Brent, *Incidents in the Life of a Slave Girl* (Boston: Author, 1861), 224.

2. Robert B. Stepto, *From Behind the Veil: A Study of Afro-American Narrative*, 2nd ed. (Urbana: University of Illinois Press, 1991); also see Hazel Carby, "It Jus Be's Dat Way Sometime: The Sexual Politics of Women's Blues," in *Feminisms: An Anthology of Literary Theory and Criticism*, ed. Robin R. Warhol and Diane Price Herndl (New Brunswick, NJ: Rutgers University Press, 1993), 751, for a discussion of Black women's use of mobility as freedom.

3. Patricia Hill Collins, *Black Sexual Politics: African Americans, Gender, and the New Racism* (New York: Routledge, 2005), 58.

4. See www.ccrjustice.org for access to reports on racial disparities in policing and information about related litigation.

4. Democratic Policy Committee, "Democrats and African Americans: Building on Past Accomplishments to Create a Stronger Nation and Safer Future," Senate Report, October 7, 2004, available at http://democrats.senate.gov/dpc/dpc-new.cfm?doc_name=sr-108-2-281.

5. Jim Hecimovich, "Affordable Housing and the Black Community," 2007 Conference Session, American Planning Association Annual Meeting. April 14–18, Philadelphia, PA.

6. Imani Perry, "Dismantling The House of Plessy: A Private Law Study of Race in Cultural and Legal History with Contemporary Resonances," *Studies in Law Politics and Society* 33 (2004): 91–159.

7. Iris Marion Young, "Impartiality and the Civic Public: Some Implications of Feminist Critiques of Moral and Political Theory," in *Feminism, the Public and the Private*, ed. Joan B. Landes (New York: Oxford University Press, 1998).

8. Catharine A. MacKinnon, "The Liberal State," in her *Toward a Feminist Theory of the State* (Cambridge, MA: Harvard University Press, 1989).

9. Patricia Hill Collins, *Fighting Words: Black Women and the Search for Justice* (Minneapolis: University of Minnesota Press, 1998), 16.

10. Carol Pateman, *The Disorder of Women* (Stanford: Stanford University Press, 1989).

11. Catharine A. MacKinnon, "Prostitution and Civil Rights," *Michigan Journal of Gender and Law* 1 (1993): 13–31.

12. See Kristin A. Kelly, *Domestic Violence and the Politics of Privacy* (Ithaca: Cornell University Press, 2003).

13. Anita L. Allen, *Why Privacy Isn't Everything: Feminist Reflections on Personal Accountability* (New York: Rowman and Littlefield, 2003), 39.

14. This concept of a privacy right that is not merely a negative right but one that ensures that people can experience privacy is also related to work by feminist theorists such as Linda McClain. Linda C. McClain, "Reconstructive Tasks for a Liberal Feminist Conception of Privacy," *William and Mary Law Review* 40, no. 3 (March 1999): 759 –794.

15. Collins, *Fighting Words*, 19.

16. 357 U.S. 449 (1958).

17. 357 U.S. 445 (1958).

18. See David Garrow, *The FBI and Martin Luther King, Jr.*, rev. ed. (New Haven: Yale University Press, 2006); Clayborne Carson and David Gallen, eds., *Malcolm X: The FBI File* (New York: Carroll and Graf, 1991); Nelson Blacstock, *Cointelpro: The FBI's Secret War on Political Freedom* (Atlanta: Pathfinder Press, 1988).

19. Here integration refers not only to the end of de jure segregation but also to the process of including African Americans in entitlement programs that occurred over the course of the twentieth century, thereby integrating them into participation in the welfare state.

20. Moreover, in the 1960s, the part of the response to Black uprisings that entailed the provision of service programs actually entailed a series of renewed interventionist oversight practices on communities. Likewise, as formal barriers to integration came down, structures of investigation for determining what kind of Black people would be admitted to integrated spaces increased in the form of testing and evaluation and the use of proxies for class as means of assessing merit.

21. Rajiv C. Shah and Jay P. Kesan, "How Architecture Regulates," *Journal of Architectural and Planning Research* 24, no. 4 (2003): 350–359.

22. Irwin Altman, *The Environment and Social Behavior* (Monterey, CA: Brooks/Cole, 1975).

23. Robert Cover, "Violence and the Word," *Yale Law Journal* 95 (1986): 1601.

24. George Gilder's 1978 conservative text "Wealth and Poverty" argued that means-tested benefits, what we popularly refer to as welfare, promoted "the value of being poor," as though the welfare state produced a population desirous of poverty. Likewise, Charles Murray, of *Bell Curve* notoriety, argued in his book *Losing Ground* that means-tested benefits created a value in being poor that caused people to remain poor, again a description of choice. If one adds to this contemporary culture of poverty arguments in which Black people are described as culturally deficient and therefore fated to lag behind in economic competition, you can begin to see the conception of the status of being poor and Black as a choice.

25. For an extending metaphorical treatment of this concept as applied to racial inequality, see Lani Guinier and Gerald Torres, *The Miner's Canary: Enlisting Race, Resisting Power, Transforming Democracy* (Cambridge, MA: Harvard University Press, 2002).

26. Lu-in Wang, *Discrimination by Default: How Racism Becomes Routine* (New York: New York University Press, 2006), 105.

27. Ibid., 95.

28. See David A. Harris, *Profiles in Injustice: Why Racial Profiling Cannot Work* (New York: Norton, 2003).

29. "Threat and Humiliation: Racial Profiling, Domestic Security and Human Rights in the United States," U.S. Human Rights Program Report, Amnesty International USA, New York, 2004.

30. See Bakari Kitwana, *The Hip Hop Generation: Young Blacks and the Crisis in African American Culture* (New York: Basic Books, 2002), 67.

31. See Ginny Kim, "Unconstitutional Conditions: Is the Fourth Amendment for Sale in Public Housing?" *American Criminal Law Review* 33 (1995): 180–184.

32. See Dorothy Roberts, *Shattered Bonds: The Color of Child Welfare* (New York: Basic Books, 2003).

33. See Anne-Marie G. Harris, "Shopping While Black: Applying 42 U.S.C. § 1981 to Cases of Consumer Racial Profiling," *Boston College Third World Law Journal* 23 (Winter 2003):1–55, and A. M. Harris, G. R. Henderson, and J. D. Williams, "Courting Customers: Assessing Consumer Racial Profiling and Other Marketplace Discrimination," *Journal of Public Policy and Marketing, Policy Watch: Commentaries and Viewpoints* 24, no. 1 (Spring 2005): 163–171.

34. See "Criminalizing the Classroom: The Over-policing of New York City Schools," New York Civil Liberties Union, March 2007, which discusses the racial disparity in school policing and the use of metal detectors in New York City. Also, according to the U.S. Department of Education, seven times as many Black tenth graders as White tenth graders attended schools with metal detectors, more than four times as many attended schools with bars on the windows, and one and a half times as many attended schools where security guards patrolled the hallways.

35. In *Ferguson v. City of Charleston*, 532 U.S. 67 (2001), the U.S. Supreme Court declared the coercive drug testing of women in public hospitals in Charleston, South Carolina, and the routine reporting of the results to the police to be a violation of the Fourth Amendment because they found no effective consent. Until then, the practice was well documented. Ongoing efforts to treat drug addiction as a form of child endangerment by a variety of state legislatures indicate that the impact of discriminatory practices related to reproduction and addiction will continue because poor women of color are more likely to be under police surveillance than women of other ethnic groups, despite comparable rates of drug use. The organization National Advocates for Pregnant Women continues to document the discriminatory treatment of African American women in particular in this context.

36. For a discussion of the Republican efforts to "discipline" Black labor rather than fully embrace free-labor ideology for the formerly enslaved, see Brian Kelly, "Black Laborers, The Republican Party and The Crisis of Reconstruction in Low Country," *South Carolina International Review of Social History* (2006) 51: 375–414.

37. See C. Vann Woodward, *The Strange Career of Jim Crow* (New York: Oxford University Press, 1955).

38. Mark R. Rank and Thomas A. Hirschl, "The Likelihood of Poverty across the American Adult Life Span," *Social Work* 44 (1999): 201–216.

39. For example, nine million African Americans receive food stamps each month, and approximately three million more are eligible. More than one in four Black families with children experiences food insecurity. Center on Budget and Policy Priorities, "Facts about African Americans in the Food Stamp Program," April 19, 2007. Moreover, much critique has been directed at the poverty line itself. See Daniel H. Weisberg, "Measuring Poverty: Issues and Approaches," in *Race, Poverty and Domestic Policy*, ed. C. Michael Henry and James Tobin (New Haven: Yale University Press, 2004).

40. W. Paul Farmer, "Affordable Housing Crisis: The "Silent Killer," Domestic Policy Watch (report issued April 2004).

41. Mary Pattillo-McCoy, *Black Picket Fences: Privileges and Peril among the Black Middle Class* (Chicago: University of Chicago Press, 1999).

42. To be clear, there's lots of theory about the culture of the African American poor, but it is posed as a theory of the intersection between race and class. On the other hand, that which gets generalized as African American frequently overrepresents the middle class in experience and perspective.

43. Rebekah Levine Coley, Ann M. Kuta, and P. Lindsay Chase-Lansdale, "An Insider View: Knowledge and Opinions of Welfare from African American Girls in Poverty—Statistical Data Included," *Journal of Social Issues* 56, no. 4 (Winter 2000): 707–726.

44. Cited in Tracy Fessenden, "The Soul of America: Whiteness and the Disappearing of Bodies in the Progressive Era," in *Perspectives on Embodiment: The Intersections of Nature and Culture*, ed. Gail Weiss and Honi Fern Haber (New York: Routledge, 1999).

45. Patricia Ann Boling, *Privacy and the Politics of Intimate Life* (Ithaca: Cornell University Press, 1996), 104.

46. Malcolm X, *The Autobiography of Malcolm X* (New York: Ballantine, 1992), 15–16.

47. Alice O'Connor, *Poverty Knowledge: Social Science, Social Policy and the Poor in Twentieth Century U.S. History* (Princeton: Princeton University Press, 2002), 293.

48. "Public Defender's Office, Attorneys for Victims of Police Abuse Seek Independent Board to Investigate Misconduct," MacArthur Justice Center, Northwestern University Law School, Press Release, April 5, 2007.

49. Jamie Kalven, "Kicking the Pigeon #9," A View from The Ground blog archive, http://www.viewfromtheground.com/archive/2005/07/ktp-9-march-29-and-30-2004.html.

50. Robert A. Moffitt, Robert Reville, and Anne E. Winkler, "Beyond Single Mothers: Cohabitation and Marriage in the AFDC Program," *Demography* 35, no. 3 (August 1998): 259–278.

51. 400 U.S. 309 (1971).

52. So. 2d 1059.

53. Jeffrey Lehman and Sheldon Danziger, "Turning Our Backs on the New Deal: The End of Welfare in 1996," in *Race Poverty and Domestic Policy*, ed. C. Michael Henry (New Haven: Yale University Press, 2004), 607.

54. Ibid., 606.

55. See Yvonne Zylan and Sarah A. Soule, "Ending Welfare as We Know It (Again): Welfare State Retrenchment, 1989–1995," *Social Forces* 79, no. 2 (December 2000): 623–665.

56. Susan T. Gooden and Nakeina E. Douglas demonstrate that strict sanctioning policies like family caps are significantly more common in states with significant Black populations. See Gooden and Douglas, "Ever Present, Sometimes Acknowledged, but Never Addressed: Racial Disparities in U.S. Welfare Policy," in *The Promise of Welfare Reform: Political Rhetoric and the Reality of Poverty in the Twenty-First Century*, ed. Keith M. Kilty and Elizabeth A. Segal (New York: Haworth Press, 2006).

57. See Rebekah J. Smith, "Family Caps in Welfare Reform: Their Coercive Effects and Damaging Consequences," *Harvard Journal of Law and Gender* 29, no. 1 (2006): 151–200.

58. See C. Kingfisher, "Poverty and Downward Mobility in the Land of Opportunity," *American Anthropologist* 103, no. 30 (2001): 824–827; and Jennifer Stuber and Mark Schlesinger, "The Sources of Stigma in Government Means-Tested Programs," *Social Science and Medicine* 63, no. 4 (2006): 933–945.

59. Susan T. Gooden, "All Things Not Being Equal: Differences in Caseworker Support toward Black and White Welfare Clients," *Harvard Journal of African American Public Policy* 4 (1998): 23–33; William Pitz and Gary Delgado, "Race and Recession," Applied Research Center, Oakland, CA, Summer 2002.

60. See John Gilliom, *Overseers of the Poor: Surveillance, Resistance and the Limits of Privacy* (Chicago: University of Chicago Press, 2001); and Lorraine Higgins and Lisa D. Brush, *Getting By, Getting Ahead: Women's Stories of Welfare and Work: A Community Literacy Project*, Pittsburgh, PA.

61. See Dennis M. Rutledge, "Social Darwinism, Scientific Racism, and the Metaphysics of Race," *Journal of Negro Education* 64, no. 3 (1995): 35.

62. David A. Harris, *Profiles in Injustice: While Racial Profiling Cannot Work* (New York: New Press, 2002), 69.

63. Ibid., 63.

64. American Civil Liberties Union, "The Persistence of Racial and Ethnic Profiling in the United States: Follow-Up Report to the U.N. Committee on the Elimination of Racial Discrimination," June 29, 2009, available at http://aclu.org/human-rights_racial justice/persistence-racial-and ethnic profiling-uniteid-states.

65. Harris, *Profiles in Injustice*, 104.

66. Ibid., 102.

67. Ibid., 58.

68. Michael K.Brown et al., *Whitewashing Race: The Myth of a Colorblind Society* (Berkeley: University of California Press, 2003), 140.

69. Harris, *Profiles in Injustice*, 77.

70. Brown et al., *Whitewashing Race*, 150.

71. 2006 National Crime Victimization Survey, Table 6, Table 42, Table 92.

72. See *HUD v. Rucker* 545 U.S. 125 (2002).

73. Harris, *Profiles in Injustice*, 84.

74. Ibid. Also see Deborah Ramirez, Jack McDevitt, and Amy Farrell, "A Resource Guide on Racial Profiling Data Collection Systems: Promising Practices and Lessons Learned" (2000), U.S. Department of Justice Monograph, Washington, DC, for a discussion of the methods of collecting data on racial profiling applied by Lamberth Consulting and other organizations.

75. Matthew Stabley, "CASA on ICE: Agents Used Racial Profiling to Meet Quota," Associated Press February 18, 2009.

76. Harris, *Profiles in Injustice*, 58.

77. Ibid., 240.

78. "The Persistence of Racial and Ethnic Profiling," 63.

79. Ibid., 51.

80. Harris, *Profiles in Injustice*, 48.

81. Ibid., 49.

82. See generally Leonard S. Rubinowitz and Imani Perry, "Crimes without Punishment: White Neighbors' Resistance to Black Entry," *Journal of Criminal Law and Criminology* 92 (2002): 335–423.

83. See Imani Perry, "Dusky Justice: Race in United States Law and Literature, 1878–1914" (Ph.D. diss., Harvard University, 2000).

84. See Ida B. Wells, *A Red Record* (Memphis, TN, 1895).

85. Brown et al., *Whitewashing Race*, 160.

86. Harris, *Profiles in Injustice*, 101.

87. Leonard Steinhorn and Barbara Diggs-Brown, *By the Color of Our Skin: The Illusion of Integration and the Reality of Race* (New York: Penguin, 1999), 174.

88. Routinely, new research comes to light that demonstrates the disproportionate and racially motivated surveillance of African American and Latino citizens. The Racial Profiling Data Collection Research Center at Northeastern University's Institute on Race and Justice, the American Civil Liberties Union's campaign against racial profiling, and Amnesty International all routinely collect information about racial profiling in areas across the United States, in confirmation of the general perception.that racial surveillance remains an issue in the United States. But the question is, of what consequence is this?

89. See Frantz Fanon, *Black Skin White Masks*, trans. Charles Lam Markman (New York: Grove Press, 1967), for a discussion of third-person consciousness.

90. See W. E. B. DuBois, *The Souls of Black Folk* (Chicago: A. C. McClurg, 1903), for the description of double consciousness.

91. Harris, *Profiles in Injustice*, 96.

92. Joseph Nevins, *Operation Gatekeeper: The Rise of the "Illegal Alien" and the Making of the U.S.-Mexico Boundary* (New York: Routledge, 2002), 113.

93. Bill Ong Hing, Defining *America Through Immigration Policy* (Philadelphia: Temple University Press, 2003), 201.

94. Charles Ogletree Jr., "America's Schizophrenic Immigration Policy: Race, Class, and Reason," *Boston College Law Review* 41, no. 4 (2000): 755–770.

95. Lizzy Ratner, "The Legacy of Guantamano," *The Nation*, July 16, 2003.

96. Jeffrey S. Passel, "Unauthorized Migrants: Numbers and Characteristics," Background Briefing for Taskforce on Immigration and America's Future, Pew Hispanic Center, June 14, 2005, 16.

97. Tomás Jimenez, "Mexican Immigrant Replenishment and the Continuing Significance of Ethnicity and Race," *American Journal of Sociology* 113, no. 6 (May 2008): 1527–1567.

98. See American Civil Liberties Union, "The Persistence of Racial and Ethnic Profiling in the United States: A Follow-up Report to the U.N. Committee on the Elimination of Racial Discrimination," August 2009.

99. Cited in Regina G. Lawrence, *The Politics of Force: Media and the Construction of Police Brutality* (Berkeley: University of California Press, 2000), 58.

100. See Tera Hunter, *To Joy My Freedom: Southern Black Women's Lives and Labors after the Civil War* (Cambridge, MA: Harvard University Press, 1997), and Perry, "Dusky Justice."

101. Nevins, *Operation Gatekeeper*, 163.

102. Jody David Armour, *Negrophobia and Reasonable Racism: The Hidden Costs of Being Black in America* (New York: New York University Press, 1997), 20.

103. Mahzarin Banaji and R. Bhaskar, "Implicit Stereotypes and Memory: The Bounded Rationality of Social Beliefs," in *Memory, Brain, and Belief*, ed. E. L. Schacter and E. Scarry (Cambridge, MA:Harvard University Press, 2000), 139–175, 144.

104. R. L. Hampton and E. Newberger, "Child Abuse Incidence and Reporting by Hospitals: Significance of Severity, Class, and Race," *American Journal of Public Health*, 75 (1985): 56–68; B. Drake and S. Zuravin, "Bias in Child Maltreatment Reporting: Revisiting the Myth of Classlessness," *American Journal of Orthopsychiatry* 68, no. 2; Thomas D. Morton, "The Increasing Colorization of America's Child Welfare System," *Policy and Practice* 57, no. 4 (December 1999): 23.

105. See Roberts, *Shattered Bonds*.

106. Ibid..

107. A. M. Harris, G. R. Henderson, and J. D.Williams, "Courting Customers: Assessing Consumer Racial Profiling and Other Marketplace Discrimination," *Journal of Public Policy and Marketing, Policy Watch: Commentaries and Viewpoints* 24, no. 1 (Spring 2005): 163–171.

108. Jody David Armour, *Negrophobia and Reasonable Racism: The Hidden Costs of Being Black in America* (New York: New York University Press, 1997), 27.

109. Also see Christina White, "Federally Mandated Destruction of the Black Family: The Adoption and Safe Families Act," *Northwestern Journal of Law and Social Policy* 1, no. 1

(Summer 2006): 303–337, for a description of how promoting adoption rather than main-tenance of kinship relationships threatens to permanently disconnect a disproportionate number of Black children from their parents.

110. Roberts, *Shattered Bonds*, 91.

111. Hortense J. Spillers, "Mama's Baby, Papa's Maybe: An American Grammar Book," *Diacritics* 17, no. 2 (Summer 1987): 64–81. In the African American political tradition, we can also see multiple instances of contestation about these racialized meanings of the body (and broader social issues) via counterinvocations of the body. These range from a figure like Homer Plessy's argument that he was both colored and White in one body to the grooming manuals of late-nineteenth- and early-twentieth-century Black civic culture and the shifting performances of Blackness over the course of the civil rights and Black Power eras.

112. Although I have chosen to talk about homelessness, there are other important concepts to explore in the treatment of female-body politics in racial surveillance. One important one is penetration, as it relates not only to rape, obviously, but also to body cavity searches for drugs, reproductive technologies, and the disparate treatment of women of color in childbirth.

113. "Homeless Children: America's New Outcasts," National Center on Family Home-lessness Report, National Family Center on Homelessness, Newton, MA, 1999.

114. Moreover, courts have in some instances failed to protect domestic privacy rights to poor citizens because they tend to live in areas easily exposed to public spaces or in homes with multiple residents. For example, see *United States v. Garcia*, 997 F.2d 1273, 1280 (9th Cir. 1993), *State v. Cloutier*, 544 A.2d 1277 (Me.1988)

115. George M. Glisson, Bruce A. Thyer, and Robert L. Fischer, "Serving the Homeless: Evaluating the Effectiveness of Homeless Shelter Services," *Journal of Sociology and Social Welfare* 28, no. 4 (December 2001): 89–97.

116. E. L. Bassuk, S. Melnick, and A. Browne, "Responding to the Needs of Low-income and Homeless Women Who Are Survivors of Family Violence," *Journal of the American Medical Women's Association* 53 (1998): 57–64.

117. S. L. Wenzel, B. D. Leake, and L. Gelberg, "Health of Homeless Women with Recent Experience of Rape," *Journal of General Internal Medicine* 15, no. 4 (2000): 265–268.

118. Ibid.

119. *People v. Thomas*, 45 Cal. Rptr. 2d 610, 613 n.2 (Cal. Ct. App. 1995) (the court argued that there was privacy expectation in cardboard box located on city sidewalk in which homeless defendant was residing); *State v. Mooney*, 588 A.2d 145, 154 (Conn. 1991) (the court said there was no privacy interest in home under a bridge); *State v. Cleator*, 857 P.2d 306, 308 (Wash. Ct. App. 1993) (the court said there was no privacy expectation in tent pitched on public land).

120. For a thorough discussion of this issue and cited cases, see Christopher Slobogin, "The Poverty Exception to the Fourth Amendment," *University of Florida Law Review* 55 (2003): 391–412.

121. Percentages calculated from data in Table 13, Department of Justice, Bureau of Justice Statistics, "Prison and Jail Inmates at Midyear 2002," April 6, 2003.

122. Race Ethnicity and Health Care Fact Sheet, July 2006, www.kff.org.

123. Christopher Mumola, *Incarcerated Parents and Their Children*, Bureau of Justice Statistics, Special Report, August 2000; Children of Incarcerated Parents Fact Sheet, Annie E. Casey Foundation, Baltimore, MD, 2008.

124. "Partnerships between Corrections and Child Welfare : Collaboration for Change, Part Two" a Report of the Annie E. Casey Foundation, Baltimore, MD, 2001.

125. See *Prison Rape Elimination Act*, signed into law September 4, 2003.

126. Margot Patterson, "Hard Truths about Prostitution," *National Catholic Reporter*, February 22, 2007, available at http://www.natcath.com/index0223.htm.

127. Ibid.

128. Dana Fris Hansen, "From Carrie's Kitchen Table and Beyond," Houston Contemporary Arts Museum, 1996.

129. See bell hooks, "Diasporic Landscapes of Longing," (Philadelphia: *The Fabric Workshop*, 1994). This essay appeared in the catalog that accompanied an exhibition of the work of Carrie Mae Weems.

130. A brilliant and beautiful example is found in Elizabeth Alexander's *The Black Interior* (Saint Paul, MN: Graywolf, 2004), 4–5, in which she writes, "The black interior is not an inscrutable zone, nor colonial fantasy . . . [it is] inner space in which black artists have found selves that go far, far beyond the limited expectations of what black is, isn't or should be."

131. While not ethnographic, this analysis of language is consistent with Melissa Harris Lacewell's call for us to listen to "everyday talk" as a source of political engagement and social thought in her work *Barbershops, Bibles and BET: Everyday Talk and Black Political Thought* (Princeton: Princeton University Press, 2004).

132. Oscar Gandy, "African Americans and Privacy: Understanding the Black Perspective in the Emerging Policy Debate," *Journal of Black Studies* 24 (1993): 178–195.

133. "Issue Brief: DNA, Forensics, and the Law," Genetics and Public Policy Center, Washington, DC, July 24, 2007.

134. Troy Duster, "Explaining Differential Trust of DNA Forensic Technology: Grounded Assessment or Inexplicable Paranoia?" *Journal of Law, Medicine and Ethics* 34, no. 2 (Summer 2006): 293–300.

135. Roberts, *Shattered Bonds*, 890.

136. Ruth Thompson-Miller and Joe R. Feagin, "Continuing Injuries of Racism," *The Counseling Psychologist* 35, no. 1 (2007): 106–115.

137. See, for example, Alfredo Mirandé, "Is There a Mexican Exception to the Fourth Amendment?" *University of Florida Law Review* 55 (2003): 367–389.

138. J. Yolande Daniels, "Black Bodies, Black Space: A-Waiting Spectacle," in *White Papers, Black Marks: Architecture, Race, Culture*, ed. Lesley Naa Norle Lokko (Minneapolis: University of Minnesota Press, 2000), 215.

139. Jeffrey Alexander, "Citizen and Enemy as Symbolic Classification: On the Polarizing Discourse of Civil Society," in Michele Lamont, ed., *Cultivating Differences: Symbolic Boundaries and the Making of Inequality* (Chicago: University of Chicago Press, 1992), 291.

140. Ibid., 292.

141. David Theo Goldberg, "Polluting the Body Politic," in *Racism, the City and State*, ed. Malcolm Cross and Michael Keith (New York: Routledge, 1993), 53.

142. R. C. Shah and J. P. Kesan, "How Architecture Regulates," *Journal of Architectural and Planning Research* 24, no. 4: 350–359.

143. Leslie Rebecca Bloom and Deborah Kilgore, "The Colonization of (M)Others in Welfare to Work Education," *Educational Policy* 17, no. 3 (2003): 365–384.

144. Alison Young, "Into the Blue: The Cinematic Possibility of Judgment with Passion," in *Laws Moving Image*, ed. Leslie J. Moran (New York: Routledge, 2004), 139.

145. Bernard E. Harcourt, *Illusion of Order: The False Promise of Broken Windows Policing* (Cambridge, MA: Harvard University Press 2001), 23.

146. Ibid., 34.

147. Allen, *Why Privacy Isn't Everything*, 196.

148. Ronald Weitzer and Steven A. Tuch, "Racially Biased Policing: Determinants of Citizen Perceptions" *Social Forces* 83, no. 3 (March 2005): 1009–1030.

149. In *Race, Crime and the Law* (New York: Vintage Books, 1998), Randall Kennedy importantly advanced the challenge of devoting attention to the disproportionate number of African Americans who are victims, rather than focusing on those who are convicted offenders. In so doing, he challenged us to enter into an accountability conversation internal to the African American community along with his argument for color-blind constitutionalism.

150. Anita Allen, "Privacy Isn't Everything: Accountability as a Personal and Social Good," 2003 Daniel J. Meador Lecture, reprinted in *Alabama Law Review* 54 (Summer 2003): 1375.

151. I understand that I have somewhat confused my argument here by relying on citizenship talk after I have previously identified the practice of racial surveillance as impacting both citizen and noncitizen. I hope the reader can forgive this transition. I believe it is important to talk about accountability structures, particularly as they are framed around the African American experience and the experience of Caribbean Latinos, who have similar kinds of experience in the Northeast. Accountability structures as they relate to communities with high rates of noncitizenship demand a distinct analysis, which depends on bodies of research and schools of political theory with which I am unfamiliar.

152. See Craig Futterman and Jamie Kalven, "The Need for Independent Civilian Review of the Chicago Police Department," University of Chicago Law School, in which they make this argument, spurred by the experience of Diane Bond and other former residents of the Stateway Gardens Housing Project. Also available through the MacArthur Justice Center, Northwestern University School of Law.

CHAPTER 6

1. W. E. B. Du Bois, *The Souls of Black Folk* (Chicago: A. C. McClurg, 1903).

2. Eric Lott, "The New Cosmopolitanism," *Transition* 72 (1996): 108–135.

3. David A. Hollinger, *Postethnic America: Beyond Multiculturalism* (New York: Basic Books, 1995).

4. Walter Benn Michaels, *Our America: Nativism, Modernism and Pluralism* (Durham: Duke University Press, 1997).

5. Stanley Crouch, *The All American Skin Game or the Decoy of Race: The Long and Short of It* (New York: Vintage Books, 1997).

6. This is perhaps a bold assertion, but, despite the fact that African Americans are consistently identified with the least desirable qualities in the eyes of all racial group, and that African American culture is rarely acknowledged for its multicultural, multiethnic, and multiregional dynamic evolution, I'm confident in making it.

7. Although Asian Americans are exceptionalized as a group, at the same time there is a very old image of the unassimilated Asian in America that has widespread currency and is used as a source of racist humor.

8. A. Leon Higginbotham, *Shades of Freedom* (New York: Oxford University Press, 1996).

9. Hanna Fenichel Pitkin, *The Concept of Representation* (Berkeley: University of California Press, 1967), 144.

10. Ibid.

11. Although there is some public discussion of conflict between groups of people of color, the discussion is generally limited to economic competition, immigration, and affirmative action, while discussions about class conflicts within groups of people of color focus on questions of authenticity and values gaps. Often, rather than exploring how divergent images of people shape experience and produce conflict, the description of the conflict subtextually relies upon the stereotypes that are part of exceptionalism.

12. See, for example, Paulette Caldwell, "A Hair Piece: Perspectives on the Intersection of Race and Gender," in *Critical Race Theory: The Cutting Edge*, ed. Richard Delgado and Jean Stefancic (Philadelphia: Temple University Press, 2000).

13. See, for example, Marianne Bertrand and Sendhil Mullainathan, "Are Emily and Greg More Employable Than Lakisha and Jamal? A Field Experiment on Labor Market Discrimination," MIT Department of Economics Working Paper No. 03-22.

14. See S. J. Ko, C. M. Judd, and I. V. Blair, "What the Voice Reveals: Within- and Between-Category Stereotyping on the Basis of Voice," *Personality and Social Psychology Bulletin* 32 (2006): 806–819, for an example of research supporting that such devaluation occurs.

15. Kenji Yoshino, *Covering: The Hidden Assault on Our Civil Rights* (New York: Random House, 2006).

16. William Petersen, "Success Story, Japanese-American Style," *New York Times Magazine*, January 9, 1966, 20.

17. "Success Story of One Minority Group in the U.S.," *U.S. News and World Report*, December 26, 1966, 73.

18. This is also tied to the color stratification in many parts of Latin America that is present in the Latin American media, as well.

19. For a discussion and critique of this line of thought, see Eduardo Bonilla Silva, "E Pluribus Unum or the Same Old Perfume in a New Bottle? On the Future of Racial Stratification in the United States," in *Racism without Racists: Color Blind Racism and the Persistence of Racial Inequality in the United States* (New York: Rowman and Littlefield, 2006).

20. Interestingly, a higher proportion of cohabiting relationships involve interracial couples than do married relationships, perhaps suggesting that people are still somewhat hesitant about embracing state-recognized interracial relationships. See Institute for Social Research, "Intimate Relationships between Races More Common Than Thought," press release, March 23, 2000.

21. Y. L. Shek, "Asian American Masculinity: A Review of the Literature," *Journal of Men's Studies* 14, no. 3 (2006): 379–391.

22. A. Uchida, "The Orientalization of Asian Women in America," *Women's Studies International Forum* 21, no. 2 (1998): 161–174.

23. However, in certain geographic regions, Puerto Ricans are often treated as racialized Americans.

24. Joanne L. Rondilla and Paul Spickard, *Is Lighter Better: Skintone Discrimination among Asian Americans* (New York: Rowman and Littlefield, 2007).

25. Ibid.; Mark E. Hill, "Color Differences in the Socioeconomic Status of African American Men: Results of a Longitudinal Study," *Social Forces* 78, no. 4 (2000): 1437–1460.

26. Ibid., 23.

27. Ibid., 9.

28. Edward E. Telles and Edward Murguia, "Phenotypic Discrimination and Income Differences among Mexican Americans," *Social Science Quarterly* 71, no. 4 (1990): 682–696; Edward Murguia and Edward E. Telles, " Phenotype and Schooling among Mexican Americans," *Sociology of Education* 69 (1996): 276–89; Walter Allen, Edward Telles, and Margaret Hunter, "Skin Color, Income and Education: A Comparison of African Americans and Mexican Americans," *National Journal of Sociology* 12, no. 1 (2000): 129–180; J. Kirschenmen and K. M. Neckerman, "We'd Love to Hire Them, But . . . ," in *The Meaning of Race for Employers Working in America: Continuity, Conflict and Change*, ed. Amy S. Wharton (Mountainview, CA: Mayfield, 1998); Mark E. Hill, "Color Differences in the Socioeconomic Status of African American Men: Results of a Longitudinal Study," *Social Forces* 78: 1437–1460.

29. Kerry Ann Rockquemore and David L. Brunsma, "Beyond Black: The Reflexivity of Appearances in Racial Identification among Black/White Biracials," in *Skin Deep: How Race and Complexion Matter in the "Color Blind" Era*, ed. Cedric Herring, Verna M. Keith, and Hayward Derrick Horton (Chicago: University of Illinois Press, 2004), 107.

30. Rita J. Simon and Rhonda M. Roorda, *In Their Own Voices: Transracial Adoptees Tell Their Stories* (New York: Columbia University Press, 2000), 160.

31. Sandra Patton, *Birthmarks: Transracial Adoption in Contemporary America* (New York: New York University Press, 2000), 77.

32. Ibid., 71.

33. See Suein Hwang, "The New White Flight," *Wall Street Journal*, November 19, 2005, Section A, 1.

34. David Dante Troutt, "The Monkey Suit," in his *The Monkey Suit and Other Short Fiction on African Americans and Justice* (New York: New Press, 1999).

35. Joe R. Feagin and Melvin P. Sikes, *Living with Racism: The Black Middle Class Experience* (Boston: Beacon Press, 1995).

36. "African Immigrants in the United States Are the Nation's Most Highly Educated Group" *Journal of Blacks in Higher Education*, no. 26 (Winter 1999–2000): 60–61.

37. Mary Waters, Black Identities: West Indian Immigrant Dreams and American Realities (Cambridge, MA: Harvard University Press, 1999).

38. See "Economic Mobility of Black and White Families," Economic Mobility Project, Pew Charitable Trusts, November 2007. Economic Mobility Project reports available at economicmobility.org/reports_and_research.

39. A. Orr, "Black-White Differences in Achievement: The Importance of Wealth," *Sociology of Education* 76, no. 4 (2003): 281–304; K. Tyson, "Weighing In: Elementary Age Students and the Debate on Attitudes toward School among Black Students," *Social Forces* 80, no. 4 (2002): 1157–1189.

40. Lawrence Otis Graham, *Our Kind of People: Inside America's Black Upper Class* (New York: Harper Perennial, 1999).

41. Emily Bernard, "Race and Power: The Real Mystery at the Heart of New England White," Slate.com, June 19, 2007.

42. Phillip J. Bowman, Ray Muhammad, and Mosi Ifatunji, "Skin Tone, Class and Racial Attitudes among African Americans," in *Skin Deep: How Race and Complexion Matter in the "Color-Blind" Era*, ed. Cedric Herring, Verna M. Keith, and Hayward Derrick Horton (Chicago: University of Illinois Press, 2004), 148.

43. S. Sue and S. Okazaki, "Asian American Educational Achievements: A Phenomenon in Search of an Explanation," *American Psychologist* 45, no. 8 (1990): 913–920.

44. See Heather Andrea Williams, *Self-Taught: African American Education in Slavery and Freedom* (Chapel Hill: University of North Carolina Press, 2005).

45. An added dimension of this is that it is uncommon for Black politicians to express the social conservatism that is so common in African American communities, perhaps because they are more sophisticated about the role policy plays in social stratification and reasonably have less faith in "bootstraps."

46. "Optimism about Black Progress Declines: Blacks See Growing Values Gap," Pew Research Center, A Social And Demographic Trends Report, November 13, 2007, 5.

47. See Leonard S. Rubinowitz and Imani Perry, "Crimes without Punishment: White Neighbors' Resistance to Black Entry," *Journal of Criminal Law and Criminology* 92 (2002): 335–427.

48. See Elaine Tyler May, "Family Values: The Uses and Abuses of American Family History," *Revue Française d'Etudes Americaines* 97 (2003): 7–22 at 15. Hence, we can see why discourses around Asian Americans' and Latinos' resistance to assimilating the nuclear family model are ambivalent. The persistence of extended-family and collective capital networks facilitate economic development and yet signify a decision not to assimilate. Traditional African American extended-family networks, in contrast, have been consistently deemed pathological, perhaps because they often do not have a married couple embedded at the center (and perhaps because all those Black people together are generally assumed to be trouble).

49. The foundational text for "other" theory is generally considered to be Edward Said, *Orientalism* (New York: Pantheon, 1978). However, earlier writers such as Frantz Fanon and Albert Memmi also constructed their own versions of "other" theory rooted in the colonial context.

50. Homi Bhabha, "Of Mimicry and Man: The Ambivalence of Colonial Discourse," in his *The Location of Culture* (London: Routledge, 1994).

51. See Deborah E. McDowell, "Recovery Missions: Imaging the Body Ideals," in *Recovering the Black Female Body: Self-Representations by African American Women*, ed. Michael Bennett and Vanessa D. Dickerson (New Brunswick, NJ: Rutgers University Press, 2001),

52. Jack Shaheen, *Reel Bad Arabs: How Hollywood Vilifies a People* (Northampton, MA: Interlink Publishing Group, 2001).

53. See S. J. Lee, "Behind the Model-Minority Stereotype: Voices of High- and Low-Achieving Asian American Students," *Anthropology and Education Quarterly* 25, no. 4 (December 1994): 413–429; William Wei, *The Asian American Movement* (Philadelphia: Temple University Press, 1993).

54. Arlene M. Davila, *Latinos Inc.: The Marketing and Making of a People* (Berkeley: University of California Press, 2001).

55. George M. Frederickson, "Self Made Hero," *New York Review of Books* 13, no. 11, June 27, 1985, available at http://www.nybooks.com/articles/archives/1985/jun/27/self-made-hero/?page=1.

56. See Leonard S. Rubinowitz and Imani Perry, "Crimes without Punishment: White Neighbors' Resistance to Black Entry," *Journal of Criminal Law and Criminology* 92 (2002): 335, 342.

57. Lindon Barrett, *Blackness and Value: Seeing Double* (Cambridge: Cambridge University Press, 1999), 12.

58. J. F. Dovidio and S. L. Gaertner, "Aversive Racism," in *Advances in Experimental Social Psychology*, ed. M. P. Zanna (San Diego: Academic Press, 2004).

59. John R. Hall, "The Capital(s) of Cultures: A Nonholistic Approach to Status Situations, Class, Gender, and Ethnicity," in *Cultivating Differences: Symbolic Boundaries and the Making of Inequality*, ed. Michele Lamont and Marcel Fournier (Chicago: University of Chicago Press, 1992), 258.

60. As Hall notes, "a dominated ethnic group may use one form of cultural capital with a currency in the wider world, while a separate kind of cultural capital establishes status within the group itself." Ibid., 270.

61. Tommie Shelby, *We Who Are Dark: The Philosophical Foundations of Black Solidarity* (Cambridge, MA: Harvard University Press, 2005).

62. Patricia J. Williams, "A Conversation on Race," Du Bois Institute, Harvard University, August 1997. 63. Nancy Fraser, "Rethinking Recognition," *New Left Review* 3 (May–June 2000).

CHAPTER 7

1. Peggy McIntosh, "White Privilege and Male Privilege: A Personal Account of Coming to See Correspondences Through Work in Womens Studies," working paper, Wellesley Center for Women, 1988.

2. David R. Roediger, *The Wages of Whiteness: Race and the Making of the American Working Class*, rev. ed. (London: Verso, 1999).

3. Cheryl Harris, "Whiteness as Property," *Harvard Law Review* 106 (1993): 1709–1795, 1710–1712.

4. Jody David Armour, *Negrophobia and Reasonable Racism: The Hidden Costs of Being Black in America* (New York: New York University Press, 2000).

5. Thomas M. Shapiro, *The Hidden Cost of Being African American* (New York: Oxford University Press, 2005).

6. Thomas Shapiro and Melvin Oliver, *Black Wealth, White Wealth: A New Perspective on Racial Inequality* (London: Routledge, 2006).

7. Evelyn Brooks Higginbotham, "African-American Women's History and the Metalanguage of Race," *Signs* 17, no. 2 (Winter 1992): 251–274, is an excellent essay for thinking through the production of race through other modes of differentiation.

8. See Ira Katznelson, *When Affirmative Action Was White: An Untold History of Racial Inequality in Twentieth Century America* (New York: Norton, 2005), chs. 4–6.

9. See generally Martin MacEwen, *Housing Race and Law* (London: Taylor and Francis, 2002).

10. Amartya K. Sen, "From Income Inequality to Economic Inequality," in *Race, Poverty and Domestic Policy*, ed. C. Michael Henry and James Tobin (New Haven: Yale University Press, 2004), 60.

11. Dalton Conley, *Being Black Living in the Red: Race Wealth and Social Policy in America* (Berkeley: University of California Press, 1999).

12. Lincoln Quillian and Devah Pager, "Black Neighbors, Higher Crime? The Role of Racial Stereotypes in Evaluations of Neighborhood Crime," *American Journal of Sociology* 107, no. 3 (2001): 717–767.

13. Heather G. Peske and Kati Haycock, "Teaching Inequality: How Poor and Minority Students Are Shortchanged on Teacher Quality," A Report and Recommendation by The Education Trust, June 2006.

14. See George Galster, Ronald Mincy, and Mitch Tobin, "The Disparate Racial Neighborhood Impacts of Metropolitan Economic Restructuring," in *Race, Poverty and Domestic Policy*, ed. C. Michael Henry and James Tobin (New Haven: Yale University Press, 2004).

15. See Samuel Bowles, Herbert Gintis, and Robert Szarka, "Escalating Differences and Elusive 'Skills': Cognitive Abilities and the Explanation of Inequality," in *Race, Poverty and Domestic Policy*, ed. C. Michael Henry and James Tobin (New Haven: Yale University Press, 2004).

16. An example of this argument as applied to legal education can be found in Richard H. Sanders, "A Systematic Analysis of Affirmative Action in Law Schools," *Stanford Law Review* 57 (2004). The May 2005 issue of the *Stanford Law Review* includes a number of articles by other legal scholars rebutting Sanders's argument and economic analysis.

17. Shapiro, *The Hidden Cost of Being African American*.

18. Devah Pager and Bruce Western, "Race at Work: Realities of Race and Criminal Record in the New York City Job Market," report prepared for the 50th anniversary of the New York City Commission on Human Rights 2006; Devah Pager, "Double Jeopardy: Race, Crime, and Getting a Job," *Wisconsin Law Review* 2 (2005): 617–660; Mark E. Hill, "Color Differences in the Socioeconomic Status of African American Men: Results of a Longitudinal Study," *Social Forces* 78, no. 4 (2000): 1437–1460.

19. Edward E. Telles and Edward Murguia, "Phenotypic Discrimination and Income Differences among Mexican Americans," *Social Science Quarterly* 71, no. 4 (1990): 682–696; Edward Murguia and Edward E. Telles, "Phenotype and Schooling among Mexican Americans," *Sociology of Education* 69 (1996): 276–89; Walter Allen, Edward Telles, and Margaret Hunter, "Skin Color, Income and Education: A Comparison of African Americans and Mexican Americans," *National Journal of Sociology* 12, no. 1 (2000): 129–180; J. Kirschenmen and K. M. Neckerman, "We'd Love to Hire Them, But . . .," in *The Meaning of Race for Employers Working in America: Continuity, Conflict and Change*, ed. Amy S. Wharton (Mountainview, CA: Mayfield, 1998); Mark E. Hill, "Color Differences in the Socioeconomic Status of African American Men: Results of a Longitudinal Study," *Social Forces* 78: 1437–1460.

20. The Discrimination Research Center (DRC) has found that temporary employment agencies in California show significant preferences for White job applicants over African American applicants. In sixty-four undercover tests conducted between May and November 2003, temporary agencies preferred White applicants four to one over African Americans in Los Angeles and more than two to one in San Francisco. DRC sent pairs of specially trained job applicants to temporary employment agencies and studied several factors, including whether one type of applicant was favored over the other in obtaining an interview, obtaining a job offer, being offered better rates of pay, and receiving longer job assignments, among other indicators. The results are strikingly similar to DRC's previous 1999 study (conducted in San Francisco only), which showed that Whites were preferred by more than three to one.

21. William A. Darity Jr., "Racial and Ethnic Economic Inequality: A Cross-National Perspective," in *Race, Poverty and Domestic Policy*, ed. C. Michael Henry and James Tobin (New Haven: Yale University Press, 2004), 83–84.

22. See Deborah Woo, *Glass Ceilings and Asian Americans: The New Face of Workplace Barriers* (Walnut Creek, CA: Altamira Press, 2000).

23. See Donald Tomaskovic-Devey, Melvin Thomas, and Kecia Johnson, "Race and the Accumulation of Human Capital across the Career: A Theoretical Model and Fixed Effects Application," *American Journal of Sociology* 111, no. 1: 58–89, for a discussion of the manner in which discrimination, social networks, and inequality impact human capital acquisition over the course of an individual's work life.

24. Shapiro, *The Hidden Cost of Being African American*, 3.

25. Michael O. Emerson, Karen J. Chai, and George Yancey, "Does Race Matter in Residential Segregation? Exploring the Preferences of White Americans," *American Sociological Review* 66, no. 6 (December 2001): 922–935, shows that race, and specifically the presence of African Americans, operates as an independent variable discouraging Whites from moving into a neighborhood. This obviously impacts home values in neighborhoods with significant numbers of African Americans.

26. See Amaad Rivera, Brenda Cotto-Escalera, Anisha Desai, Jeannette Huezo, and Dedrick Muhammad, *Foreclosed: State of the Dream*, Institute for Policy Studies, United for a Fair Economy, 2008. This report reveals the explicit targeting of Blacks and Latinos for subprime mortgage loans and the unprecedented wealth loss that is expected for people of color as a result of the mortgage crisis. Also see Calvin Bradford, "Risk or Race? Racial Disparities and the Subprime Refinanc Market," Center for Community Change, May 2002.

27. Sen, "From Income Inequality to Economic Inequality," 70.

28. See Ian Ayres, *Pervasive Prejudice: Unconventional Evidence of Race and Gender Discrimination* (Chicago: University of Chicago Press, 2001).

29. Anne-Marie G. Harris, "Shopping While Black: Applying 42 U.S.C. § 1981 to Cases of Consumer Racial Profiling," *Boston College Third World Law Journal* 23 (Winter 2003): 1–55.

30. See Kerwin Kofi Charles, Erik Hurst, and Nikolai Roussanov, "Conspicuous Consumption and Race," NBER Working Paper No. W13392, September 2007, http://www.nber.org/authors/nikolai_roussanov. The authors show that African Americans and Latinos spend more on visible goods compared to other groups but that consumption pattern can be explained by class (low income people in general spend a greater proportion of their income on visible consumer groups relative to other groups) rather than race.

31. The work of Charles, Hurst, and Roussanov supports this supposition, given that it shows that low-income people in general compensate for their low status by purchasing visible consumer goods.

32. Sen, "From Income Inequality to Economic Inequality," 61.

33. Equal Employment Opportunity Commission Compliance Manual, Section on Race and Color Discrimination, Section 15, V, example 4.

34. Ibid., Section 15, VI, Recruiting.

35. "Wanted: Caucasian College Women as Egg Donors," *Journal of Blacks in Higher Education* no. 27 (Spring 2000): 55. Also see Debora Spar, "Designing Babies," in her *The Baby Business: How Money Science and Politics Drive the Commerce of Conception* (Allston, MA: Harvard Business Press, 2006). 36. Michele Goodwin, "The Free Market Approach to Adoption: The Value of a Baby," *Boston College Third World Law Journal* 26 (2006): 61–79.

37. Kristal Brent Zook, "Have You Seen Her? While the Families of the Missing Struggle to Bring National Attention to Their Lost Loved Ones, They Sift through the

Clues and Pray for a Miracle," *Essence,* July 2005, 128; Eugene Robinson, "(White) Women We Love," *Washington Post,* June 10, 2005, A23. Also see Sean Gardiner, "NYPD Inaction over a Missing Black Woman Found Dead Sparks a Historic Racial-Bias Lawsuit," *Village Voice,* May 6, 2008, detailing litigation in New York courts in response to police bias in responding to missing persons.

38. "Sex Workers: Perspectves in Public Health and Human Rights," Sexuality Information and Education Council of the United States (SIECUS) Report 33, no. 2 (Spring 2005): 5–7.

39. Glen C. Loury, *The Anatomy of Racial Inequality* (Cambridge, MA: Harvard University Press, 2002), 25.

40. In 2005, 75.8 percent of Whites, 60.1 percent of Asians, 58.2 percent of Native Americans, 49.5 percent of Hispanics, and 48.2 percent of African Americans owned their homes (U.S. Census Bureau).

41. Thomas P. Boehm and Alan M. Schlottmann, "Mortgage Pricing Differentials across Hispanic, African-American, and White Households: Evidence from the American Housing Survey," *Cityscape* 9, no. 2 (2007): 105.

42. In 2002, for example, the median net worth for African Americans was $5,988 and for Hispanics $7,932, whereas for Whites it was $88,561. Hispanic immigrants from Central American and Caribbean countries had a median net worth of $2,508. Rakesh Kochhar, "The Wealth of Hispanic Households 1996–2002," a Pew Hispanic Center Report, October 2004. For an extensive discussion of the racial wealth gap between African Americans and Whites, see Dalton Conley, *Being Black Living in the Red: Race Wealth and Social Policy in America* (Berkeley: University of California Press, 1999).

43. Michael K. Brown et al., *Whitewashing Race: The Myth of a Color Blind Society* (Berkeley: University of California Press, 2003).

44. "Racism out of Place: Thoughts on Whiteness and an Antiracist Geography in the New Millenium," *Annals of the Association of American Geographers* 90, no. 2 (2000): 392–403.

45. George Galster, Ronald Mincy, and Mitch Tobin, "The Disparate Racial Neighborhood Impacts of Metropolitan Economic Restructuring," in *Race, Poverty and Domestic Policy,* ed. C. Michael Henry and James Tobin (New Haven: Yale University Press, 2004), 210.

46. Richard Brooks, "Covenants and Conventions," Northwestern Law and Economics Research Paper No. 02-8, September 2002, demonstrates the durable current inequality produced by the history of racially restrictive covenants and segregationist social conventions. Also see Patricia J. Williams, "A Conversation on Race," Du Bois Institute, August 1997, describing how she caused property values to drop as she purchased her own home.

47. David Delaney, "The Space That Race Makes," *The Professional Geographer* 54, no. 1 (February 2002): 6–14.

48. Randall Kennedy, in his book *Race, Crime and the Law* (New York: Random House, 1997), 161, makes the point that the disproportionate emphasis on Blacks as perpetrators of crimes distracts attention from the fact that African American are disproportionately victims of crimes.

49. Centers for Disease Control, "Infant Mortality Statistics from the 2005 Period Linked to Birth/Infant Death Data Set," *National Vital Statistics Reports* 57, no. 2, Table 2, 2008.

50. U.S. Department of Justice, Bureau of Justice Statistics, "Homicide Trends in the United States," *Trends in Race*, 2007.

51. James Alan Fox and Marianne W. Zawitz, "Homicide Trends in the United States," *Age Gender and Race Trends*, U.S. Department of Justice, Bureau of Justice Statistics, 2007.

52. Pierre Bourdieu, *Distinction: A Social Critique of the Judgment of Taste* (Cambridge, MA: Harvard University Press, 1984).

53. See, for examples of research on this subject, Audrey Devine Eller, "Rethinking Bourdieu on Race: A Critical Review of Cultural Capital and Habitus in the Sociology of Education," *Qualitative Literature* (unpublished paper); Matthijs Kalmijn and Gerbert Kraaykamp, "Race, Cultural Capital, and Schooling: An Analysis of Trends in the United States," *Sociology of Education* 69, no. 1 (January 1996): 22–34, but also note the following works for their critique of the notion that the only form of racialized cultural capital is that which is found among Whites. These authors identify capital that operates within communities of color and facilitates resilience for members of those communities when dealing with social inequality: Prudence Carter, "Black Cultural Capital, Status Positioning, and Schooling Conflicts for Low-Income African American Youth," *Social Problems* 50, no. 1 (2003): 136–155; Tara J. Yosso, "Whose Culture Has Capital: A Critical Race Theory Discussion of Community Cultural Wealth," *Race, Ethnicity and Education* 8, no. 1 (March 2005): 68–91.

54. Leticia Saucedo, "The Employer Preference for the Subservient Worker and the Making of the Brown Collar Workplace," *Ohio State Law Journal* 67 (2006): 961–1022; also see Philip Moss and Chris Tilly, *Stories Employers Tell: Race, Skill and Hiring in America* (New York: Russell Sage Foundation, 2001), showing employers give Blacks more positive reviews in jobs as cleaners and drivers.

55. Kanye West, featuring Jay Z, "Diamonds from Sierra Leone," *Late Registration*, Island Def Jam, 2005.

56. The Delcambre, Louisiana, ordinance carries a penalty of up to six months in jail and a $500 fine. "Cajun Town Bans Saggy Pants in Bid to Cover Up Private Parts," Associate Press, June 13, 2007. Similar ordinances have been passed or initiated in towns in Texas, Virginia, South Carolina , Georgia, and Connecticut.

57. "Asian Americans Provide Opportunities for Marketing," *National Research Network*, no. 17, June 2009; "Shopping Habits of U.S. Hispanics Differ from Those of U.S. Adults Overall," *Retailer Daily*, January 12, 2009; "African American Market in the U.S.," *Packaged Facts*, February 2008.

58. John McKnight, "Human Service Systems," in his *The Careless Society: Community and its Counterfeits* (New York: Basic Books, 1996).

59. Ibid.

60. Ibid.

61. See Elijah Anderson, "The Mating Game," in *Code of the Street: Decency, Violence and the Moral Life of the Inner City* (New York: Norton, 1994).

62. Daryl Michael Scott, *Contempt and Pity: Social Policy and the Image of the Damaged Black Psyche 1880–1996* (Chapel Hill: University of North Carolina Press, 1997).

63. Andrew Coyle, Allison Campbell, and Rodney Neufeld, eds., *Capitalist Punishment: Prison Privatization and Human Rights* (Atlanta: Clarity Press, 2003). Also see Angela Y. Davis, *Are Prisons Obsolete* (St. Paul: Open Media, 2003), and Ruth Wilson Gilmore, *Golden Gulag: Prisons, Surplus, Crisis, and Opposition in Globalizing California* (Berkeley: University of California Press, 2007).

64. Brian Grow and Keith Epstein, "The Poverty Business: Special Report," *Business Week*, May 21, 2007, 56–67.

65. For example Douglas Massey and Nancy Denton, *American Apartheid: Segregation and the Making of the Underclass* (Cambridge, MA: Harvard University Press, 1998).

66. See generally Tamara Beauboeuf-Lafontant and D. Smith Augustine, *Facing Racism in Education*, 2nd ed. (Cambridge, MA: Harvard Educational Review, 1996).

67. See for a general overview "Housing Discrimination and Residential Segregation: Where Are We Now?," National Fair Housing Alliance, May 2008. This report showed race-based steering in 87 percent of tests conducted in twelve metropolitan areas. Also see specific examples in municipalities: "Westchester Real Estate Brokers to End Racial Discrimination: State Investigation Reveals Violation of Fair Housing Laws," press release, Office of the New York State Attorney General Eliot Spitzer, September 21, 2005; U.S. Department of Justice "Justice Department Settles Race Discrimination Case against Milwaukee Re/Max Offfice, Real Estate Agent and Homeowner," press release, February 29, 2008.

68. See Edward Shihadeh and Raymond.Barranco, "Low-skilled Jobs and Black Violence: Is Hispanic Competition Leading to Higher Crime Rates for Blacks?" Paper presented at the annual meeting of the American Society of Criminology, Atlanta, Georgia, November 14, 2007, in which the authors tie African Americans' high reserve wage to labor displacement by Hispanics, which then leads to higher crime rates.

69. Douglas S. Massey, "Geography of Inequality in Urban America," in *Race, Poverty and Domestic Policy*, ed. C. Michael Henry and James Tobin (New Haven: Yale University Press, 2004), 185.

CONCLUSION

1. Elizabeth Anderson, "What Is the Point of Equality" *Ethics* 109, no. 2 (January 1999): 287–337 at 289.

2. Ibid., 287.

3. Interest convergence and other theories have argued that change was coming anyway. I think interest convergence offers an accurate analysis, but the idea that it happens because of the will of the powerful is mistaken. The lesson should be that those advocates of equality look for ways to make the interest intersect with a broader pool of people and do so without taking on the agendas of others instead of their own.

4. Derrick Bell and Mary Dudziak have argued that the transformations had a great deal to do with interest convergence. Derrick A. Bell Jr., "*Brown v. Board of Education* and the Interest Convergence Dilemma," in *Critical Race Theory: The Key Writings That Formed the Movement*, ed. Kimberlé Crenshaw et al. (New York: New Press, 1996), 20 22; Mary Dudziak, *Cold War Civil Rights: Race and the Image of American Democracy* (Princeton: Princeton University Press, 2002). I agree with them, at the level of courts and legislation, but I also believe that the nation ratified the narrative shift as a result of the argumentative impact of the activism of African Americans in the civil rights movement.

5. Eric Zachary and Shoya Olatoye, "Community Organizing for School Improvement in the South Bronx: A Case Study," prepared as part of the Institute for Education and Social Policy's Community Involvement Program, New York University, Institute for Education and Social Policy, 2001.

6. Good film resources for "narrative shifting" can be found in the films produced by the landmark production company Blackside, as well as in those distributed by California Newsreel and Media Rights.

7. I. V. Blair and M. R. Banaji, "Automatic and Controlled Processes in Stereotype Priming," *Journal of Personality and Social Psychology* 70 (1996): 1142–1163; I. V. Blair, "The Malleability of Automatic Stereotypes and Prejudice," *Personality and Social Psychology Review* 6 (2002): 242–261.

8. Anderson, "What Is the Point of Equality?" 316.

9. Ibid.

10. "America's Cradle to Prison Pipeline," report, Children's Defense Fund, Washington, DC, 2007, 17.

11. Toni Terling Watt, "Factors Contributing to Differences in Substance Use among Black and White Adolescents," *Youth and Society* 39, no. 1 (2007): 54–74.

12. Roberto Mangabeira Unger and Cornel West, *The Future of American Progressivism* (Boston: Beacon Press, 1998), 30.

13. See Eddie S. Glaude, Jr. *In a Shade of Blue: Pragmatism and the Politics of Black America* (Chicago: University of Chicago Press, 2007), and Tommie Shelby, We Who Are Dark: The Philosophical Foundations of Black Solidarity (Cambridge, MA: Harvard University Press, 2005), for examples.

14. See Randall Kennedy's *Sellout: The Politics of Racial Betrayal* (New York: Pantheon, 2008), for a discussion of this phenomenon.

15. Alan Wolfe, "Democracy versus Sociology: Boundaries and Their Political Consequences," in *Cultivating Differences: Symbolic Boundaries and the Making of Inequality*, ed. Michele Lamont and Marcel Fournier (Chicago: University of Chicago Press, 1992), 319.

Index

About the Author

IMANI PERRY is an interdisciplinary scholar of race, cultural studies, and American law. Professor Perry holds a Ph.D. in American civilization and a J.D., both from Harvard, and has published articles and essays in a range of fields. Her first book, *Prophets of the Hood: Politics and Poetics in Hip Hop*, has been adopted widely in college-level courses in ethnomusicology and African American studies. Currently she is a professor at the Center for African American Studies at Princeton University.

Made in the USA
Middletown, DE
10 July 2020